Metropolitan Management

EDI Series in Economic Development

Metropolitan Management
The Asian Experience

K. C. Sivaramakrishnan
and
Leslie Green

Published for the Economic Development Institute
of
The World Bank
OXFORD UNIVERSITY PRESS

Oxford University Press

NEW YORK OXFORD LONDON GLASGOW
TORONTO MELBOURNE WELLINGTON HONG KONG
TOKYO KUALA LUMPUR SINGAPORE JAKARTA
DELHI BOMBAY CALCUTTA MADRAS KARACHI
NAIROBI DAR ES SALAAM CAPE TOWN

First printing April 1986

Library of Congress Cataloging-in-Publication Data

Sivaramakrishnan, K. D., 1935–
   Metropolitan management.

   Includes index.
   1. Metropolitan areas—Asia.   2. Metropolitan
government—Asia.   3. Community development, Urban—
Asia.   4. Urban policy—Asia.   I. Green, Leslie.
II. Economic Development Institute (Washington, D.C.)
III. Title.
HT334.A8S58   1986   307.7′64′095   86-821
ISBN 0-19-520508-1

Foreword

THE MOST DRAMATIC CHANGE in urban structure in the world has been among the largest cities. According to recent U.N. estimates and projections of urban population, thirty-five cities in the world today have 5 million or more inhabitants. Of these cities, twenty-one are in developing countries, where thirty years ago there were only three of that size. It is clear that a growing number of the world's largest urban agglomerations will be in the less developed regions.

In a developing country a large metropolitan area is usually a primary center of industry, commerce, and trade that provides a substantial share of gross national product and many of the goods and services required for the development of the other sectors. Accompanying economic and physical growth of the city is a growing demand for transport, water supply and sanitation, shelter, communications, and other essential services. The brunt of the urban challenge thus falls on the great cities of developing countries, which are hard pressed to find the requisite funds, skills, and institutional capacities to meet the task.

The World Bank has been involved for more than a decade in projects to develop urban infrastructure. Initial efforts concentrated on the provision of services, but now the emphasis is shifting to institutional issues and managerial approaches to their solution. Inevitably, this is a learning process, for the Bank as well as its borrowers. Courses and seminars on urban management presented by the Economic Development Institute (EDI) of the Bank have been an important part of this process.

This book arises from a seminar on metropolitan management that the EDI organized in 1981 in Manila in collaboration with the Asian Development Bank (ADB). Twenty-five metropolitan officials with direct experience in the management of sixteen cities of South and East Asia participated along with senior EDI, other World Bank, and ADB staff. The chief objectives of the seminar were to identify the critical tasks of metropolitan management and determine the extent to which the institutional, financial, and other constraints to performance can be eased.

In this book K. C. Sivaramakrishnan and Leslie Green review the planning and development exercises as well as the institutional initiatives of eight cities in South and East Asia. They compare and contrast the experiences of the cities and explore possible new responses to the tasks facing metropolitan management in the region. Managerial processes and operating styles are emphasized rather than the creation of elaborate organizational structures.

Although the World Bank had been involved in funding single- or multiple-sector projects in all of the eight cities surveyed, the Manila seminar was the first opportunity for senior managers from these cities to share their experiences with each other. Two years later a similar seminar in Rio de Janeiro was organized by the EDI and the U.N. Centre for Human Settlements. Representatives from eleven metropolitan cities in eight countries of the Latin American region participated. Because the problems and solutions discussed at the two seminars are strikingly similar, a brief resume of the findings of the Rio meeting is appended to this book.

The EDI hopes that all those concerned with the arduous task of managing metropolitan growth in the developing countries will find this study of relevance and use.

Christopher R. Willoughby
Director
Economic Development Institute

Contents

Acknowledgments   *xi*

Abbreviations   *xiii*

Part I. Survey and Analysis   *1*

  1. The Metropolitan Dimension   *3*

     Trends in Urbanization   *3*
     The Premetropolitan Phase   *4*
     The Metropolitan Challenge   *5*
     The Sectoral Response   *6*
     The Multisectoral Response   *8*
     Experiments in Metropolitan Government   *9*
     Persistent Problems   *10*

  2. Tasks of Metropolitan Management   *23*

     Provision of Services   *23*
     Programming of Projects   *26*
     Economic Development   *27*
     Spatial Planning   *30*
     Overcoming Constraints   *32*
     Developing Managerial Processes   *32*

  3. Financial Constraints   *34*

     Allocation of Resources   *34*
     Scale of Demand   *35*
     Interagency Consistency   *36*
     Assessing Needs and Resources   *37*
     Determining Priorities   *38*
     Internal Efficiency   *41*
     Cost Recovery   *42*
     Tax Policies   *43*
     Resource Mobilization   *45*

4. Institutional Constraints   *47*

Lack of Metropolitan and Long-Term Perspectives   *47*
Urban Bureaucracies and Development Administration   *49*
Social and Political Development   *51*
Coping with Uncertainty   *54*
Adopting New Perspectives   *56*

5. The Search for Alternatives   *58*

Integrating the Planning and Administration of Development   *59*
Reconciling Development Administration and Urban Bureaucracies   *62*
Responsive Networking   *65*
Using the Private Sector   *71*
Using Voluntary Groups   *72*
Roles of the Public and Private Sectors   *73*

6. Manpower Needs and Development   *75*

Manpower Needs   *75*
Training   *77*

7. Effective Metropolitan Management   *82*

Minimum Organizational Needs   *82*
Management Team and Investment Budget   *83*
Interorganizational Relations   *84*
Management and Local Representation   *86*
The Role of International Agencies   *88*

Part II. City Profiles   *91*

8. Bangkok   *93*

Growth of the City   *93*
Metropolitan Problems   *94*
Structure of Government   *100*
Fiscal Situation   *103*
Response to Metropolitan Problems   *107*
Pending Issues   *114*

9. Bombay   *119*

Growth of the City   *119*
Metropolitan Problems   *126*
Structure of Government   *127*
Fiscal Situation   *131*
Response to Metropolitan Problems   *133*
Pending Issues   *136*

10. Calcutta   *140*

Growth of the City   *140*
Metropolitan Problems   *141*
Structure of Government   *149*
Fiscal Situation   *151*
Response to Metropolitan Problems   *152*
Pending Issues   *167*

11. Colombo   *171*

    Growth of the City   *171*
    Metropolitan Problems   *172*
    Structure of Government   *178*
    Fiscal Situation   *181*
    Response to Metropolitan Problems   *183*
    Pending Issues   *186*

12. Jakarta   *189*

    Growth of the City   *189*
    Metropolitan Problems   *196*
    Structure of Government   *198*
    Fiscal Situation   *200*
    Response to Metropolitan Problems   *201*
    Pending Issues   *206*

13. Karachi   *209*

    Growth of the City   *209*
    Metropolitan Problems   *210*
    Structure of Government   *215*
    Fiscal Situation   *219*
    Response to Metropolitan Problems   *223*
    Pending Issues   *224*

14. Madras   *228*

    Growth of the City   *228*
    Metropolitan Problems   *233*
    Structure of Government   *234*
    Fiscal Situation   *237*
    Response to Metropolitan Problems   *239*
    Pending Issues   *242*

15. Manila   *245*
    Growth of the City   *245*
    Metropolitan Problems   *246*
    Structure of Government   *252*
    Fiscal Situation   *255*
    Response to Metropolitan Problems   *259*
    Pending Issues   *263*

Appendix A. Managing Metropolitan Growth in Latin America   *265*

Appendix B. Asian Development Bank–Economic Development
            Institute Seminar on Metropolitan Management   *283*

Index   *286*

Acknowledgments

THE STORY OF ANY ONE CITY is difficult enough to tell, but a comparative account of eight Asian metropolises is, to say the least, ambitious. The inspiration to undertake this effort came from a seminar in Manila on metropolitan management sponsored by the Asian Development Bank and the Economic Development Institute (EDI) of the World Bank. The insights and experiences expressed by the participants in that seminar have left their mark on this book. To these participants, therefore, must go the first acknowledgment.

Anthony Churchill, director, Water Supply and Urban Development Department of the World Bank, has been a consistent source of encouragement and advice throughout this endeavor. The authors gratefully acknowledge his support.

A comparative account of this kind has to draw upon information from numerous sources, both documentary and personal. The assistance received in this regard from the staff of the South and East Asia urban projects division in the World Bank has been invaluable. We are indebted to Daud Ahmad, Douglas Graham, Patrick McCarthy, Gerhard Menckhoff, Braz Menezes, Sven Sandstrom, Paul Stott, Inder Sud, Fred Temple, and David Williams for sharing with us the material pertaining to the eight cities examined in this book. Leonie Menezes has been responsible for most of the research in the preparation of the city profiles.

The authors have benefited greatly from the comments and advice of several colleagues and friends who took time to read the preliminary drafts: Annmarie H. Walsh, president, and Janice Hopper and Randolph L. Marshall of the Institute of Public Administration; John D. Herbert, Neil E. Boyle, Evan Rotner, and Rakesh Mohan of the World Bank; M. G. Kutty and Kalyan Biswas of Calcutta; and several others.

K. J. Davy of the Institute of Local Government Studies in Birmingham, England, has made valuable contributions to chapter 3 in his capacity as resource person at the Manila seminar. Thanks are also due to Irving Sirken of the EDI and K. L. Luthra of the Asian Development Bank for their encouragement and to Christopher Willoughby for writing the foreword to this book.

The tale of any city needs maps and pictures. Ulrich Boegli and his colleagues in the World Bank's Cartography Division, in particular Christine Windheuser, Pilar Garcia, and Yung Koo, have done an excellent job in assembling the sources and preparing the maps for the publication. James Flatness of the U.S. Library of Congress has been helpful in locating historical maps of some cities. Photographs of the cities were assembled with the valuable assistance of John Courtney and Evan Rotner of the World Bank, the Ceylon Tourist Board, and the Indonesian Embassy.

Amy Glades of the World Bank, Cassandra Reynolds of the Institute of Public Administration, and Gopal Das and Shyamal Guhamazumdar of Calcutta have rendered unstinting secretarial help. Venka Macintyre tended with diligence and speed the editing of this manuscript. The authors appreciate her patience and faith.

Abbreviations

BEST Bombay Corporation's Electric Supply and Transport
BDP Basic Development Plan (Calcutta)
BMA Bangkok Metropolitan Administration
BMC Greater Bombay Municipal Corporation
BMRDA Bombay Metropolitan Regional Development Authority
BOC Barangay Operations Center
CIDCO City and Investment Development Corporation (Maharashtra)
CIF Capital investment folio
CIT Calcutta Improvement Trust
CMD Calcutta Metropolitan District
CMDA Calcutta Metropolitan Development Authority
CMPO Calcutta Metropolitan Planning Organization
CMWSA Calcutta Metropolitan Water and Sanitation Authority
CUDP Calcutta Urban Development Project
GCEC Greater Colombo Economic Commission
HFC Home Finance Commission (Philippines)
HIT Howrah Improvement Trust
JABOTABEK Acronym for Jakarta, Bogor, Tangra, and Bekasi
KDA Karachi Development Authority
KIP Kampung Improvement Program
KMC Karachi Metropolitan Corporation
KWSB Karachi Water Supply and Sewerage Board
MC Madras Corporation
MDP Municipal Development Program (Calcutta)
MFC Municipal Finance Commission (Calcutta)
MIDC Maharashtra Industrial Development Corporation
MHADA Maharashtra Housing and Area Development Authority
MMA Madras Metropolitan Area
MMC Metropolitan Manila Commission

MMDA Maharastra Metropolitan Development Authority
MMWSSB Madras Metropolitan Water Supply and Sewerage Board
MWSS Metropolitan Water and Sewerage System (Manila)
NEDA National Economic and Development Authority (Philippines)
NESDB National Economic and Social Development Board (Thailand)
NHA National Housing Authority (Philippines and Thailand)
NHDA National Housing Development Authority (Sri Lanka)
PAM Perusatan Air Minum (Jakarta)
RGS Revised Grants Structure
RTG Royal Thai Government
SIICOM State Industrial and Investment Corporation of Maharashtra
STC State Transport Corporation (West Bengal)
UDA Urban Development Authority (Colombo)
WSDB Water Supply and Drainage Board (Sri Lanka)

PART I

Survey and Analysis

1

The Metropolitan Dimension

THIS IS A STUDY of the management problems experienced by selected metropolitan cities in South and East Asia and of the approaches adopted in resolving them. Although the region contains many of the world's developing countries, it is not an exception to the universal trends in urbanization, which have had a massive impact on its metropolitan cities. Apart from Tokyo, the cities concerned tend to dominate the economic and political scene in their respective countries, but for the purposes of this discussion it is not inappropriate to refer to them and the problems they face as being broadly metropolitan. To the ancient Greeks, the term "metropolis" meant the mother city and principal seat of government of a state or colony. Urban geographers and planners now tend to use the term "metropolitan" to refer to a large identifiable area of continuous urbanization consisting of several administrative jurisdictions. Demographers today often classify cities with populations of more than 1 million people as metropolitan, and in common usage the term is widely employed to symbolize social, economic, and political status. All of these characteristics apply to the cities studied here.

Trends in Urbanization

Between 1920 and 1960, the world's population rose by 60 percent (from 1,860 million to 3,000 million).[1] The number of people living in towns and cities having more than 20,000 inhabitants rose from 270 million to 760 million, or 180 percent. The urban proportion of the world's population

---

1. These and the following statistics are from *World Urbanization Trends, 1920–1960* (New York: United Nations, Bureau of Social Affairs, 1966); Homer Hoyt, *World Urbanization*, Technical Bulletin no. 43 (Washington, D.C.: Urban Land Institute, 1962); and World Bank, *Annual Report, 1970* (Washington, D.C., 1970).

grew from 14 percent to 25 percent. This increase was three times more rapid in the developing countries than in the developed countries. As a result, by 1960 the developing countries had experienced the sharpest increases in both population and urbanization even though they still had the lowest percentages of urban population. Furthermore, urban growth in the developing countries as a whole had been concentrated overwhelmingly in cities with more than 50,000 inhabitants. By 1960, these cities had absorbed half of the urban growth in East Asia, a third in South Asia and in Latin America, and a fourth in Africa. Moreover, 37 percent of the world's cities of this size were located in the developing countries, compared with only 13 percent in 1920.

If the current trend toward an increasing concentration of population in large cities continues, by the year 2000, 38 percent of the world's population will be living in towns and cities with 20,000 or more inhabitants. Most of these people will be in urban agglomerations with a population of a million or more.[2] Today there are 225 of these metropolitan cities, 116 of which are located in the developing countries. By the end of the century, there will be close to 414 such cities, of which 264 will be in the developing countries. Among these, some 60 are expected to have populations in excess of 5 million by the year 2000, and 32 of them will be located in South and East Asia in the region that stretches eastward from Pakistan and India, by way of Thailand and the Malay Peninsula, to the countries bordering the western rim of the Pacific Ocean (see tables 1-1 to 1-6 at the end of this chapter). The implications of this increase weigh heavily on urban management.

The Premetropolitan Phase

For many years before this massive urbanization, city management in South and East Asia consisted of a few day-to-day functions such as the delivery of essential public services (health care, water supply, sanitation, primary education, and so on), the provision and upkeep of related public works, and the regulation of certain private activities (trades, professions, house building, land uses, traffic, markets, and places of entertainment). To finance these functions, city managements levied a limited range of local taxes.

Whether in Karachi or Bombay, Bangkok or Jakarta, the machinery of public administration for the discharge of these routine tasks had become organized on traditional departmental and hierarchical lines, which were sanctioned and defined by a slowly growing but substantial maze of rules and regulations. Some of the institutions were national in status and scope, some were provincial, and some local. As a result, all large cities were ad-

2. These statistics are from *Trends and Prospects in the Population of Urban Agglomerations, 1950–2000* (New York: United Nations, Department of Economic and Social Affairs, 1975).

ministered by a web of long-established bureaucracies that had been legitimized by history and seemed impervious to change.

Despite their geopolitical and historical importance, the principal cities of South and East Asia remained relatively small until the Second World War. Of the thirty-two Asian cities expected to reach the 5 million mark by the end of the century (see table 1-2), only six—namely, Tokyo, Osaka, Shanghai, Beijing, Calcutta, and Bombay—could then be classed as metropolitan. Typically, urban management in these cities continued to concern itself with the general administration of traditional, long-standing functions. Economically, politically, and socially, these cities remained colonial in character. More often than not, a wealthy elite made up of both Europeans and indigenes held the reins of power in business, government, and society and lived in fashionable and well-provided local enclaves. Most of the remaining population inhabited urban villages that encircled the enclaves and were built and maintained in essentially rural ways, and they retained strong family ties with the communities of the rural hinterland.

The Metropolitan Challenge

By 1950, nineteen of the thirty-two cities had populations of 1 million or more (see table 1-2). By 1980, ten had passed the 5 million mark. Tokyo, for example, had reached 19.7 million, Osaka 9.7 million, Calcutta 9.6 million, Seoul 9.4 million, Bombay 8.7 million, and Jakarta 7.2 million. Except for Hong Kong, not one was now colonial. Independence and subsequent industrialization had brought high population growth rates nationwide and vast migrations of people from rural to urban areas. Stability had been replaced by explosive change.

Almost immediately, urban management was beset by unprecedented problems far beyond the historical experience and capability of established institutions. Socially—mainly because of rapid migration on a very large scale from distant as well as surrounding areas—the linguistic and cultural diversity of cities increased, the age and sex structure of their populations skewed progressively in favor of males and young persons, family life and the stability it promotes deteriorated, and irreversible changes occurred in the organization of urban life in general. Physically and functionally, old city boundaries were quickly eroded by the rising flood of people, which overwhelmed existing health, sanitary, environmental, and educational facilities and services. Moreover, as the cities grew, congestion and the lack of access to industrial and commercial locations became serious problems. Furthermore, despite the employment provided by organized trade and industry and the few new jobs created by small-scale and unorganized enterprises, unemployment and poverty escalated because the labor force was steadily expanding.

The conventional machinery of public administration was thus confronted with social, physical, functional, and economic crises demanding urgent, large-scale, and unconventional responses. The physical and functional problems were plainly visible, particularly the conflicting and chaotic use of land and the fast-spreading slums, to which an immediate response needed to be made. City officials therefore felt an urgent need to build huge numbers of dwellings and to provide related services. The urban infrastructure that had been assembled slowly over several years had to be doubled and in some cases trebled within a decade. The daily upkeep of basic services—whether of water supply, drainage, transportation, street cleaning, or refuse removal—became almost an impossible task. The scale altered the very nature of the problem.

The countries of South and East Asia sought answers to these problems in the experience of already developed countries. As they studied the technology and administrative and financial methods used elsewhere to deal with these problems, the governments of this region adopted a project-oriented, sectoral approach, along with the appropriate technology, managerial machinery, and financial procedures that such an approach implied. They were encouraged to do so by the international aid agencies, which argued that this approach—service sector by service sector, and project by project—would promote technical efficiency, make it easier to quantify needs and deficiencies, utilize local engineering skills, produce perceptible and politically acceptable results in the short term, and facilitate the identification of beneficiaries and the recovery of costs.

The Sectoral Response

The first response of many Asian cities was to address their water supply and drainage problems and to provide housing. Typically, these cities undertook large-scale projects that were formulated, financed, and managed sectorally by special housing, water, and sanitation or other public works authorities with either regional or local jurisdiction. Their powers and finances were defined in special statutes, and from the outset they tended to be independent of city councils or municipalities. Some metropolitan areas set up special authorities for subsectoral purposes, such as sites and services projects or slum upgrading within the housing sector.

The sectoral response to the metropolitan challenge was successful in many respects. Although social and economic issues received relatively little attention, no city succumbed to the onslaught of urbanization. Even Calcutta—of which an international team of experts had said in 1966, ''We have not seen human degradation on a comparable scale in any other city in the world''[3]—not only survived but began to rehabilitate itself in the early 1970s. Nevertheless, some institutional, financial, and political weaknesses in this response soon became evident.

3. Concluding Statement, International Planning Seminar on Calcutta Metropolitan Plan, Calcutta, 1966.

First, the number of public corporations, statutory bodies, and parastatal agencies (that is, statutory or other types of public organizations formed by the government for special purposes) created in each sector mounted rapidly. In Calcutta, where the Metropolitan District was already fragmented into thirty-three municipalities, thirty-seven nonmunicipal urban units, two improvement trusts, and two city corporations, the initial effort to improve the infrastructure included the creation of yet another water, sewerage, and drainage authority. The planners had also proposed a series of functional authorities (see the Calcutta city profile, Part II). By the end of the 1960s, many Asian countries had set up special provincial or national housing authorities to undertake large-scale programs for building new houses in metropolitan cities such as Madras, Bangkok, and Manila (see the relevant city profiles in Part II). Some examples of sectoral authorities are the water supply companies formed in Jakarta; the Metropolitan Water Authority in Bangkok; the Metropolitan Water Supply and Sewerage Board in Manila; and the Metropolitan Transport authorities in Bangkok, Manila, and Jakarta.

These special bodies were mainly concerned with financing and installing capital works or with handling certain aspects of service systems. (In Karachi and Madras, for example, new water supply projects were confined to headworks and primary distribution, whereas existing municipal governments were responsible for secondary distribution and house connections.) Traditional local governments looked after most of the capital assets created and the day-to-day operation of the upgraded consumer service. Yet little if any attempt was made to ensure that these governments would be able to muster the greatly enlarged financial, administrative, and technical resources needed to discharge the duties thrust upon them, and thus maintenance deficiencies soon became a serious problem for all. In sum, because of the emphasis on short-term sectoral plans, projects, and special authorities, insufficient attention was given to the long-term impact on existing institutions, other sectors, and the overall availability of resources.

Furthermore, as the developed countries had already discovered, the proliferation of new special authorities tended to enhance the role of the appointed professional in urban management rather than that of the elected representative.[4] Not only was a consensus of opinion more difficult to obtain than in the premetropolitan city, but it was arguably a luxury to be forgone in the face of massive urban problems demanding urgent attention. The issue of public access and participation thus remained low on the list of priorities and was generally unresolved, except, for example, in Tokyo (because of the special, prefectural and federal status of its metropolitan government) and in Singapore (which had become a city-state in 1965).

Problems of interagency relations at the metropolitan level multiplied as the web of authority grew more complex, both functionally and territorially.

4. See, for example, L. Wingo, ed., *Reform of Metropolitan Government* (Washington, D.C.: Resources for the Future, 1972), pp. 36–38.

Since so many of the special bodies were created at the national or provincial level of government, there was little intersectoral coordination either in formulating policies or executing projects. The metropolitanwide raising, allocation, and programming of capital investment, sector by sector and agency by agency, became increasingly difficult, too. For the same reason, within the broad functional sectors themselves, a hiatus became evident between pricing or operating policies and new investments. For instance, in Calcutta, there was little coordination between the construction of road improvements and the expansion, routing, or intermodal adjustments of the bus fleet. Similar intrasectoral distortions occurred in Jakarta's road-passenger system and persisted in service and fleet operations in Bombay, Madras, and Bangkok.

The Multisectoral Response

Because of these interagency problems, during the past decade or so more and more attention has focused on the need for an additional, multisectoral response to the metropolitan challenge. An early example of this kind of response was the establishment of the Calcutta Metropolitan Planning Organization (CMPO) in 1961 as an advisory, noncorporate agency of the West Bengal state government. But this model has not found favor elsewhere in South and East Asia. Although its Basic Development Plan of 1966 had laid the foundations for the intersectoral coordination of programs and projects, the CMPO was only a planning instrument and wielded no executive or financial powers. Thus, the typical response in Pakistan, India, the Philippines, and Sri Lanka was to set up strong, command-type development authorities with metropolitanwide jurisdictions. These entities were given the power to formulate multisectoral programs and budgets and to fund, coordinate, and supervise their implementation by and through the sectoral and local authorities. Some examples are the Karachi Development Authority (created in 1962), the Calcutta Metropolitan Development Authority (1970), the Madras Metropolitan Development Authority (1973), the Bombay Metropolitan Region Development Authority and Metropolitan Manila Commission (1975), and the Sri Lanka Urban Development Authority for Colombo and other urban areas (1978).

The initial emphasis on intersectoral coordination and supervision has now given way, however, to a direct involvement in sectoral implementation. In many cases such a refocusing of operations has led these authorities to neglect their multisectoral planning, programming, and budgeting responsibilities. In Calcutta, for example, the Development Authority has increasingly assumed the responsibilities of large sectoral agencies, including the management of the Metropolitan Water and Sanitation Authority and the Howrah Improvement Trust; it absorbed the CMPO and until recently was operating as a public works agency under the control of the State Public Works (Metropolitan) Department. In Karachi, the Development Authority has always been in charge of project implementation and until 1984 it was the metropolitan bulk-water supply agency. The Metropolitan Region Development Authority of Bombay has also been drawn into sectoral project roles despite comprehensive legislation providing it with a representative metropolitan board to undertake goal setting, policy and program formulation, and interagency coordination. In spite of the thorough reorganization it underwent in 1983, the Authority's presence is yet to be felt in metropolitan policy.

Although the Metropolitan Manila Commission initially concentrated on multisectoral capital budgeting throughout the city and also undertook a number of studies and provided technical assistance in the spheres of taxation and administrative reform for the local governments, it too eventually assumed some sectoral responsibilities such as garbage collection and disposal and traffic control. Similarly, in Madras the Metropolitan Development Authority originally concentrated on assembling a multisectoral urban development program, seeking the resources needed for program execution, and performing an important staff function for the state government by providing advice on the allocation of public investment to projects and agencies active in the metropolitan area. In this case, however, efforts have continued to focus on interagency coordination and technical support for program implementation, in spite of growing involvement in land use control and implementation of some special projects such as new towns in the metropolitan periphery. But its activities have been atypical.

Where development authorities have increasingly assumed the responsibilities of sectoral agencies or moved into project implementation themselves, they have failed to bridge the gap between the institutions responsible for creating assets and those responsible for maintaining and improving them. Furthermore, they have tended not only to foster centralization of power (both functionally and territorially), but also to undermine still further traditional local governments already weakened by the loss of sectoral responsibilities, finances, and manpower to the special ad hoc authorities. As a result, sensitivity to locally expressed needs at the submetropolitan level has declined; another more common problem, however, is that there is less public access to and public participation in urban management.[5]

Experiments in Metropolitan Government

An alternative multisectoral response has been to create metropolitan governments with special provincial powers and status. Such governments have been established in Tokyo, Jakarta (1964), Karachi (1973), Bangkok (1972), and Manila (1975). Their performance has been mixed.

The Bangkok Metropolitan Administration, for example, was created as a metropolitan government with an elected assembly and governor. Six

5. See Harry J. Friedman, "Other Asia," in *International Handbook on Local Government Reorganization*, ed. Donald C. Rowat (Westport, Conn.: Greenwood Press, 1980).

years later its autonomy was severely curtailed, and since then it has been engaged mainly in looking after street cleaning, street lighting, primary education, and health care services normally handled by more localized municipal authorities. Sectoral organizations created for housing, electricity, industrial estates, and water works have continued to act independently, programming and executing their own major capital investments. Similarly, Karachi's Metropolitan Corporation has a limited range of municipal functions; furthermore, its performance has been adversely affected by a fragmented organization and inadequate revenue base, and its relationship with the Development Authority has been ambiguous. Although the Metropolitan Manila Commission is sometimes referred to as a metropolitan government, its responsibilities continue to be restricted to only a few capital programs that are metropolitan in scope.

By contrast, Tokyo's metropolitan government exercises the powers of both a city and a prefecture over twenty-three special wards, seventeen cities, twelve towns, and one village. Not only has the metropolitan organization provided for widespread public representation and participation (including a 120-member metropolitan assembly), but it has also enabled the metropolitan government to control and supervise nonnational sectoral authorities as well as submetropolitan local governments units. Only recently has a problem developed between agencies (outside of transportation), because the population has spread into adjacent prefectures.[6]

A similar problem has arisen in Jakarta, where the population has begun to spill over into West Java province. The Special Capital Territory of Jakarta (known as DKI-Jakarta) was created in 1964 to give the city government provincial powers, greater revenue resources, and better access to central funds and technical assistance. As a province, it also gained a BAPPEDA or state-level planning organization and a centrally appointed governor with powers of coordination and control over all central units functioning in the metropolitan area. Even so, Jakarta is plagued by deficiencies in civic services, and its financial resources are dwindling. Despite the government's provincial status, new sectoral authorities have been established to handle some of the city's problems. In 1973, for example, the urban expansion into adjacent areas of West Java beyond the jurisdiction of the Jakarta governorate led to the creation of the JABOTABEK Development Planning Board, which is responsible for metropolitan planning in these areas.

Persistent Problems

Even though a substantial effort has been made to cope with the metropolitan challenge in South and East Asia, considerable institutional, financial, and planning problems persist in all the cities of the region. By and

6. See, for example, Masamichi Royama, "Tokyo and Osaka," in *Great Cities of the World*, ed. W. R. Robson and D. E. Regan (London: Allen and Unwin, 1971).

large, these problems stem from the fact that most metropolitan cities of this region are passing through a phase of urbanization in which they are growing much faster than other national or provincial centers and are far surpassing them in size. Furthermore, their resident population is increasing at a high rate, and they are expanding rapidly into largely rural hinterlands. Thus, their economies have to sustain and service ever-widening areas as well as ever-increasing populations. In the process, their economic, financial, and institutional problems are being exacerbated. Because of their great national or provincial importance, however, basic questions about their economic development lie beyond their purview. And, for much the same reason, national policies tend to restrict industrial and social investment in them, in the pursuit of more balanced interprovincial development and the dispersal of industry and population. Since the 1960s India, for example, has consistently enforced a ban on the location of new, large-scale industries in its five largest metropolitan complexes. Despite these restrictions, cities such as Calcutta, Bangkok, and Manila have continued to act as the principal centers of medical care, higher education, and professional and financial services for their expanding hinterlands. Yet they are not permitted to make use of the financial resources of their hinterlands and instead must rely on their own resources to support such services.

Mainly because of the primacy of the region's metropolitan cities and the absence of a metropolitan ethos, the fundamental issues of public access to, participation in, and control over their management continue to await, and possibly defy, resolution in many cases. The organizational experiments carried out thus far demonstrate a deep reluctance on the part of national and provincial governments in the region to confer significant political and financial powers on metropolitan institutions. Existing forms of metropolitan government appear to be inapplicable to such fast-growing and expanding urban agglomerations and inappropriate for dealing with conflicts between national and city objectives. The political and economic dominance of these metropolitan complexes thus distinguishes them from the cities of developed countries and also renders solutions to their problems more complicated.

One aim of the present study is to assess the institutions that eight metropolitan cities of South and East Asia have established in recent years to resolve these persistent issues of metropolitan management. The cities reviewed are Bangkok, Bombay, Calcutta, Colombo, Jakarta, Karachi, Madras, and Manila. Major exercises have been undertaken in all of them, particularly since the 1960s, including comprehensive planning in Calcutta and Manila, the creation of metropolitan governments in Jakarta and Bangkok, and the setting up of urban development authorities in Bombay, Karachi, and Colombo. The similarity of approach has been significant, although there has been no grand international design to that end. In all of the eight cities save Colombo, the World Bank has been concerned with the funding of sectoral or multisectoral projects; nevertheless, until the 1981 seminar on metropolitan management held in Manila by the Asian Development Bank and the Economic Development Institute, no conscious attempt had been made to enable these cities to begin to share their experience.

In addition to comparing the initiatives taken in selected cities, the study explores possible new directions of response to the tasks and constraints facing the region's metropolitan managements. These new directions emphasize managerial processes and operating styles rather than the creation of new institutions and organizational structures. They are based on the belief that urban management should be concerned with the incremental, routine provision and maintenance of essential public works and services as much as with innovative planning and execution of development projects. They also recognize the special constraints to which urban management is subjected by the relative scarcity of available finance and manpower, the particular importance of political and social concerns, and the intricate and complex nature of the government of metropolitan cities in South and East Asia. Part II of this study presents detailed profiles of the eight cities selected.

Table 1-1. Trends in Size and Distribution of Cities, 1950–2000: Developed and Developing Countries

Area and size group (population in thousands)	Number of cities						
	1950	1960	1970	1975	1980	1990	2000
World total							
5,000	6	12	20	21	25	40	50
2,000–4,999	24	31	39	55	71	101	133
1,000–1,999	41	67	98	105	128	101	222
500–999	101	136	179	220	269	303	396
200–499	281	355	554	659	730	877	1,059
100–199	453	654	841	907	998	1,192	1,460
Developed nations							
5,000	5 ⎫	10	11	11	11 ⎫	15	16
2,000–4,999	15 ⎬48	16	20	24	31 ⎬109	41	50
1,000–1,999	28 ⎭	38	54	56	67 ⎭	77	84
500–999	61	22	94	110	116	131	152
200–499	173	221	288	327	353	387	406
100–199	275	350	437	453	453	532	553
Developing nations							
5,000	1 ⎫	2	9	10	15 ⎫	25	43
2,000–4,999	9 ⎬23	15	19	31	40 ⎬116	60	83
1,000–1,999	13 ⎭	29	44	49	61 ⎭	104	138
500–999	40	54	80	110	131	172	206
200–499	108	104	266	332	377	490	655
100–199	178	304	404	454	515	660	897
	Population in cities (thousands)						
World total							
5,000	47,364	95,951	167,219	195,761	251,519	414,403	646,485
2,000–4,999	73,026	92,219	114,011	161,706	106,072	297,200	403,079
1,000–1,999	56,314	94,591	137,429	148,378	173,533	243,965	309,962
500–999	69,062	95,949	124,336	153,646	171,701	208,403	273,641
200–499	84,568	117,838	168,667	198,040	222,250	276,458	330,575
100–199	61,713	90,845	118,858	125,503	138,130	167,711	203,788
Developed nations							
5,000	41,583	83,019	103,145	112,169	121,354	159,486	182,552
2,000–4,999	48,306	43,744	57,659	70,485	90,619	115,850	147,637
1,000–1,999	39,434	54,272	75,016	79,590	91,504	103,835	114,603
500–999	41,630	56,839	68,715	78,752	81,083	89,456	103,784
200–499	53,286	68,339	86,955	99,018	106,354	120,803	128,268
100–199	37,535	48,950	61,698	63,147	66,168	73,296	79,487
Developing nations							
5,000	5,781	12,932	64,074	83,592	130,165	254,917	463,933
2,000–4,999	24,720	48,475	56,352	91,221	115,453	181,331	255,442
1,000–1,999	16,880	40,319	62,413	68,788	82,029	140,130	195,359
500–999	27,432	39,110	55,621	75,096	90,618	118,947	169,857
200–499	31,262	49,499	81,702	99,022	115,896	153,655	202,307
100–199	24,178	41,895	57,160	62,356	71,962	94,017	124,301

Source: United Nations, Department of Economic and Social Affairs, *Trends and Prospects in the Population of Urban Agglomerations 1950–2000*, ESA/P/WP50 (New York, November 1975).

Table 1-2. Number of Cities by Size in Developing Regions

Size group (population in thousands)	1980	1985	2000	2025
4,000 +	22	28	50	114
2,000–3,999	28	30	72	145
1,000–1,999	69	88	157	227
500–999	147	177	243	n.a.
250–499	255	274	n.a.	n.a.
100–249	414	n.a.	n.a.	n.a.

n.a. Not available.

Note: The variations between the figures in this table and those in table 1-1 are due to changes in administrative boundaries and intercensal definitions.

Source: United Nations, *Estimates and Projections of Urban, Rural and City Populations, 1950–2025: The 1982 Assessment* (New York, January 1985).

Table 1-3. Population Trends, 1950–2000: Urban Agglomerations Expected to Have Populations Greater than 5 Million by 2000

City (country)	Population (millions)			City population in 1950 at a percentage of	
	1950	1990	2000	National population	Total urban population
Africa					
Alexandria (Egypt)	0.9	2.9	5.6	6.9	13.0
Cairo (Egypt)	2.4	5.4	16.4	20.0	39.0
Casablanca (Morocco)	0.6	2.3	5.2	11.3	27.0
Kinshasa (Zaire)	0.2	3.0	9.1	10.7	35.0
Lagos (Nigeria)	0.3	2.9	9.4	4.0	20.0
Latin America					
Belo Horizonte (Brazil)	0.4	2.6	5.7	2.1	3.0
Bogotá (Colombia)	0.7	4.4	9.5	14.6	22.0
Buenos Aires (Argentina)	1.5	10.4	14.0	38.4	47.0
Caracas (Venezuela)	0.7	3.2	6.0	22.7	76.0
Guadalajara (Mexico)	0.4	2.6	6.2	3.7	6.0
Lima-Callao (Peru)	0.6	5.2	12.1	29.4	49.0
Mexico City (Mexico)	2.9	13.9	31.6	19.9	30.0
Rio De Janeiro (Brazil)	2.9	10.0	19.4	7.9	12.0
Santiago (Chile)	1.3	3.5	5.1	31.3	36.0
São Paulo (Brazil)	2.5	12.5	26.0	9.9	16.0
North America					
Chicago (United States)	4.9	7.5	9.3	3.3	4.0
Detroit (United States)	2.8	4.5	5.7	2.0	3.0
Los Angeles (United States)	4.0	10.7	14.8	4.8	6.8
New York (United States)	12.3	17.9	22.2	8.0	10.0
Philadelphia (United States)	2.9	4.5	5.6	2.0	3.0

| City (country) | Population (millions) | | | City population in 1950 at a percentage of | |
	1950	1990	2000	National population	Total urban population
East Asia					
Baotou (China)	n.a.	2.0	5.3	0.2	1.0
Beijing (China)	2.2	10.2	19.1	1.1	4.0
Hong Kong (Hong Kong)	1.6	4.3	5.5	96.0	100.0
Lanzhou (China)	0.1	2.4	5.1	0.3	1.0
Osaka-Kobe (Japan)	3.8	9.7	12.6	8.2	11.0
Pusan (Rep. of Korea)	0.5	2.9	5.1	7.8	15.0
Seoul (Rep. of Korea)	1.0	9.4	18.7	25.1	27.0
Shanghai (China)	5.8	12.0	19.2	1.3	5.0
Tianjin (China)	2.4	4.7	7.5	0.5	2.0
Tokyo-Yokohama (Japan)	6.7	19.7	26.1	16.7	21.0
Wuban (China)	1.1	3.4	5.8	0.4	1.0
South Asia					
Ahmedabad (India)	0.9	2.5	5.5	0.4	2.0
Ankara (Turkey)	0.3	2.3	5.3	5.1	11.0
Baghdad (Iraq)	0.6	4.6	10.9	35.1	53.0
Bangalore (India)	0.8	2.5	5.4	0.4	2.0
Bangkok-Thonburi (Thailand)	1.0	4.3	11.0	8.7	48.0
Bombay (India)	2.9	8.7	19.1	1.3	5.0
Calcutta (India)	4.4	9.6	19.7	1.4	6.0
Delhi (India)	1.4	5.7	13.2	0.8	4.0
Dhaka (Bangladesh)	0.4	2.1	5.9	2.0	32.0
Faisalabad (Pakistan)	0.2	2.0	6.2	2.4	8.0
Hanoi (Viet Nam)	0.2	1.9	5.1	3.9	20.0
Ho Chi Minh City (Viet Nam)	1.0	2.4	5.1	4.9	26.0
Istanbul (Turkey)	1.0	4.0	8.3	8.9	19.0
Jakarta (Indonesia)	1.6	7.2	16.9	4.6	22.0
Karachi (Pakistan)	1.0	6.0	15.9	7.2	24.0
Lahore (Pakistan)	0.8	3.1	7.7	3.7	12.0
Madras (India)	1.4	4.7	10.4	0.7	3.0
Manila (Philippines)	1.5	5.6	12.7	10.7	28.0
Rangoon (Burma)	0.7	3.1	7.4	8.8	35.0
Surabaja (Indonesia)	0.7	2.3	5.0	1.5	7.0
Tehran (Iran)	1.0	5.8	13.8	15.1	32.0
Europe					
Leningrad (U.S.S.R.)	2.6	4.6	6.1	1.7	3.0
London (United Kingdom)	10.2	11.0	12.7	19.0	25.0
Madrid (Spain)	1.6	4.1	5.9	11.0	15.0
Milan (Italy)	3.6	6.5	8.3	11.5	17.0
Moscow (U.S.S.R.)	4.8	8.2	10.6	3.1	5.0
Paris (France)	5.4	9.9	12.3	18.0	23.0
Rhein-Ruhr (Fed. Rep. of Germany)	6.8	9.9	11.3	16.0	19.0

n.a. Not available.
Source: See table 1-1.

Table 1-4. World's 35 Largest Agglomerations, Ranked by Population in Millions, 1950–2000

Rank	Agglomeration and country	Population in 1950	Agglomeration and country	Population in 1955	Agglomeration and country	Population in 1960
1	New York/Northeastern New Jersey, U.S.A.	12.4	New York/Northeastern New Jersey, U.S.A.	13.3	New York/Northeastern New Jersey, U.S.A.	14.2
2	London, United Kingdom	10.4	Shanghai, China	10.6	London, United Kingdom	10.7
3	Shanghai, China	10.3	London, United Kingdom	10.5	Tokyo/Yokohama, Japan	10.7
4	Rhein-Ruhr, Fed. Rep. of Germany	6.9	Tokyo/Yokohama, Japan	8.6	Shanghai, China	10.7
5	Tokyo/Yokohama, Japan	6.7	Rhein-Ruhr, Fed. Rep. of Germany	7.7	Rhein-Ruhr, Fed. Rep. of Germany	8.7
6	Beijing, China	6.7	Beijing, China	7.1	Beijing, China	7.3
7	Paris, France	5.5	Paris, France	6.3	Paris, France	7.2
8	Tianjin, China	5.4	Greater Buenos Aires, Argentina	6.1	Greater Buenos Aires, Argentina	6.9
9	Greater Buenos Aires, Argentina	5.3	Tianjin, China	5.8	Los Angeles/Long Beach, U.S.A.	6.6
10	Chicago/Northwestern Indiana, U.S.A.	5.0	Moscow, U.S.S.R.	5.5	Moscow, U.S.S.R.	6.3
11	Moscow, U.S.S.R.	4.8	Chicago/Northwestern Indiana, U.S.A.	5.5	Chicago/Northwestern Indiana, U.S.A.	6.0
12	Calcutta, India	4.4	Los Angeles/Long Beach, U.S.A.	5.2	Tianjin, China	6.0
13	Los Angeles/Long Beach, U.S.A.	4.1	Calcutta, India	4.9	Osaka/Kobe, Japan	5.7
14	Osaka/Kobe, Japan	3.8	Osaka/Kobe, Japan	4.7	Calcutta, India	5.5
15	Milan, Italy	3.6	Rio de Janeiro, Brazil	4.2	Mexico City, Mexico	5.2
16	Rio de Janeiro, Brazil	3.5	Milan, Italy	4.0	Rio de Janeiro, Brazil	5.1
17	Mexico City, Mexico	3.1	Mexico City, Mexico	4.0	São Paulo, Brazil	4.8
18	Philadelphia/New Jersey, U.S.A.	3.0	São Paulo, Brazil	3.7	Milan, Italy	4.5
19	Greater Bombay, India	2.9	Greater Bombay, India	3.4	Greater Bombay, India	4.0
20	Detroit, U.S.A.	2.8	Philadelphia/New Jersey, U.S.A.	3.3	Cairo/Giza/Imbaba, Egypt	3.7
21	São Paulo, Brazil	2.8	Detroit, U.S.A.	3.2	Philadelphia/New Jersey, U.S.A.	3.7
22	Naples, Italy	2.8	Leningrad, U.S.S.R.	3.0	Detroit, U.S.A.	3.6
23	Leningrad, U.S.S.R.	2.6	Cairo/Giza/Imbaba, Egypt	3.0	Leningrad, U.S.S.R.	3.5
24	Manchester, United Kingdom	2.5	Naples, Italy	3.0	Naples, Italy	3.2
25	Birmingham, United Kingdom	2.5	Birmingham, United Kingdom	2.6	Jakarta, Indonesia	2.8
26	Cairo/Giza/Imbaba, Egypt	2.5	Manchester, United Kingdom	2.5	Hong Kong	2.7
27	Boston, U.S.A.	2.3	Shenyang, China	2.3	Birmingham, United Kingdom	2.7
28	Shenyang, China	2.3	Boston, U.S.A.	2.3	Manchester, United Kingdom	2.5
29	West Berlin, Fed. Rep. of Germany	2.2	San Francisco/Oakland, U.S.A.	2.2	Shenyang, China	2.5
30	San Francisco/Oakland, U.S.A.	2.0	Jakarta, Indonesia	2.2	San Francisco/Oakland, U.S.A.	2.5
31	Leeds-Bradford, United Kingdom	1.9	Hong Kong	2.2	Katowice, Poland	2.4
32	Glasgow, United Kingdom	1.9	Berlin, Fed. Rep. of Germany	2.2	Boston, U.S.A.	2.4
33	Jakarta, Indonesia	1.8	Katowice, Poland	2.1	Seoul, Rep. of Korea	2.4
34	Hamburg, Fed. Rep. of Germany	1.8	Madrid, Spain	2.0	Manila, Philippines	2.3
35	Wien, Austria	1.8	Rome, Italy	1.9	Madrid, Spain	2.3

Rank	Agglomeration and country	Population in 1965	Agglomeration and country	Population in 1970	Agglomeration and country	Population in 1975
1	New York/Northeastern New Jersey, U.S.A.	15.4	New York/Northeastern New Jersey, U.S.A.	16.3	Tokyo/Yokohama, Japan	16.4
2	Tokyo/Yokohama, Japan	12.6	Tokyo/Yokohama, Japan	14.9	New York/Northeastern New Jersey, U.S.A.	15.9
3	Shanghai, China	10.8	Shanghai, China	11.4	Mexico City, Mexico	12.1
4	London, United Kingdom	10.8	London, United Kingdom	10.6	Shanghai, China	11.6
5	Rhein-Ruhr, Fed. Rep. of Germany	9.2	Rhein-Ruhr, Fec. Rep. of Germany	9.3	London, United Kingdom	10.3
6	Paris, France	8.0	Mexico City, Mexico	9.2	São Paulo, Brazil	10.3
7	Greater Buenos Aires, Argentina	7.7	Greater Buenos Aires, Argentina	8.5	Rhein-Ruhr, Fed. Rep. of Germany	9.3
8	Beijing, China	7.6	Los Angeles/Long Beach, U.S.A.	8.4	Greater Buenos Aires, Argentina	9.3
9	Los Angeles/Long Beach, U.S.A.	7.5	Paris, France	8.3	Los Angeles/Long Beach, U.S.A.	9.0
10	Mexico City, Mexico	6.9	Beijing, China	8.3	Beijing, China	8.9
11	Moscow, U.S.S.R.	6.8	São Paulo, Brazil	8.2	Paris, France	8.6
12	Osaka/Kobe, Japan	6.7	Osaka/Kobe, Japan	7.6	Calcutta, India	8.2
13	Chicago/Northwestern Indiana, U.S.A.	6.4	Rio de Janeiro, Brazil	7.2	Rio de Janeiro, Brazil	8.2
14	São Paulo, Brazil	6.4	Moscow, U.S.S.R.	7.1	Osaka/Kobe, Japan	8.0
15	Calcutta, India	6.3	Calcutta, India	7.1	Moscow, U.S.S.R.	8.0
16	Tianjin, China	6.2	Tianjin, China	6.9	Tianjin, China	7.6
17	Rio de Janeiro, Brazil	6.1	Chicago/Northwestern Indiana, U.S.A.	6.8	Greater Bombay, India	7.4
18	Milan, Italy	5.0	Greater Bombay India	5.9	Seoul, Rep. of Korea	7.2
19	Greater Bombay, India	4.9	Milan, Italy	5.6	Chicago/Northwestern Indiana, U.S.A.	7.0
20	Cairo/Giza/Imbaba, Egypt	4.6	Seoul, Rep. of Korea	5.4	Milan, Italy	6.8
21	Philadelphia/New Jersey, U.S.A.	3.9	Cairo/Giza/Imbaba, Egypt	5.4	Cairo/Giza/Imbaba, Egypt	6.2
22	Detroit, U.S.A.	3.8	Jakarta, Indonesia	4.5	Jakarta, Indonesia	5.5
23	Leningrad, U.S.S.R.	3.8	Philadelphia/New Jersey, U.S.A.	4.0	Manila, Philippines	5.0
24	Jakarta, Indonesia	3.5	Detroit, U.S.A.	4.0	Delhi, India	4.6
25	Seoul, Rep. of Korea	3.5	Leningrad, U.S.S.R.	4.0	Leningrad, U.S.S.R.	4.3
26	Naples, Italy	3.4	Delhi, India	3.6	Tehran, Iran	4.3
27	Hong Kong	3.3	Naples, Italy	3.6	Philadelphia/New Jersey, U.S.A.	4.1
28	Manila, Philippines	2.9	Manila, Philippines	3.6	Karachi, Pakistan	4.0
29	Delhi, India	2.9	Hong Kong	3.5	Madrid, Spain	4.0
30	Birmingham, United Kingdom	2.8	Madrid, Spain	3.3	Hong Kong	4.0
31	Madrid, Spain	2.8	Tehran, Iran	3.3	Detroit, U.S.A.	3.9
32	San Francisco/Oakland, U.S.A.	2.7	Bangkok/Thonburi, Thailand	3.3	Istanbul, Turkey	3.9
33	Bangkok/Thonburi, Thailand	2.7	Karachi, Pakistan	3.1	Bangkok/Thonburi, Thailand	3.9
34	Shenyang, China	2.6	Madras, India	3.1	Naples, Italy	3.9
35	Katowice, Poland	2.6	San Francisco/Oakland, U.S.A.	3.0	Baghdad, Iran	3.8

(Table continues on the following page.)

17

Table 1-4 (continued)

Rank	Agglomeration and country	Population in 1980	Agglomeration and country	Population in 1985	Agglomeration and country	Population in 1990
1	Tokyo/Yokohama, Japan	17.0	Mexico City, Mexico	18.1	Mexico City, Mexico	21.3
2	New York/Northeastern New Jersey, U.S.A.	15.6	Tokyo/Yokohama, Japan	17.2	São Paulo, Brazil	18.8
3	Mexico City, Mexico	15.0	São Paulo, Brazil	15.9	Tokyo/Yokohama, Japan	17.2
4	São Paulo, Brazil	12.8	New York/Northeastern New Jersey, U.S.A.	15.3	New York/Northeastern New Jersey, U.S.A.	15.3
5	Shanghai, China	11.8	Shanghai, China	11.8	Calcutta, India	12.6
6	Greater Buenos Aires, Argentina	10.1	Calcutta, India	11.0	Shanghai, China	12.0
7	London, United Kingdom	10.0	Greater Buenos Aires, Argentina	10.9	Greater Bombay, India	11.9
8	Calcutta, India	9.5	Rio de Janeiro, Brazil	10.4	Greater Buenos Aires, Argentina	11.7
9	Los Angeles/Long Beach, U.S.A.	9.5	Seoul, Rep. of Korea	10.2	Seoul, Rep. of Korea	11.5
10	Rhein-Ruhr, Fed. Rep. of Germany	9.3	Greater Bombay, India	10.1	Rio de Janeiro, Brazil	11.4
11	Rio de Janeiro, Brazil	9.2	Los Angeles/Long Beach, U.S.A.	10.0	Los Angeles/Long Beach, U.S.A.	10.5
12	Beijing, China	9.1	London, United Kingdom	9.8	Cairo/Giza/Imbaba, Egypt	10.0
13	Paris, France	8.8	Beijing, China	9.2	London, United Kingdom	9.5
14	Greater Bombay, India	8.5	Rhein-Ruhr, Fed. Rep. of Germany	9.2	Beijing, China	9.5
15	Seoul, Rep. of Korea	8.5	Paris, France	9.2	Jakarta, Indonesia	9.3
16	Moscow, U.S.S.R.	8.2	Moscow, U.S.S.R.	8.7	Moscow, U.S.S.R.	9.2
17	Osaka/Kobe, Japan	8.0	Cairo/Giza/Imbaba, Egypt	8.5	Delhi, India	9.2
18	Tianjin, China	7.7	Osaka/Kobe, Japan	8.0	Rhein-Ruhr, Fed. Rep. of Germany	9.1
19	Cairo/Giza/Imbaba, Egypt	7.3	Jakarta, Indonesia	7.9	Paris, France	9.0
20	Chicago/Northwestern Indiana, U.S.A.	6.8	Tianjin, China	7.8	Tehran, Iran	9.0
21	Jakarta, Indonesia	6.7	Delhi, India	7.4	Baghdad, Iraq	8.9
22	Milan, Italy	6.6	Baghdad, Iraq	7.2	Istanbul, Turkey	8.4
23	Manila, Philippines	6.0	Tehran, Iran	7.2	Manila, Philippines	8.3
24	Delhi, India	5.9	Manila, Philippines	7.0	Karachi, Pakistan	8.2
25	Baghdad, Iraq	5.7	Milan, Italy	7.0	Tianjin, China	8.0
26	Tehran, Iran	5.6	Chicago/Northwestern Indiana, U.S.A.	6.8	Osaka/Kobe, Japan	7.8
27	Istanbul, Turkey	5.3	Istanbul, Turkey	6.8	Milan, Italy	7.3
28	Karachi, Pakistan	5.2	Karachi, Pakistan	6.8	Chicago/Northwestern Indiana, U.S.A.	6.9
29	Leningrad, U.S.S.R.	4.7	Lima-Callo, Peru	5.7	Lima-Callo, Peru	6.8
30	Bangkok/Thonburi, Thailand	4.6	Bangkok/Thonburi, Thailand	5.5	Dhaka, Bangladesh	6.5
31	Lima-Callo, Peru	4.6	Madras, India	5.2	Bangkok/Thonburi, Thailand	6.5
32	Madrid, Spain	4.6	Hong Kong	5.1	Madras, India	6.1
33	Hong Kong	4.6	Madrid, Spain	5.1	Kinshasa, Zaire	5.8
34	Madras, India	4.4	Leningrad, U.S.S.R.	5.1	Hong Kong	5.6
35	Philadelphia/New Jersey, U.S.A.	4.1	Dhaka, Bangladesh	4.9	Madrid, Spain	5.5

Rank	Agglomeration and country	Population in 1995	Agglomeration and country	Population in 2000
1	Mexico City, Mexico	24.2	Mexico City, Mexico	26.3
2	São Paulo, Brazil	21.5	São Paulo, Brazil	24.0
3	Tokyo/Yokohama, Japan	17.1	Tokyo/Yokohama, Japan	17.1
4	New York/Northeastern New Jersey, U.S.A.	15.3	Calcutta, India	16.6
5	Calcutta, India	14.5	Greater Bombay, India	16.0
6	Greater Bombay, India	13.8	New York/Northeastern New Jersey, U.S.A.	15.5
7	Seoul, Rep. of Korea	12.7	Seoul, Rep. of Korea	13.5
8	Shanghai, China	12.5	Shanghai, China	13.5
9	Greater Beunos Aires, Argentina	12.5	Rio de Janeiro, Brazil	13.3
10	Rio de Janeiro, Brazil	12.3	Delhi, India	13.3
11	Cairo/Giza/Imbaba, Egypt	11.5	Greater Buenos Aires, Argentina	13.2
12	Delhi, India	11.1	Cairo/Giza/Imbaba, Egypt	13.2
13	Jakarta, Indonesia	11.0	Jakarta, Indonesia	12.8
14	Tehran, Iran	10.9	Baghdad, Iraq	12.8
15	Los Angeles/Long Beach, U.S.A.	10.9	Tehran, Iran	12.7
16	Baghdad, Iraq	10.8	Karachi, Pakistan	12.2
17	Istanbul, Turkey	10.2	Istanbul, Turkey	11.9
18	Karachi, Pakistan	10.1	Los Angeles/Long Beach, U.S.A.	11.2
19	Beijing, China	9.9	Dhaka, Bangladesh	11.2
20	Moscow, U.S.S.R.	9.7	Manila, Philippines	11.1
21	Manila, Philippines	9.7	Beijing, China	10.8
22	London, United Kingdom	9.3	Moscow, U.S.S.R.	10.1
23	Paris, France	9.1	Bangkok/Thonburi, Thailand	9.5
24	Rhein-Ruhr, Fed. Rep. of Germany	8.9	Tianjin, China	9.2
25	Dhaka, Bangladesh	8.6	Paris, France	9.2
26	Tianjin, China	8.5	Lima-Callo, Peru	9.1
27	Lima-Callo, Peru	8.0	London, United Kingdom	9.1
28	Bangkok/Thonburi, Thailand	7.8	Kinshasa, Zaire	8.9
29	Osaka/Kobe, Japan	7.7	Rhein-Ruhr, Fed. Rep. of Germany	8.6
30	Milan, Italy	7.5	Lagos, Nigeria	8.3
31	Kinshasa, Zaire	7.3	Madras, India	8.2
32	Madras, India	7.1	Bangalore, India	8.0
33	Chicago/Northwestern Indiana, U.S.A.	7.0	Osaka/Kobe, Japan	7.7
34	Bangalore, India	6.5	Milan, Italy	7.5
35	Lagos, Nigeria	6.4	Chicago/Northwestern Indiana, U.S.A.	7.2

Source: United Nations, *Estimates and Projections of Urban, Rural, and City Populations, 1950–2025: The 1982 Assessment* (New York, January 1985).

Table 1-5. *Selected Characteristics of Countries with Agglomerations Expected to Reach 5 Million by 2000*

| Country | Population 1980 (millions) | | Growth rate 1930–80 (percent) | | 1976 population of largest city as percentage of | | Gross domestic product 1976 (U.S. dollars) | | Income inequality (10 million rupees[a]) | |
	Total	In cities larger than 100,000	Total	In cities larger than 100,000	Population in next three largest cities	Total population	Total (millions)	Per capita	Regional (1976)	National
Africa										
Egypt	42.1	11.0	105	210	164	11.1	14.9	349	n.a.	0.436
Morocco	20.4	4.9	127	250	126	9.7	8.1	455	n.a.	n.a.
Nigeria	72.6	3.1	137	292	63	1.2	28.5	445	n.a.	n.a.
Zaire	28.0	1.9	146	533	405	3.4	3.7	145	n.a.	n.a.
North America										
United States	224.1	130.7	48	96	195	7.8	1,701.7	7,911	0.134	0.407
Latin America										
Argentina	27.1	16.5	58	312	155	39.0	47.4	1,844	0.313	0.411
Brazil	126.4	42.8	143	370	81	7.7	144.7	1,325	1.620	0.647
Chile	11.2	4.1	84	356	482	27.4	11.3	1,075	n.a.	0.376
Colombia	30.2	11.7	167	485	109	11.8	14.8	608	0.307	0.562
Mexico	70.0	23.8	171	386	263	17.8	79.1	1,270	0.534	0.583
Peru	17.7	4.2	113	367	338	18.4	13.4	840	n.a.	0.594
Venezuela	14.1	5.1	176	410	123	20.2	31.1	2,510	0.533	0.477
East Asia										
China	907.6	130.7	62	222	76	1.1	n.a.	n.a.	n.a.	n.a.
Hong Kong	4.5	4.5	125	181	—	100.0	9.2	2,099	n.a.	0.430
Japan	117.5	66.2	41	198	152	11.9	555.2	4,922	0.301	0.287
Korea, Rep. of	37.4	12.1	82	290	154	14.6	25.4	707	0.308	0.372

Southeast Asia									
Burma	35.2	87	140	188	4.4	3.5	113	n.a.	0.381
Indonesia	154.9	104	307	134	3.8	37.3	267	n.a.	0.453
Philippines	52.2	157	232	75	10.7	17.8	407	n.a.	0.466
Thailand	49.5	153	225	271	5.8	16.3	379	0.678	0.448
Viet Nam	48.6	116	154	163	4.4	7.6	156	n.a.	n.a.
Southwest Asia									
Iran	38.5	136	203	234	11.5	66.8	1,988	0.923	0.502
Iraq	13.1	152	400	199	14.3	15.7	1,363	n.a.	0.629
Turkey	45.4	118	394	98	7.4	41.1	999	n.a.	0.568
South Central Asia									
Bangladesh	92.5	232	n.a.	n.a.	n.a.	7.9	85	n.a.	n.a.
India	694.3	96	144	67	1.4	86.0	141	0.185	0.477
Pakistan	83.0	235	130	97	2.8	14.5	200	n.a.	0.330
Europe									
France	55.1	32	116	128	16.9	346.6	6,552	0.243	0.518
Germany, Fed. Rep. of	62.0	22	37	74	11.0	445.8	7,249	0.135	0.394
Italy	56.3	20	75	69	5.4	170.8	3,040	0.272	n.a.
Poland	35.3	41	88	70	7.3	98.2	2,856	n.a.	0.264
Spain	37.2	33	85	113	9.1	104.7	2,908	n.a.	0.393
United Kingdom	57.5	14	13	264	20.5	219.2	3,922	0.109	0.339
U.S.S.R.	268.1	49	125	97	2.9	708.2	2,759	n.a.	n.a.

— Not applicable.
n.a. Not available.
a. A rupee equals about US$0.80 in 1985 dollars.

Table 1-6. Profile Cities: Demographic Concentration, 1977

City	Metro-politan population (millions)	Total urban population of country (millions)	Metro-politan population as percentage of total urban population of country	National population (millions)	Metro-politan population as percentage of national population	Rate of population growth 1970–77	
						Metro-politan region	Country
Bangkok	4.8	8.1	60	43.8	11.0	5.0	2.9
Bombay	7.6	132.6	6	631.7	1.2	3.7	2.1
Calcutta	8.8	132.6	7	631.7	1.4	2.2	2.1
Colombo	2.1	3.5	60	14.1	14.9	2.9	1.7
Jakarta[a]	6.2	24.0	26	133.5	4.3	4.6	1.8
Karachi	5.0	19.5	26	74.9	6.6	5.0	3.1
Madras	4.4	132.6	3	631.7	0.7	4.0	2.1
Manila	5.3	15.1	35	44.5	12.0	3.8	2.7

a. DKI-Jakarta only (not JABOTABEK metropolitan region).
Source: World Bank data.

2

Tasks of Metropolitan Management

THE PRINCIPAL TASK of metropolitan management—to identify and attack the critical metropolitan issues—is easy enough to describe, but extremely difficult to carry out. Whether, at any particular time, management should emphasize the economic aspects of urban development; the spatial, social, or organizational aspects; the creation of new assets and services as opposed to the improvement of existing ones; or immediate or longer-term issues—all depends on the total situation. What that total situation is, however, cannot be fully determined through any existing managerial system. The task encompasses too many people and is too intricate, too susceptible to change, and too fraught with uncertainty to be readily discharged. Therefore, decisions on metropolitan goals and priorities ultimately resolve themselves into exercises in leadership, will, judgment, and intuition in which contemporary political and societal values become the final arbiters of choice.

Nevertheless, coping with growth, change, and uncertainty remains a central task of metropolitan management. It must strive progressively to improve its ability to understand and resolve the many problems posed by rapid urbanization, massive population increase, and radical social and economic transformations. An understanding of the principal tasks arising from these problems is a first step in the process of improvement.

Provision of Services

One important task of metropolitan management is to deliver essential services. Despite recent efforts to improve such services in the leading cities of South and East Asia, gross deficiencies still exist in sector after sector owing to the rapid growth and enormous size of these cities. Karachi, for example, now accounts for at least 25 percent of the population of Sind province, Manila for 41 percent of the total urban population of the Philippines, and Bangkok for 10 percent of the entire population of Thailand. The central problem here is that most urban dwellers belong to low-income groups (see table 2-1) or are very poor, and few can afford even the minimum of water, shelter, light, and sanitation needed to exist in the now crowded and congested urban areas. In Bangkok and Jakarta, for example, less than one-third of the inhabitants have house connections to the water supply system. Many systems were designed for a much smaller clientele and cannot meet the demands of today. One such system is Calcutta's sewerage network, which was installed in 1910 in the relatively wealthy central area of the old municipality. It must now serve a population twice the size of the one for which it was originally designed.

Another problem is that the real cost of providing city services has been rising rapidly. Many of these services are labor intensive and most are municipally operated. As a result, they have come under the influence of municipal labor unions, which recently have become well organized and have sought and won wage increases in keeping with provincial or national trends. Salaries thus constitute a high proportion of most municipal budgets. Obsolescence (with respect to both equipment and operating practices) coupled with inefficiency has added to unit costs. Aging water supply plants, leakage in the distribution networks, underutilization of garbage trucks, and poor maintenance of storm drainage all aptly illustrate the point. Moreover, cost recovery procedures have failed to keep in step, largely because consumer resistance to user charges is widespread, supplies are poorly measured, and dues seldom collected. In Bangkok, for example, 70 percent of the water meters do not function, and in Calcutta supplies have never been metered on a significant scale.

Table 2-1. Profile City Countries: Income and GNP, 1980
(U.S. dollars)

City and country	Per capita income group[a] (1979)	GNP (millions)	Per capita GNP	GNP annual growth rate[b] 1970–79 (percent)
Bangkok, Thailand	330–759	31,140	670	4.4
Bombay, Calcutta, and Madras, India	Less than 330	159,430	240	1.6
Colombo, Sri Lanka	Less than 330	3,990	270	2.5
Jakarta, Indonesia	330–759	61,770	420	4.6
Karachi, Pakistan	Less than 330	24,870	300	1.5
Manila, Philippines	330–759	34,350	720	3.9
Industrial countries[c]	3,250 and over		9,440[d]	

Note: GNP data are preliminary, at market prices.

a. Per capita income groups range as follows: less than $330; $330–$759; $760–$3,249; $3,250–$7,589; $7,590 and over.

b. Real.

c. As defined in World Bank, *Accelerated Development in Sub-Saharan Africa* (Washington, D.C., 1981), Statistical Annex, table 1.

d. 1979.

Source: World Bank Atlas, 1981 (Washington, D.C., 1981).

Urban management's response to these continuing deficiencies has varied widely from city to city. What were formerly straightforward, limited types of services and delivery systems confined to local areas, have often needed urgent expansion on a vast, metropolitan scale. Faced with such a scale of demand but severely limited funds, some cities in the region have responded by scaling down standards and adopting innovative approaches. Shelter programs, for example, are no longer limited to providing built-up dwelling units but include, increasingly, the preparation of serviced sites and conservation of existing housing stock through the upgrading of slums. This was the approach adopted by the National Housing Authority of Thailand, which between 1976 and 1980 supplemented its program for the construction of 120,000 dwelling units with sites and services schemes. Going a step further, Manila has virtually abandoned its policy of bulldozing slums (initiated in 1976 for the 200,000 slum households of Tondo) and is now planning to upgrade 15,000 slum households annually. Since 1970 Calcutta, too, has focused on the progressive upgrading of slums in its urban development projects and in so doing has brought services to some 1.5 million people. Similarly, Madras has moved increasingly toward a metropolitanwide program of servicing sites and providing basic services to the city's widespread slum areas.

Investments in other urban services have been equally massive. Water supply and sanitation investments account for close to one-third of the metropolitan infrastructure program in Bombay and Karachi, and up to 45 percent of Calcutta's five-year program for 1984–89. Traffic and transportation, both for the transport infrastructure and augmentation of the transit fleet, constitute another large investment in the cities under consideration, particularly in Bombay, Calcutta, Madras, Bangkok, and Jakarta. The design, implementation, and management of these massive sectoral projects have varied from city to city, but in most cases—except in Bombay, where the Municipal Corporation has been the principal executing agency—the projects have been initiated and executed by special-purpose agencies.

Although such authorities have been able to mobilize the resources needed for the execution of projects, it is seldom recognized what factors contribute to the success of a project. In a water supply project, as was amply illustrated in Karachi, it is not enough to focus on the construction of the treatment plants and the distribution networks alone. Steps must be taken to measure quality, charge tariffs, bill consumers, enforce payment, charge connections, and determine the appropriate mix of house connections and standpipes.

Similarly, highway construction projects such as the one in Manila cannot succeed unless attention is paid to the problems of land acquisition, property values, displacement and relocation, maintenance methods, and financing. These "software" elements of a project are often more difficult to deal with than its physical aspects, or "hardware." In Calcutta, for example, a large sewage treatment facility has remained idle because house connections have not yet been made. It was merely assumed that houses would automatically be connected, and no effort was made to obtain the financing or to make the administrative arrangements necessary to ensure house connections. Another case in point comes from Madras, where the distribution of titles to slum households has lagged far behind the pace of physical improvements.

The success of the current Calcutta transport project further illustrates the value of attending to the software elements. Although the principal objective of this project has been to improve the state-owned bus and tram fleets, little headway would have been made without due attention to the internal operations of the bus and tram companies, rationalization of routes and tariffs, better traffic management, and other software items. Furthermore, because a number of government departments, parastatals, and regulatory agencies have been involved and because passenger transport in Calcutta is both a private and a public service, considerable time has been spent on analyzing the project's impact on the private sector (particularly on the bus companies providing 65 percent of all services); identifying the related problems that will determine whether the project will operate efficiently; developing alternatives to resolve these problems (such as alternative fare formulas); and assigning tasks to the several agencies. This approach has made it possible to organize an interagency committee capable of steering and coordinating project activities toward success. The outcome was far different in an earlier (1971–73) transport improvement project that focused on hardware only. These experiences serve to illustrate the various associated tasks that need to be undertaken to secure the ultimate success of a project. A critical responsibility of metropolitan management is to establish a process in which tasks are first identified and organizational arrangements are subsequently determined by those tasks.

Programming of Projects

Until recently, relatively few attempts have been made to identify and quantify the heavy public investments being incurred in the establishment and operation of large-scale services and delivery systems in the metropolitan areas of South and East Asia. One attempt to prepare input-output tables[1] for the Calcutta Metropolitan District in the early 1960s failed for want of published data, particularly with respect to local government services. Since the Calcutta Metropolitan Development Authority came into being, however, capital budgets covering at least the state government agencies have been prepared annually. In Madras, too, the Metropolitan Development Authority has been assembling investment packages for the city's five-year plans annually; and in Bombay, as that city's profile indicates, investment estimates were compiled for 1977–78, although ongoing project programming did not take place. Even so, outside of Tokyo and the city-states of Hong Kong and Singapore, Manila is probably the only city

---

1. By R. H. Dhar for the Institute of Public Administration, New York.

in South and East Asia to have attempted capital budgeting on a continuing basis. (For the details of Manila's capital investment folio [CIF], see its city profile.)

Initiated by the Ministry of Public Works in 1978, the CIF exercise became the responsibility of the Metropolitan Manila Commission in 1981. During 1979 and 1980, Manila's sectoral agencies were given an opportunity to coordinate the level and location of their investments by identifying potential and actual areas in which they overlapped or conflicted. The CIF also made it possible to exercise collective judgment on the timing of investment; thus some projects were brought forward and some others were deferred. Criteria were not yet sufficient, however, to determine whether a project should be included in or eliminated from the folio. Today, projects continue to be formulated and designed by the sectoral agencies, partly because no updated regional development plan is available to reinforce investment strategy. In the past two years, however, the commission has been refining the socioeconomic criteria and indicators by which projects are selected for the CIF and monitored, and is now responsible for preparing a regional development plan. In addition, the Management Coordination Board—set up in March 1980 with the commission's vice-governor as the chairman—coordinates action on the various development projects assisted by the World Bank. Thus both the opportunity and the requisite organizational mechanism are available to develop the capital investment folio into an effective instrument for metropolitan decisionmaking.

Although Manila has been able to maintain this interagency exercise on a continuing basis, it still fails to include municipal investment and the funds needed for maintenance. Nor does it have data on major private investments, whose impact on a metropolitan economy cannot safely be ignored by any policymaking public authority. The question is whether the kind of information needed to coordinate at least all public investment projects, and preferably major private ones, too, can be made available readily, periodically, and on a metropolitan scale. An alternative would be to focus on the programming of private and public projects in selected service sectors that are critical to metropolitan development strategy over given periods of time. So far, this alternative has not been attempted, and although the need for programming in investment projects is becoming increasingly evident in the region's cities, metropolitan management has failed to fulfill this task in most of them.

Economic Development

The role of metropolitan management in promoting employment and improving incomes is possibly the least understood—not to mention the least recognized—of all its functions. In many of the region's cities employment cannot keep pace with the growth of the labor force, and a high percentage of the population lives below the poverty-income level (see table 2-2). Metropolitan Manila accounts for 30 percent of the urban poor in the Philippines;

Table 2-2. Profile Cities: Urban Poverty-Income Levels, 1976–77

City	Year	Urban poverty-income level (U.S. dollars)		Urban population below poverty level[a] (percent)
		Absolute	Relative	
Bangkok	1977	126	115	10[b]
Bombay	1977	83		45[c]
Calcutta	1977	83		61
Colombo	1977	52		23
Jakarta	1976	194		66
Karachi	1977	77		45
Madras	1977	83		50[c]
Manila	1977	250	132	35[d]

Note: Based on annual per capita income at current U.S. prices. The operative urban poverty-income level is the higher of relative and absolute poverty-income levels. For some countries, only one or the other type of poverty-income level has been estimated to date. This reflects the judgment that the type of poverty-income level estimated is clearly the operative one for the country concerned. The relative urban poverty-income level is one-third of per capita personal income adjusted for urban-national cost-of-living differences, and the absolute level is the income level at which a country-specific expenditure pattern yields minimum caloric requirements.

a. Refers to population below the higher of the absolute and relative poverty-income levels.

b. Because of the relatively high employment level, absolute poverty appears to be less widespread in Bangkok than in other Asian cities.

c. Estimates.

d. Metropolitan Manila accounts for 30 percent of the urban poor in the Philippines.

Source: World Bank data, April 1979.

61 percent of Calcutta's inhabitants fall below the urban poverty level for India; in 1971, 38 percent of Colombo's male workers aged 20–25 were unemployed; close to 1 million persons are chronically underemployed in Jakarta. Even in Bombay, Madras, and Karachi, where employment in industry and trade has kept pace with the growth in the labor force, low incomes continue to be a problem. Yet urban management has barely addressed these basic economic issues.

One reason that such fundamental problems are overlooked is the tendency to regard employment promotion or poverty alleviation programs as provincial or national tasks and therefore to consider them beyond the purview of metropolitan management. Another reason is that in many countries of the region the provision of urban services is regarded as a social overhead. Although it is certainly necessary to distinguish between directly productive and supportive investment, funding to remove service deficiencies should not be regarded as having only a social objective. Water shortages and traffic congestion, for example, obviously affect industrial production and commercial activities just as much as they do health and the quality of the urban environment. Besides, metropolitan service authorities can and do contribute specifically to the generation of income and jobs through sectoral investments. According to a World Bank assessment, 30,000 construction jobs would be available directly from the Calcutta Urban Development Project over a five-year period and another 20,000 jobs over the operational life of the utilities created.

Such direct job creation should not be regarded as the only economic task of metropolitan management, however. All over the world, city authorities are responsible for public service delivery, infrastructure investment, and various regulatory functions that affect the city economy. Although national policy will remain a major determinant of employment and incomes, it is largely at the city level that "the economies and externalities of agglomeration can be promoted and inefficiencies minimized."[2] There are several ways by which metropolitan management can accomplish this, such as the provision of land and infrastructure, direct business support (for example, credit for small-scale enterprises), vocational training, review of regulations, and so on.

The provision of serviced land for industry or business has been a method of economic promotion for several years. In a number of cases, however, such schemes have been taken up independently of metropolitan needs and constraints. For example, the decision to set up a free-trade zone near the Katunayake airport in Colombo and create a Greater Colombo Economic Commission to administer the zone was made at the national and not the metropolitan level. The location is also not part of the metropolitan development plan, although the zone is to provide 40,000 jobs and transport linkages with Colombo City are grossly inadequate. In Madras, a number of factory workshops in one of the sites and service areas remained vacant because the electricity supply agency had not budgeted for a needed transformer substation and the metropolitan authority did not have the funds for financing the item itself.

Other cities have had similar experiences, but in recent years there has been increasing evidence that metropolitan authorities regard such schemes as an essential part of urban development programs. The City and Industrial Development Corporation of Bombay, which is responsible for developing New Bombay across the harbor, is developing warehouses and wholesale markets for agricultural products and is constructing telephone exchange buildings to expedite economic development in the area.

Direct business support measures are also being taken up. A credit scheme for small enterprises is a part of the Calcutta Urban Development Programme. Vocational training and technical assistance to entrepreneurs are components of the Madras urban development project. Although the scale of these efforts has been modest, there is enough evidence to demonstrate adequate economic returns and income and employment generation. Another way in which metropolitan management can help in the development of small business is to enable city authorities to review and adjust regulations and procedures for business location and construction,

2. Friedrich Kahnert, "Improving Urban Employment and Labor Productivity" (Washington, D.C.: World Bank, Water Supply and Urban Development Department, February 1985), processed.

licensing, the purchase of materials for municipal use, and the payment of bills. The establishment of economic-development or business-promotion offices as part of metropolitan management bodies or in association with business and industry will also help.

In circumstances where the planning of economic development has been preempted by national and regional governments, metropolitan management should be able to identify a city's economic ills, research its economic advantages and opportunities, and formulate relevant action programs that can be incorporated, in whole or in part, in national and regional development plans. If the action programs are sensitive to the informal as well as the formal needs of the business sector, are coordinated with supporting social and physical programs, and are viable (both institutionally and financially), a city should be able to prepare strong development briefs that regional and national governments cannot ignore in the long run. In some respects, the Calcutta Basic Development Plan of 1966 formed such a brief. Although at first it had little impact on higher levels of government, four years later it became the agenda of the Calcutta Metropolitan Development Authority with the backing of the central and state governments.

Spatial Planning

Scarcity of land has long been a problem for every metropolis in the region. The geomorphology of city sites has also seriously impeded physical development and the provision of services. Few Asian cities have been founded on ideal sites. Many are located in swamps and marshes because strategic or trading considerations in colonial times made proximity to the sea or to a major waterway an overriding priority. Calcutta has emerged as a vast metropolis in spite of being set in a low-lying area that is annually inundated. Jakarta was founded on marshy land, and with five rivers flowing seaward through its metropolitan area, it continues to be subject to flooding. Bangkok, which is less than three feet above sea level, faces severe problems of seasonal flooding, a high water table, impervious soil, and a lack of natural drainage. Bombay originally consisted of seven marshy and malarial islands. The Kelani river normally floods the coastal plain surrounding Colombo, which lacks a natural harbor but gave colonial traders access to the former capitals of Kandy and Kottee (see the city profiles in Part II).

Massive urbanization has seriously compounded these natural disadvantages. Major reclamation work has had to be done and expensive communication networks built to maintain urban access. Some cities (such as Karachi, Bombay, and Madras) have even had to bring in potable water from distant sources to avoid contamination or to supplement local supplies. Such large-scale public works have tended to influence the spatial pattern of subsequent urban growth, regardless of the consequences for other sectors or for overall urban form.

Spatial planning should thus have been introduced in the early stages of metropolitan urbanization, if only to prevent arbitrary land development. Some cities—such as Madras, Bangkok, Manila, and Bombay—have in fact prepared elaborate town plans from time to time. In Calcutta and Colombo, however, the absence of town planning has been conspicuous. In the mid-1960s planners in Calcutta deliberately decided to defer land use planning and focus instead on deficiencies in the physical infrastructure. Apart from considering the broad metropolitan configuration that might be desirable, they made little effort to plan even for important parts of the metropolis where sectoral investments were sure to induce new construction. The current situation clearly indicates that this deferment of land use planning was a costly decision since construction, whether private or public, has become even more arbitrary and haphazard than before. At the other end of the spectrum are Hong Kong and Singapore, where spatial planning has been the centerpiece of development in putting scarce land to optimum use.

According to the city profiles for the region, the public sector has played mainly a passive role in land use development, merely nodding its approval or disapproval of private initiatives. Except where legislation has permitted the creation of new town corporations or authorities, as in Madras or Bombay, public action has been directed to functional sectors only—such as water, housing, power, transport, and industrial estates—as opposed to more comprehensive spatial development.

Critical spatial decisions have often been based on narrow sectoral requirements, with little heed paid to wider urban concerns or the capacities of supporting agencies to provide the services required. Industrial and housing estates have usually been located where land and power are readily available rather than on sites that are suitable from a spatial-planning point of view. Wherever land development has been more comprehensive than required by the needs of the sectoral agency involved, it has generally been incidental to the main project, as in Manila, where the construction of a container port led to the reclamation of Dagat Dagatan for resettlement. In some cases, location has been determined by the most economic site for major new sectoral investment, as in the case of a refining and petrochemicals complex in Madras and the consequent northern expansion of that city. At other times, it has been subsidiary to the redevelopment of a dilapidated local area, as in the case of Echelon Square in Colombo. Spatial planning has seldom been perceived as a means of deliberately initiating desirable urban growth, other than in the New Territories of Hong Kong or the new towns of Singapore, where it has been a pronounced success.

These circumstances emphasize that the location of infrastructure and the provision of services should not be divorced from spatial planning, especially in cities where usable land is scarce. Such planning can at least help identify distortions that need to be avoided. In other words, cities should have some means of assembling, analyzing, and disseminating relevant information area by area as well as sector by sector in order to guide decisionmaking. Urban management should use such systems of information to coordinate intersectoral and interagency activities on a planned spatial basis.

Overcoming Constraints

The discharge of these urgent and wide-ranging tasks has been subjected to severe constraints in many cities. Stringent financial restrictions and institutional deficiencies have jeopardized many programs, seriously curtailed some, and brought others to a virtual standstill. Many of the constraints are not new, nor, in principle, are they confined to this region, as pointed out by a 1969 study of thirteen cities throughout the world (two of which were Calcutta and Karachi).[3] The study defined five categories of administrative problems restricting the ability of the public sector to respond to urban issues of that time:

- Inability of tradition-bound bureaucracies to cope with continuously shifting demographic, social, and economic factors of life in large cities
- Inability to augment public expenditure, particularly capital expenditure, at rates commensurate with rising needs for public investment in urban areas
- Inadequate skills and manpower to deal with the increasingly technical and complex job of managing a large and rapidly growing city
- Strain on organizational arrangements ill-suited to new tasks and to broadening geographic and functional responsibilities of government (in particular, new modes of communication, joint planning, and intergovernmental leadership and cooperation were needed)
- Inadequate time perspectives in urban planning, budgeting, financing, and decisionmaking.

Today, relief from these constraints remains an important task of urban management in all the cities of this region.

Developing Managerial Processes

In all of the cities reviewed, there has been a growing understanding of the principal tasks of metropolitan management and of the resulting need to identify and institutionalize more appropriate managerial processes than have been used so far. The establishment, maintenance, and updating of information systems for decisionmaking constitute one such management process that is most urgently needed. The existing systems are barely adequate for the formulation, monitoring, and evaluation of single-sector proj-

3. Annmarie Hauck Walsh, *The Urban Challenge to Government* (New York: Institute of Public Administration, 1969), pp. 9–40.

ects, and few such systems even exist for interagency or interarea communication. The system required here is not the mere compilation of a mass of data; rather, it consists of consolidated and readily retrievable information providing an updated overview of the social, economic, physical, and financial condition of the metropolitan area. Such a system will make possible ''systematic forethought''—in the words of the Herbert Commission[4]— which is essential for evaluating the efficiency and likely economic impact of proposed investments.

The mobilization, planning, and control of scarce resources of land, finances, manpower, and materials constitute another important managerial process to be established. The investment budget exercises undertaken in Manila and Madras are the first efforts toward this, but much more needs to be done in optimizing the use of scarce manpower and material resources among competing metropolitan demands. The systematic review of the day-to-day operation and maintenance of essential urban facilities and of the improvements needed constitutes another managerial process that should be developed.

In developing and institutionalizing these managerial processes, governments clearly need to recognize that a strong contrast exists between monolithic and formalized metropolitan institutions, on the one hand, and the heterogeneous communities, on the other. Generally speaking, the requisite variety and flexibility of institutional structures are seldom to be found. The political procedures through which institutions of metropolitan management can secure public access and participation are still deficient. There is also a need to reconcile institutionally two basic processes of urban management: the traditional or orthodox public administration, on the one hand, and the more recently introduced development administration, on the other. Issues such as these are discussed in the succeeding chapters and possible solutions put forward.

4. *Report of the Royal Commission on Local Government in Greater London (Herbert Commission)* (London: Her Majesty's Stationery Office, 1961).

3

Financial Constraints

LIKE MANY METROPOLITAN CITIES of the world, those of South and East Asia are often accused of either preempting or unfairly competing with other urban centers and rural areas in the allocation of scarce financial resources. Frequently, they are also accused of making disproportionate demands on their national economies for all kinds of capital investments. Underlying these perceptions is a combination of traditional animus against large cities, a persistent political bias against them, an attitude that because they are big they should be able to look after themselves, and fear of a progressive drain on national resources.

The contributions that the metropolitan cities do make to the region's national economies are less frequently weighed in the balance. Yet, undoubtedly, all of the cities being discussed here are principal engines of industry, commerce, and finance in their respective countries: one-third of Thailand's gross domestic product (GDP) originates in Bangkok; Bombay has only 5.3 percent of India's urban population but accounts for 10 percent of the country's industrial jobs and for 21 percent of the value added by its manufacturing sector; more than 60 percent of the manufacturing firms in the Philippines are located in Manila; and nearly 50 percent of Sri Lanka's employment in commercial, financial, and transport services is accounted for by Colombo alone. The metropolitan cities also contribute substantially to public revenues. Despite its recent economic decline, Calcutta is still responsible for about 15 percent of India's corporate tax revenues. Bombay accounts for nearly 80 percent of all Maharashtra State tax revenues and for about one-quarter of the country's income tax receipts.

Allocation of Resources

In most cities of the region, however, the taxes generated have to be shared disproportionately with either the province or the nation. In many cases, receipts from income tax, customs, or excise duties are not distributed to the city administration at all. In most countries the allocation of tax yields is the executive responsibility of national governments, although provincial governments may have a say in the case of some taxes. The tax resources assigned to the cities are usually insignificant. Shanghai, the biggest metropolis in China, retains no more than 11.2 percent of all the taxes and fees it collects for the country. Only in Singapore and Hong Kong, which are city-states, are distinctions between metropolitan and national needs and resources blurred. Nevertheless, the resources available for urban development in either of these cities are not limitless. Out of revenues totaling some US$5.5 billion[1] in Hong Kong in 1980-81, only about US$823 million, or 15 percent, was made available on both capital and recurrent accounts for expenditure on items of urban infrastructure, which included mainly public works and land development.

It is not so much the size of the resources being allocated to urban purposes that is important as the recognition that a great city, if it is to sustain its function as a principal generator of wealth, must be permitted to absorb a sufficient portion of the wealth it creates for its own upkeep and further development, whether state and city are identical or not. That is certainly the case in the metropolitan cities of South and East Asia, which need much of this money to maintain their economic role as the principal centers of production and trade in the region. The scale of such expenditure is not necessarily out of proportion to the wealth they generate. For instance, in 1980–81, the total investment in major items of public infrastructure in Bombay (613 million rupees [Rs]) represented only about 5 percent of the net value added by its manufacturing sector in that year.

Scale of Demand

Although it has not been proved conclusively that a correlation exists between increases in city size and rising unit service costs,[2] there is no doubt that the quality and scale of services needed in metropolitan cities significantly exceed those appropriate to smaller urban areas. The growing density of settlements (see table 3-1) also exerts pressure on water supply systems, communication networks, sanitation, refuse disposal, and road maintenance services. The generation of solid wastes, for example, is 25–30 percent greater per head in the larger and more densely packed cities. The high rate of population growth also bears directly on the technology and costs of urban services, particularly with respect to housing, power supply, and health. Karachi—the population of which has been growing at twice the national average—experiences an influx of some 200,000 persons every

1. Billion refers to a thousand million throughout.
2. See Harry W. Richardson, *City Size and National Spatial Strategies in Developing Countries*, World Bank Staff Working Paper no. 252 (Washington, D.C., April 1977).

Table 3-1. Profile Cities: Metropolitan Population Densities, 1981

City	Metropolitan region area		Metropolitan population (millions)	Metropolitan density	
	Square miles	Square kilometers		Per square mile	Per square kilometer
Bangkok	618	1,600	5.0	8,090	3,125
Bombay[a]	1,700	4,400	11.3	6,651	2,568
Calcutta	546	1,414	10.0	18,315	7,072
Colombo[b]	700	1,813	4.0	5,714	2,206
Jakarta[c]	216	560	6.2	28,704	11,071
Karachi	135	349	6.1	45,185	17,479
Madras	450	1,166	5.1	11,333	4,375
Manila	246	637	8.2	33,333	12,873
Average	576	1,492	7.0	12,153	4,692

a. Greater Bombay: area 170 square miles (440 square kilometers); population 8.0 million; density 47,059 per square mile (18,182 per square kilometer).

b. Colombo urban core: area 91 square miles (236 square kilometers); population 1.7 million; density 18,681 per square mile (7,203 per square kilometer).

c. DKI-Jakarta only (not JABOTABEK metropolitan region).

Source: See tables in the city profiles in Part II of this volume.

year, all requiring shelter, heat, light, and nutrition; and metropolitan Bombay must provide for about 45,000 new households annually. The physical infrastructure created in many cities before the Second World War will have to be doubled within the next decade.

The scale of demand for resources is also affected by adverse location. As already noted, Bangkok, Calcutta, Manila, and Colombo are all in low-lying coastal areas prone to flooding. Thus their drainage systems require expensive networks of pipes, pumps, and canals. The fact that Bombay is on a peninsula adds considerably to the city's transport costs, and in Karachi as well as in Bombay and Madras, further costs are incurred in transporting supplies of fresh water from distant sources. Land values, too, are affected by adverse location.

Finally, the status of most metropolitan cities in South and East Asia as provincial or national capitals and the long presence of substantial expatriate communities have given rise to high service standards that are not affordable. This is particularly the case where population growth is rapid and low-income groups are predominant. The cumulative effect of these various factors on the scale of demand for resources greatly alters the nature of the financial problems encountered by metropolitan management.

Interagency Consistency

One important consequence of the fragmentation of executive responsibility for metropolitan services between levels of government and sectoral agencies in most of the region's cities is that certain agencies may have better access to funds than others. Their precedence is generally based on institutional or historical reasons rather than the priority of an agency's functions and needs. Long-established water supply authorities such as Manila's operate on much larger capital budgets than other agencies because of retained earnings and earlier borrowings. In some cases, external funding also contributes to the imbalance. Manila's capital investment folio illustrates the value of subjecting agency proposals to some form of collective judgment in the interest of interagency equity, in this case securing the deferment of selected water supply investments.

Fragmentation is also responsible for the lack of consistency between agency investments. The development of Manila's container port, for example, has depended on a housing scheme to relocate squatters on the access road right of way; in Karachi, storm water drainage depends on the schemes of the Port Trust; in Calcutta, major road improvements and extensions are contingent on drainage programs; and in Colombo, the success of downtown redevelopment is dependent on the program for relocating warehousing facilities. These dependencies are not merely of a planning nature. In essence, they are critical aspects of programming in general and of budgeting in particular. Failure to perceive or consider such problems is usually due to inadequate budgetary procedures rather than any lack of goodwill among agencies.

The reconciliation of investment in capital projects with the capacity to operate and maintain them is a further problem to be faced in many developing countries. There is more excitement and glamour in construction than in maintenance, and often less real difficulty. The problem has been particularly severe in metropolitan areas, where government and parastatal agencies have built the service facilities but transferred them to municipal authorities for operation and upkeep. The constraints on municipal maintenance have not always been taken into account in the design of such capital projects.

A related financial problem resulting from fragmented organizational responsibilities is that operational policies may reduce the intended benefits of a capital investment. Poor traffic enforcement or inadequate parking regulations can drastically reduce the benefit of improvements to a road network, as in Calcutta and Bangkok. Sewerage or water supply investments will not be fruitful unless operational practices, pricing, and special financing arrangements are designed to facilitate house connections. Subsidized commuter fares in Bombay have had the unintended effect of linear residential spread and acute traffic congestion in the central urban core.

Assessing Needs and Resources

Perhaps no city can hope to eliminate these problems. Indeed, many of the problems are the natural outcome of dynamic growth. But mechanisms are needed to reduce their severity, and an effort must be made to identify and resolve interagency conflicts. A first step in this direction would be to assess the overall investment needs and available resources at the metropolitan level. For cities such as Singapore and Tokyo—both of which have virtually self-contained financial systems based on established revenue sources (which, in the case of Tokyo, include central government allotments according to a predictable formula) and very little external borrowing—this is largely a matter of projecting trends in revenue sources. For most of the metropolitan cities reviewed in this study, however, the exercise is fraught with uncertainty.

Typically, these cities have to compete for an uncertain share of the national budget. Even if they believe that a well-prepared scheme having obviously high priority will attract greater funds from the central government, they must also beware that in practice financial support from provincial or central governments is often modified by political and economic considerations. Thus, for example, the initial capital folio efforts of the Metropolitan Manila Commission were essentially a practical and politically sensitive compromise between the historical projection of expenditure and the sum total of ranked project proposals. By contrast, until 1969, infrastructure investments for the Calcutta metropolitan district formed part of the budgets of sectoral departments and parastatals and were not clearly earmarked for that district. Since the inception of West Bengal's fourth five-year-plan, which established a separate head of account for Calcutta development schemes, it has been possible not only to assess the outlay for the metropolitan district in relation to that for the state as a whole, but also to ensure a continuity of state funding. An earmarked tax—the octroi (a tax on goods entering the metropolitan district)—the proceeds of which are applied in part to service market borrowings, has also made it easier to assess resources.

Determining Priorities

The overall shortage of resources necessitates selectivity. The problem has been approached in different ways in South and East Asia. One aproach, for example, has been to recognize that public investment should be directed only to those sectors or functions that are not well served by the private sector. Bus operations in Calcutta are a case in point. Until about 1960, the State Transport Corporation (STC), owned by the West Bengal government, was the principal bus operator in the city. High operating costs, low fares, and a deteriorating fleet led to a steady decline, and privately owned buses were allowed to operate on temporary permits. By 1979, private operators were providing nearly 65 percent of city transit. A major transport improvement project was begun in 1980 with World Bank assistance. Rather than expand the service of the State Transport Corporation, this project has focused on consolidating its operations and improving its performance, recognizing that the STC can continue to provide only a limited proportion of the required transit. More significantly, the project has sought to confirm the franchises of private bus operators and to improve their services through a more rational route structure. Similarly, Manila, after some attempts to increase government-owned bus operations, now recognizes that "jeepneys" provide nearly 40 percent of the city's transit and, as such, need to be encouraged rather than discouraged.

The issue here is not one of the private versus the public sector; rather, it is a question of directing scarce public resources to where they are needed most. Many of the region's cities already accept this approach in housing and thus their public programs concentrate on the lower-income groups, leaving middle- and higher-income housing to the private sector. When public sector investments are restricted, it may also be necessary to intervene where private sector service costs fall disproportionately upon one group. By increasing the frequency of standpipes in Jakarta, for instance, the heavy cost of carting water to low-income households without house connections has been substantially reduced.

Measuring Costs and Benefits

Even when public sector investments are restricted to specific fields, priorities have to be established between different public sector programs. Quantitative analysis, in particular the measurement of costs and benefits, has only recently become a part of urban infrastructure projects. A principal reason is that the benefits of an urban project have to be measured from the standpoint of an entire economy, and this is a much more complicated task than calculating the profitability of a private investment. Still, cost-benefit analysis is feasible and has been done in a variety of urban projects, particularly in those connected with transportation and water supply.

In metropolitan areas, especially where a number of projects are proposed within one sector or among many sectors and where scarce resources demand a rigorous selection, cost-benefit analysis can be valuable. At the least, it will impart a discipline to the process of identifying all the costs. Thus the cost of dislocation in existing services or alternative arrangements during construction, which is usually ignored in many projects, will not be overlooked. The laying of water and sewer networks in a built-up area is an apt illustration. A more striking example is the underground railway under construction in Calcutta, where the computation of costs has been limited to items directly connected with the project and has failed to take into account the dislocation caused by reduced access to shops and businesses on the alignment, discontinued transport services, and the like.

Urban freeways, transport systems, and drainage and flood control projects are all being increasingly subjected to cost-benefit analysis. Even in low-income shelter projects where the expected benefits are considered nonmeasurable, internal rates of return have been worked out. In a recent Bombay program negotiated for World Bank assistance, for example, the economic benefits of a land and infrastructure scheme and a slum-upgrading program have been measured on the basis of estimated rental value of serviced residential, commercial, and small industrial plots. The IRR in this case was calculated to be 20.4 percent. There is increasing evidence that quantitative analysis is being used in the cities of South and East Asia, although the degree of analysis appears to vary, depending on the agency to which the project proposal is addressed for financing.[3]

Cost-Effectiveness

Where the measurement of economic costs and benefits is clearly not possible, priorities can be established on the basis of cost-effectiveness. The benefits are assumed to be given and a choice is made between the costs of alternative schemes. On this basis, as already mentioned, Manila, Jakarta, Bangkok, Madras, Calcutta, and several other cities decided to abandon policies of slum clearance and stop rehousing displaced families in expensive tenements in favor of upgrading their slums and providing sites and services. In the field of transport, road-based systems are preferred because they have been found to be more cost-effective and flexible than subway systems. The assessment of cost-effectiveness does depend, however, on the range of costs considered. For instance, the costs of providing sites and services vary with location, which in turn affects the costs of transportation and employment.

Impact

A third approach to determining priorities is to measure potential impact, not only in evaluating options within each sector, but also in choosing between different sectoral programs. Manila's capital investment folio has used a matrix to weigh each scheme according to its impact on a variety of social and economic factors and thereby to rank it in overall priority. Among the many indicators used in such impact analysis are health, sanitation, safety, employment, labor intensity, increased productivity, energy consumption, and foreign exchange savings. In the initial years of the exercise, a scoring methodology was developed and applied through consensus. More recently, the system has been under careful review, and more precise scoring techniques are now being developed to promote objectivity in and greater understanding of the weighting procedure.

Minimum Standards

With varying success, many countries and some cities in South and East Asia have attempted to determine priorities on the basis of minimum needs and standards. The concept of minimum needs was used in formulating India's fourth and fifth five-year plans, whereby a proportion of central and state resources was earmarked for specific programs such as drinking water, primary health care, and slum upgrading. Because of the vast size of

3. Metropolitan Manila Commission and Halcrow Fox and Associates, "Metropolitan Manila Capital Investment Folio Study" (Manila: Office of the Commissioner for Planning, November 1982).

the population, however, to fulfill even minimum needs demanded an equally vast scale of resources. Nevertheless, in city infrastructure programs, standards expressed in terms of targets such as per capita consumption of potable water, maximum response time by fire engines, or per capita square meterage of open space have often been a basis for both the design and justification of programs. Once unit costs are calculated and the current scale and location of service deficits identified, a conventional program-budgeting approach can be used in allocating resources to each service sector and setting output targets. This technique can be effective if the standards are realistic because even the so-called minimum standards may be damagingly rigid. A realistic relationship has to be set and *maintained* between the standards prescribed, the extent of the existing deficits, the rate of population growth, and the scale of resources available. It is also important to identify the possible tradeoffs within the limits of such resources, for example, between the amount of open space to be left and the dimension of internal roads in a sites and services layout.

Internal Efficiency

A number of metropolitan development programs are emphasizing the more efficient use of existing stock. Better use of existing road space as opposed to expensive additions has been the underlying theme in the design of transport schemes for Bangkok and Bombay. Improving the performance of the current fleet of vehicles, decreasing the percentage of their downtime, reducing manning and improving vehicle speeds through better traffic management have been the central goals of the transportation programs in Madras and Calcutta. In the field of water supply, Manila, Karachi, and Jakarta now regard the reduction of water leakage (as low as 3 percent in Singapore but as high as 30–40 percent in several other cities) as a serious challenge undermining demands for further investment in this sector. The slum-upgrading approach—whether employed in Manila, Jakarta, or Calcutta—clearly considers slums to be part of the existing housing stock and hopes to make them function more efficiently as residential settlements. Efficiency must also be a prime concern of new investments in housing or serviced sites, however. The use of the least encumbered and therefore cheapest land has often incurred the heaviest costs in the provision of infrastructure. The choice of appropriate technology (particularly in reducing the need for imported materials), the phasing of construction to allow for future need without anticipating it in actual expenditure, the use of designs and materials that minimize maintenance costs—all are important considerations of design and efficiency.

The use of any or all of these approaches often depends on the initiative of the agency most concerned with the particular project. In a metropolitan context, however, a choice has to be made between projects of comparable efficiency, impact, and cost effectiveness. Program budgeting approaches and interdepartmental project teams have been tried in many of the cities reviewed, and coordination and control have been sought through central programming (as in Jakarta, Madras, and Calcutta), but with varying degrees of success. In the absence of such mechanisms (as in Bangkok, Colombo, and Karachi), it has been difficult even to identify the main features of a metropolitan program. Manila is an exception, however, in that it recently formalized the process that began as a capital investment folio exercise, the initial emphasis of which—as noted earlier—was on subjecting agency proposals to some form of collective judgment and on using group pressure rather than formal authority to achieve better cooperation and balance. An interagency technical working group has now been set up, and the process is regarded as an instrument of the National Economic and Development Authority in Sanctioning priorities and allocating funds.

Cost Recovery

Cost recovery is a central issue in most development projects, but in a metropolitan context it assumes additional importance because institutional fragmentation can create rigidities in the pattern of cost recovery. That is to say, costs will be charged to the consumers where the agency is a utility corporation, to the urban taxpayers at large where the agency is a municipality, and to the national taxpayers where the central government is involved, regardless of which group can or should pay for the service in question. In the absence of a rational basis of cost recovery, services may suffer from gross neglect or may receive arbitrary and ad hoc subsidies. From a geographic standpoint, cost recovery can be analyzed as to the source: the local beneficiaries or consumers, the metropolitan city taxpayers at large, and the national taxpayers. It should be remembered that these are concentric rather than exclusive groups, and that the metropolitan dweller or business conceivably makes contributions to each.

Public transport, water supplies, and housing are the principal areas of urban expenditure that are traditionally charged directly to the consumer. Even so, the opportunity to recover full costs varies widely between cities and sectors, depending on political sensitivity, the varying costs of provision, and the ability of lower-income groups to pay for minimum levels of consumption. Most housing programs are fully self-sufficient, although initial land costs are only partly recovered from public housing tenants in Hong Kong, and sites and services recoveries in Madras exclude the capital costs of water supply. Cross-subsidization within housing schemes to assist lower-income residents is common.

Water supply charges are particularly sensitive, and attempts to increase them frequently encounter severe resistance. The Karachi Metropolitan Corporation has so far (1982) refused to increase charges, although they cover only one-third of the cost of bulk supply and one-eighth of the cost of marginal extensions (see the Karachi city profile). Tokyo and Hong Kong provide a basic family level of consumption at below cost, but charge excess consumption on a progressively rising tariff. This approach clearly offers a possible solution, but it requires the installation of meters and the delinking of water charges from the property tax structure. Public transport is heavily subsidized in Calcutta, as in many cities in developed countries. In Madras it has shown the potential to be self-sufficient, but population expansion and the policy of providing subsidies for specific groups have already begun to create deficits, as indicated in the city profile.

Fixing charges for such essential services depends not only on actual costs, but on what people perceive to be fair. Calcutta delayed fare increases to the second year of its transportation program so that improvements in service could be perceived. Water tariff increases in Dhaka and Manila have been prefaced by carefully worded public statements of the reasons and expected improvements in coverage. Some services do provide a surplus for subsidizing other services, land development in Karachi being one example. The Karachi Development Authority has thus been able to offset deficits in the water supply account from surpluses in the land development account. Removing responsibilities from municipal governments to national sectoral agencies has deprived cities of resources available for cross-subsidization.

Tax Policies

The metropolitan cities covered in this review face three types of problems with respect to taxation policies and practices. In the first place, most of them are made up of several municipal jurisdictions. Karachi, Greater Bombay, Bangkok, and Jakarta are less fragmented than the others, however, in the sense that the core as well as a substantial part of the metropolitan area fall under the jurisdiction of a single municipality. Calcutta probably represents municipal fragmentation in its most acute form, followed by Manila, Madras, and Colombo.

Although some form of metropolitan-level planning or development authority exists in all these cities, there are gross disparities in the levels of taxation from district to district within the metropolitan area because the municipal jurisdictions are divided. In Manila, which comprises seventeen separate municipal areas, per capita revenues range from US$2 to $10 in four municipalities of similar status. In Calcutta, they range from US$0.80 to $10. Typically, city cores are better financed and serviced than the peripheries, because of both historical development and central concentrations of highly taxable property and businesses. Older industrialized cities in many developed countries are beginning to experience the reverse phenomenon: that is, business, industry, and upper-class residents in those countries are moving to the suburbs, but this is yet to happen in the cities of South and East Asia, except perhaps for Tokyo. The relations between core and periphery have very important revenue implications and they remain a thorny issue in most metropolitan jurisdictions.

Some cities have set up equalization funds to which all municipal jurisdictions contribute and from which the financially weaker ones receive additional grants. In Manila, for example, all municipalities contribute 20 percent of their revenues to the Metropolitan Manila Commission. Assistance to weaker municipalities is one of the commission's main objectives, although most of the municipal contributions are used for its own operations.

A second factor limiting metropolitan revenues in South and East Asia is the nature of local taxation itself (see table 3-2). Traditionally, the urban tax base has been dominated by property taxation. The standardization of codes, reform of valuation systems, training of staff, and stricter enforcement of collection have all helped to improve yields substantially in several cities. Nevertheless, mainly for administrative and political reasons, the property tax is a relatively inelastic tax source in times of rapid population growth and inflation. If metropolitan government is to finance a substantial part of the large range of urban services from local taxes, a wider tax base is required. Tokyo meets 70 percent of its general account from its own taxation, but this includes surcharges on national corporations and income taxes, as well as automobile taxes. Bangkok relies heavily on taxes on business, which it shares with the national government. Less industrialized countries depend more heavily on indirect taxes and levies such as octroi. A surcharge on the sales tax (as proposed in Madras) may offer cities more buoyant revenues, although the solution is attended by problems of equity and efficient collection.

A third important limiting factor is the vulnerability of city taxation to national and provincial governments—Bangkok's tax rates, for example, are set by the central government, and Jakarta recently lost its gambling tax resources when the casinos were closed. National and provincial governments usually monopolize the most buoyant tax sources and derive considerable revenue from the metropolitan areas. Yet the benefit of much of the investment in the cities, particularly in capitals and large ports, is felt primarily at the national rather than local level. Thus a substantial contribution from the national taxes is both necessary and justified, and in cities

Table 3-2. Profile Cities: Metropolitan Revenues, 1979–80
(percentage distribution)

Source	Bangkok	Bombay	Calcutta	Colombo	Jakarta[a]	Karachi	Madras	Manila
Local taxation	15–20	70	68	61	62	79	80	73
Property	n.a.	56	78	90	n.a.[b]	30	73	49[c]
Octroi	n.a.	38	16	n.a.	n.a.	68	n.a.	n.a.
Other	n.a.	6	6	10	n.a.	2	27	51
Nontax receipts	40–50	24	11	12	9	21	14	15
Government grants and tax allotments	30–40	6	21	27	29	n.a.	6	12
Total	100	100	100	100	100	100	100	100

n.a. Not available.

a. DKI-Jakarta.

b. Business taxes account for 41 percent of Metropolitan Manila's local taxation sources.

c. In Jakarta, the property tax is an item of shared revenue.

Sources: Budgets for 1978–79 or 1979–80, and World Bank data.

such as Tokyo national expenditures are comparable in size to those of the metropolitan government. Fixed shares of national income earmarked for cities, as in Japan and, to a lesser extent, in the Philippines, help to increase predictability and metropolitan-level budgeting, although these most commonly benefit state or provincial rather than municipal revenues. The metropolitan cities under review all suffer from this problem; despite their contributions to the national economy and to national and provincial tax revenues, the shares allocated to them continue to be grossly inadequate to meet their needs (see table 3-2).

Resource Mobilization

Revenue sharing and the additional allocation of funds from higher levels of government continue to be the favored methods of mobilizing resources in metropolitan cities, whether in less or more developed countries. The arguments repeated year after year at the U.S. Conference of Mayors illustrate the universality of this approach. Yet, for most cities of South and East Asia its potential is very limited, as the national competition for resources can become only increasingly severe if country populations continue to expand at a rapid rate. Thus, although advocacy for additional resources is and will remain a vital task at the metropolitan level, it must be supported by demonstrable evidence that the locally available resources have already been tapped to the hilt and that the resources so mobilized are being used effectively and efficiently.

Improving the flow and utilization of resources at the metropolitan level typically involves a series of tasks. First, as mentioned above, an inventory must be made of the resources already available to the wide range of agencies concerned with metropolitan development. Such an inventory will enable authorities to assess needs and deficits sectorally and on a metropolitan basis. Preparing such inventories should be a first step in any negotiations for resources. At the same time, it is important to quantify, at least approximately, the investment being made by the private sector for both new and operational purposes. Mention has already been made (see also chapter 5) of the private sector's substantial involvement in transport, hospital care, and education services in many of the region's cities. An inventory of such investments will help to determine in which areas, and for what time periods, scarce public sector resources will be required in addition to private sector efforts.

Second, the utilization of existing resources can also be improved by measuring the benefits, cost effectiveness, impact, and internal efficiency of services. Furthermore, management must recognize that every service has a financial component in the form of cost recovery. Given the scale of demand, metropolitan managements can ill afford to disregard this element. Indeed, the level of consumer charges for services and the effectiveness of billing and collections by the various agencies concerned need to be reviewed frequently. There is a similar need to improve assessment systems and the collection of city taxes; to review and possibly standardize the city's legal codes and tax rates; to persuade sectoral agencies and municipal authorities to improve their financial performance; and to provide them with necessary technical assistance. The successful experience of the Metropolitan Manila Commission in working with the constituent municipal units toward tax code reform and tax mapping illustrates what can be done.

To repeat, advocacy is a vital task at the metropolitan level. An analysis of the resources generated within a metropolitan area and applied to its current needs in comparison with national expenditures will at least dispel the common perception of disproportionate allocations, as demonstrated in the case of Madras. Such analysis will provide metropolitan managements with a legitimate basis on which to press their claims upon provincial and national governments for a fairer share of their budgets, for the conferment of more tax sources on city governments, and for the allocation of resources and securing of external funds. But even the fairest of the formulas for revenue sharing or grants-in-aid are unlikely to change a poor city into a rich one. With few exceptions, the cities of South and East Asia will have to bear the brunt of the fiscal challenge by utilizing existing internal resources more efficiently.

4

Institutional Constraints

THE CITY PROFILES and the overview in chapter 1 indicate that the sectoral response to urbanization in South and East Asia has had too limited a time horizon as well as too narrow a vision. More often than not, management has focused on only one or two major functions at a time, with the result that development has become more fragmented, both sectorally and territorially. In addition, in the absence of a historical perspective, too little attention has been paid to long-term side effects on other sectors and areas, and on the human, material, and financial resources still available to institutions that are responsible for the day-to-day provision of services.

Lack of Metropolitan and Long-Term Perspectives

The metropolitanwide assessment of needs and resources and the establishment of sectoral and area priorities have seldom been undertaken on a continuing basis. Even where metropolitan development authorities have been created, either they have not been mandated to undertake these specific tasks or their structure has not been designed to enable them to develop the metropolitan perspective. For example, a functional analysis of Colombo's urban management in 1977 (see the city profile in Part II) could find no existing institution or legislation that could be used for the overall planning and coordination of metropolitan development without extensive modification. Even though Karachi has its Development Authority and Metropolitan Corporation, a metropolitan policy continues to be lacking, and there is little coordination of spatial and socioeconomic planning for the metropolis at any level of government. In Bangkok, urban development proceeds on an ad hoc basis in the absence of any policy guidelines whatsoever, whether metropolitan, provincial, or national. In Calcutta, Madras, and Bombay, where development planning did begin with a metropolitan perspective, the process of relating sectoral projects and operational policies to that perspective is yet to be properly established. Manila's capital investment folio and the Regional Development Framework Plan are only now beginning to contend with the self-protective attitude of the sectoral agencies. The same is true of the JABOTABEK plans. (JABOTABEK is an acronym for Jakarta, Bogor, Tangra, and Bekasi, the areas forming the region.)

A basic reason for this sectoral emphasis is that the metropolis itself has remained a planner's delineation and is yet to emerge as a platform for integrating planning, administrative, and fiscal activities. Unlike Hong Kong and Singapore—where the city and the country coincide, and the policies, programs, and executive activities of sectoral ministries, departments, and parastatal organizations have been coordinated and ultimately controlled on corporate lines by a central organ of the island's government (the governor-in-council or the cabinet)—there is no such coincidence elsewhere in the region. The central government's broad national concern has not compensated at the metropolitan level for the narrower concerns of its sectoral ministries, departments, and other public agencies with multiple jurisdictions. Even when a metropolitan city has been given provincial status (as in the case of Bangkok and Jakarta) the needed consolidation and perspective have not necessarily been achieved. Except in Madras and Manila, the multisectoral development authorities set up at the metropolitan level have not succeeded in compensating for higher-level tunnel vision. Either they have failed to make an effective impression, as in Bombay, or they have tended to adopt and maintain sectoral roles themselves, as in Karachi and Calcutta.

As for the emphasis on the short term, a major reason has been urban management's concern with the economic and political climate. Even in Hong Kong and Singapore, for example, a high sensitivity to the vagaries of international trade has necessarily focused attention on the short term.[1] Other cities have either placed a premium on immediate action programs to maintain popular support (as in Calcutta) or have ignored the longer term altogether (as, apparently, in Colombo, where the Abercrombie Plan of 1949 has provided the only regional development guidelines available, and subsequent urban development schemes have been unrelated even to that framework). As the city profiles show, metropolitan management has severely restricted its horizons jurisdictionally, functionally, and temporally. Furthermore, within these confines, the newly created institutions whose ostensible purpose has been to emphasize metropolitan planning have often strayed from their original goals and adopted new roles as they have struggled to accommodate themselves to their changing political environment.

If a principal objective of management is to sustain a truly metropolitan perspective, other directions need to be explored beyond the sectoral and multisectoral paths followed so far. Past experience strongly suggests that,

1. *Report on the Joint ADB/EDI Regional Seminar on Metropolitan Management in Manila, January 12–16, 1981* (Washington, D.C.: World Bank, Economic Development Institute, 1981).

instead of creating a welter of entirely new institutions, cities should develop processes of management within and between organizations capable of adopting and sustaining such a perspective.

Urban Bureaucracies and Development Administration

Traditional public administration and innovative development administration differ substantially in their style, procedures, and organization. These differences have not been adequately recognized whenever the region's major cities have set up or changed institutions. As a cyclical, project planning, programming, and implementing process, development administration is concerned primarily with identifying and resolving the large-scale problems of urban growth and change that typically demand new and innovative responses. Traditional public administration is concerned primarily with the application of existing legislation and regulations to the routine operation, maintenance, and incremental improvement of established services, and with the control and regulation of public and private activities.

These contrasting functions call for contrasting forms of organization. Development administration requires a nonhierarchical and often collegial structure, which—as illustrated in the city profiles of Madras and Manila in connection with investment programming—are often informal, nonlegalistic, relatively flexible, and impermanent. The personnel are usually highly professional individuals who take an intersectoral approach to urban issues. The organization emphasizes mobility (as opposed to security of tenure), merit (as opposed to seniority), and the recognition of authority and responsibility as functions of individual expertise and performance. By contrast, traditional public administration calls for hierarchical forms of organization that are typically legalistic, relatively inflexible, formal, and permanent. The personnel here are bureaucrats who are organized through a detailed division of labor that engenders a sectorally or functionally limited approach to urban issues. The organizational emphasis is on seniority, security (or orderly promotion), and the idea that authority and responsibility rest in the office instead of the person.

Urban bureaucracies as such should not be denigrated, however. In principle, if not always in practice, the bureaucratic form of organization has great potential when it comes to the efficient delivery of essential services, the maintenance of physical infrastructure, and the regulation of public and private sector activities in urban areas. It can provide a formal and permanent administrative structure that is logically organized around clearly defined institutional goals. The power and authority needed by the chief administrators or executives to achieve these goals can be granted through the appropriate functional departments that they direct. Traditionally, the chief administrators or executives of the municipal departments in South and East Asia have been made responsible to the public by being subordinate either to locally elected representatives or to appointees of higher levels of government, who are in turn responsible to the public either regionally or nationally. Today, the long-established municipal institutions combining departmental bureaucracies and elected or appointed representative bodies remain the universal means of public administration throughout the cities of South and East Asia.

However, the modernization and upgrading of these institutions have been seriously neglected, despite the growing need for the services, infrastructure, and controls. Undoubtedly, the urban bureaucracies could begin to satisfy these needs much more effectively and efficiently if their capacities were to be expanded by systematic restructuring of internal organization and by the allocation of requisite financial and human resources, which are currently being denied to them. Such restructuring should be based on the classical administrative principles. Typically, each municipal department should consist of a hierarchy of offices, each exercising powers and duties considered appropriate to a limited category of activities. In principle, for the efficient division of labor, powers and duties should be clearly defined and distinguished by rules and regulations to ensure that individual issues or cases will be classified and treated according to the categories of activity allocated to each office. These categories should be comprehensive, detailed, and thoroughly analyzed and defined, and persons should be trained and appointed accordingly, job by job. Efficient performance on the job should be motivated by maximizing tenure of office, vocational security, and better service conditions. But solutions that follow the classical route have also to be reconciled with institutional solutions to problems of development planning and administration on a metropolitan scale.

The failure to understand the contrasting need for both traditional and innovative administration in the region's cities has certainly contributed to the difficulties of metropolitan management. Metropolitan development authorities set up to initiate and undertake citywide development planning and administration have tended to become little more than special public works agencies (as in Calcutta) that are organized on orthodox bureaucratic lines and that are sector specific. In some cases, as in Madras, they have been given responsibility under town planning legislation for the regulation and control of land use, buildings, and other structures for which they are functionally inappropriate. Undoubtedly, a principal reason for this confusion has been the changing nature of the concepts of planning and administration briefly referred to in chapter 2 and discussed later in this chapter. Because these functions have progressively converged and overlapped, implementation has come within the purview of planning, and planning within the purview of routine administration. The role of development administration—the managing of development—still needs clarification at the metropolitan level, so that it can be institutionalized effectively and reconciled with the more traditional activities of local municipal authorities.

In Colombo, for instance, the preamble to the legislation establishing the Urban Development Authority describes its objective as being ''to promote integrated planning and implementation of economic, social and physical development.'' Similar intentions are expressed in the legislation setting up some of the other metropolitan development authorities; but their powers and responsibilities do not specifically include economic and social planning. Rather, they usually focus on land use planning and funding, and on implementing or coordinating infrastructure projects. The local public impression in Colombo is that the authority has been set up primarily to execute commercially profitable ventures by undertaking (on a self-financing basis) the development of strategically located and valuable urban land.[2] Similar conclusions have been a regular feature of discussion on development authorities in India. The role of the Delhi Development Authority as a large-scale real estate developer is most frequently cited.

This limited role is a far cry from the concept of urban and regional planning as a continuous process of initiating and coordinating action on programs and projects within the framework of consistent metropolitan strategies for the promotion of development. Moreover, it does not imply a consequent need for continuously updated information and monitoring systems to provide data on changes in urban structure and growth rates, social priorities, and economic circumstances. Nor does it appreciate the need for planning to become an integral element of urban management, which encompasses the review of institutional roles, organizations, and procedures at metropolitan and more local municipal levels.

Social and Political Development

The legitimacy of metropolitan management derives ultimately from the community's sanction; its effectiveness should therefore be judged by its response to the community's expressed needs and desires. As already mentioned, management must be able to identify the changing physical, socioeconomic, and political problems accompanying progressive urbanization. It must be able to modify the existing institutional systems wherever necessary to deal with these problems and to create new systems where the present ones still fail. The tactic of every profile city, as noted earlier, has been to seek short-term answers through the piecemeal creation of special authorities appointed by the central and provincial governments to which they are responsible. As a result, local government institutions have become progressively weaker, and, more often than not, the public's direct or indirect participation in these critical processes of urban management has declined. To restore the type and degree of access and participation that existed before may be neither possible nor desirable at the metropolitan level, in view of the greatly changed circumstances. The point at issue is whether the authority of government itself, which flows from the consent of the governed, is being imperiled.

2. People's Bank, Colombo, *Economic Review* 16, no. 1 (April 1980): 4–5.

Access and participation are both double-edged. If the urban community has little access to the relevant corridors of managerial power and seldom participates in its exercise, both government and public are the losers. Access provides the public with information about relevant government activities and with the means of influencing them; it provides government with information about relevant social needs and priorities that it can otherwise obtain only with difficulty or not at all. Participation provides the public with the means of sharing in government decisions; it provides government with political insight into the ways and means of implementing them. On a day-to-day basis, participation also provides the government with an opportunity to assess the effectiveness of its actions and with a possible platform for recovering the cost of the public services. The problem for most urban managements in South and East Asia today is that public access in a socially heterogeneous metropolitan context has not become adequately institutionalized.

The preferred approach in many cities so far has been to treat metropolitan management as an intermediate level of administration inserted between the national and provincial levels on the one hand and municipal government on the other. The Madras Metropolitan Development Authority, for example, consists of seventeen members, but only one represents a local government authority, and he is a state-appointed administrative officer. The entire Metropolitan Manila Commission is state-appointed and has no local representative. The Urban Development Authority in Colombo has a state-appointed board of management of which only two out of sixteen members are nominated by the minister of local government to represent local government authorities. Although the assembly of the Bangkok Metropolitan Administration (BMA) originally consisted of elected and appointed members in roughly equal numbers and the BMA's governor or chief executive officer was to be elected for a four-year term, all are now appointed. Moreover, as the Bangkok city profile concludes, the BMA functions as little more than an agency of the Ministry of the Interior, with a limited range of municipal responsibilities. In Bombay, furthermore, the most recent reorganization of the Metropolitan Authority ended up by reducing representation from the Municipal Corporation. Apart from the atypical examples of Hong Kong and Singapore city-states, only Tokyo seems to have clearly accepted a participatory organizational design by creating an elected, two-tier or federal structure of metropolitan government.

It is not clear, however, whether Tokyo's solution is applicable elsewhere in South and East Asia. Recommendations for a two-tier structure—part appointive and part indirectly elective—have found little favor in Calcutta, principally because of political and administrative apprehensions. A recent recommendation for a two-tier reorganization of metropolitan administration in Bangkok, to bring the BMA and other public authorities under the umbrella of a coordinating council headed by a minister for the capital region, is considered unacceptable for even more sensitive political reasons. The nation-state is a dominant political myth of the contemporary world, even though the largest nations are too small to govern the world and too large to govern the cities. The city may be a conspicuous battlefield for national politics, but it seldom gains any political power for itself from the battles.[3]

In many instances, the region's metropolitan cities are national capitals. They are seats of national or provincial governments that will not permit their authority to be challenged by other organizations in the capital city itself. The governments are also not willing to provide metropolitan-level organizations with more autonomy or opportunities that would make them highly visible political platforms for potential opponents. This phenomenon is not confined to Asian countries. The powers and resources of the metropolitan governments of greater London, Paris, and Toronto, for example, have always been subject to limitations. (There is already a proposal to abolish the Greater London Council in 1986, and the decision to replace the fragmented administration of Mexico City with one federal district, three state governments, and several municipalities is deliberate and not merely an outcome of history.) Thus the issue of representative government at the metropolitan level is indeed fraught with many practical difficulties.

New suggestions for resolving the problems of access and participation in South and East Asia are beginning to emerge, however. The Metropolitan Manila Commission, for example, has been asked to study "the feasibility of increasing barangay (neighborhood) participation in the affairs of their respective local governments," and to propose "definite programs and policies for implementation." Barangays are not only the primary social and political institutions in Manila, but they are also the oldest, having roots in the city's precolonial past; barangay captains or chairmen and executive committees are locally elected. In Jakarta, there are two informal levels of government below the official hierarchy: the rukun warga (RW) community groups of some 150 families each, and the rukun tetangga (RT) community groups of some 30 families each. These two groups—which, among other things, disseminate government information—have volunteer heads who, together with the chief executive officers of the lowest level of formal government units, form kampung (that is, neighborhood) committees to assess local development priorities, organize self-help labor, and collect funds for special improvement programs. Like barangays, kampungs are made up of traditional urban villages and primary social and political units. In both cases, systematic remodeling and strengthening of these indigenous institutions may provide a possible bottom-up solution to the problem of political and social development in the metropolitan context. Such a solution needs to be complemented by imaginative top-down solutions that likewise systematically create opportunities for access and partici-

3. See Robert T. Norman, "Urban Political Development in India," in *The City in Indian Politics*, ed. Donald B. Rosenthal (Delhi: Thomson Press, 1976).

pation. Initially, however, institutional arrangements can be informal and information systems exploratory and flexible rather than definitive.

An alternative solution to the problem of access and participation is to revive representative municipal government and to decentralize appointed metropolitan development authority staff with a view to helping the municipalities, both technically and professionally, to undertake a much greater volume of local development activities themselves. Recent and current initiatives taken by the West Bengal government are predicated on this alternative. After two decades of experience with centralized institutions, the municipal administrations (including Calcutta Corporation) are being reformed, reorganized, and strengthened by the restoration of elections, extension of powers, and enhancement of financial resources on both revenue and capital accounts. For its part, the Metropolitan Authority is undergoing a fundamental reorganization in order to revive its original metropolitan planning, programming, and budgeting functions. Some of the changes will decentralize technical and financial personnel to two new regional coordinating and monitoring offices and five zonal offices set up by West Bengal's Metropolitan Development Department to provide groups of municipalities with professional assistance in project preparation and implementation. In addition, the Institute of Local Government and Urban Studies has been set up by the state government to provide opportunities for training and research.

As a result of this upgrading of municipal institutions and simultaneous breakup of the monolithic structure of the Development Authority, the state government intends to funnel substantial development funds directly to the municipalities, which will be charged with the responsibility of preparing and executing local projects as planned and programmed by the Development Authority (within the framework of urban development strategies laid down by the state government and subject to its financial controls, which directly link annual capital programs to actual revenue performance). At the metropolitan level, the Water, Sewerage, and Drainage Authority and the Improvement Trusts are to be freed from the Development Authority's management and strengthened so that they will be able to perform their assigned tasks of providing services and developing land.

Coping with Uncertainty

The financial and institutional constraints discussed thus far indicate that the existing managerial systems are incapable of handling the overall problems confronting metropolitan management in South and East Asia today. As argued in chapter 2, this does not imply that it is neither possible nor desirable to set metropolitan goals, policies, and priorities. It does imply, however, that goals, policies, and priorities must always be open to modification and substitution in the light of new information about these problems. In style and character, metropolitan management must be an active learning process in which the authorities continuously identify the critical metropolitan issues being thrown up by the forces of urbanization and try to reduce the penumbra of uncertainty.[4]

It is true that international assistance to the cities under discussion has helped to reduce uncertainty about the continuity of funding for their metropolitan development programs. In Calcutta, for instance, there was some doubt as to whether the initial package of central and state government funding arrangements put together in 1970–71 would be continued during the fifth five-year plan commencing in 1975–76. It was largely because of the likelihood of external assistance for a considerable part of the program that its continuity from the fourth to the fifth five-year plan and from the fifth to the sixth plan could be ensured. The first loan was a credit from the International Development Association (IDA), an affiliate of the World Bank. At the time the loan was made, the Bank declared that this was the first of a series of credits, and throughout three urban development projects and one urban transport project it continued to maintain a strong, supportive interest in the Calcutta program. As a result, the central and the state governments were able to embark on a wide range of fiscal and institutional reforms in the medium and long terms. Similarly, in both Jakarta and Manila, a series of projects aided by the World Bank has in each case helped to strengthen both metropolitan and long-term perspectives and to secure the progress of a metropolitanwide planning and development effort. To the extent that uncertainty about the continuity of ongoing projects has thus been reduced, it has been possible for national, regional, and local administrations to initiate and carry through complex organizational changes and institutional reforms.

In spite of this kind of assistance, it still needs to be stressed that uncertainty remains a central challenge to metropolitan management in South and East Asia. It should also be emphasized that uncertainty is not confined to the present time or to the projects currently under way. Increasingly, urban management in South and East Asia is being forced to face problems concerning the future consequences of present actions. The large-scale public facilities being demanded require immediate investment decisions that will inevitably have long-term and widespread future ramifications of uncertain dimensions. For example, new highway and rail networks, industrial areas, commercial centers, housing projects, and water, sewerage, and power systems will all have powerful and permanent repercussions on the direction, pattern, and density of future metropolitan development. These repercussions cannot be determined in advance except as broad possibilities; they are unlikely to be limited to specific localities or service sectors; and, in the years to come, many of the investment decisions taken now will be reversible only at prohibitive cost.

Of course, the broad spatial planning undertaken in many cities of South and East Asia—particularly the 1966 basic development plan of Calcutta—has set public goals and priorities from time to time. The policies

4. See Ruth P. Mack, *Planning on Uncertainty* (New York: Institute of Public Administration, 1971), pp. 177–87, 188–209.

formulated by these exercises have concentrated on the progressive provision of basic or minimum services to all areas and sections of the city, as in Tokyo and Hong Kong; on the spatial zoning of metropolitan development for residential, industrial, commercial, and recreational purposes, particularly to regulate and control private and public initiatives, as in Singapore and Karachi; and, to a more limited extent, on the creation of job opportunities and income, as in the case of Calcutta, Madras, and Colombo.

However, no city in South and East Asia appears to have been able to set overall development goals and to attack overall development problems with enough appropriate information about the metropolitan population, economy, and land uses; about revenues, expenditures, and projected investments of the agencies involved; or about the local public's felt needs and aspirations as well as the plans and policies of regional and national governments. A central problem of metropolitan management has remained its inability to institutionalize a learning process that will reduce the gaps in knowledge to acceptable proportions, and to bring as much relevant information as possible to bear where it is most needed for decisionmaking.

Adopting New Perspectives

Faced with such great tasks, the region's metropolitan managements must adopt fresh perspectives in planning and administering urban development. For example, in recent years theory and practice have increasingly concentrated on urban and regional planning as a dynamic, organizational process of pursuing moving goals and objectives in conditions of uncertainty and accelerating change. This perception has encouraged a shift of emphasis from town planning as conventionally understood (that is, the designing of comprehensive land use plans) toward the initiation of wide-ranging and policy-oriented research and analysis requiring contrasting and changing clusters, patterns, and flows of activity not necessarily focused on land uses. This differently oriented activity may in fact be concerned mainly with defining development problems and goals in the economic and social context; such activity includes the design and appraisal of related action projects and schemes and it extends to learning by assessing performance.

There is also a growing recognition that planning the actual implementation of urban and regional development policy is as essential as formulating the programs and projects. It has become clear that the final payoff is not simply the approval of a plan or program, but some concrete act under a plan or program that has a tangible effect on everyday public life. Moreover, feedback about and evaluation of this concrete action are both integral to the success of the development planning process.

Such a philosophy of planning needs general adoption in South and East Asia because it recognizes the intimate interrelationship of the planning of development and its administration. Indeed, the methodologies of both activities are converging toward the increasing sophistication of the tools and techniques used, progressive substitution of science for art, and a growing concern for explicit validation. The validation of plans and policies is no longer mainly a function of a planner's or administrator's reputation or intuitions. Attempts are now being made to evaluate alternatives systematically in terms of conflicting norms, differing degrees of uncertainty, and varying potential futures. At the same time, the impact of politics on the process of administration—the influence of public interest groups, political parties, constituency interests, public opinion, and internal pressures and conflicts within and between administrative departments—is increasingly being viewed as a critical factor in effective urban management.[5] Undoubtedly, political leadership with vision, energy, and zeal is an essential ingredient of success.

5. See, for example, W. D. Broadnax, "Public Policy: Its Formulation, Adoption, Implementation and Evaluation," *Public Administration Review* 36, no. 6 (November–December 1976): 699–703.

5

The Search for Alternatives

MOST METROPOLITAN DEVELOPMENT authorities in the profile cities have been built on exclusive lines with minimal, if any, concessions to access and participation by other institutions and the general public. In addition to wielding significant powers of finance and control over other agencies, they have also been mandated to assume the latter's functions, either in default or in substitution. In practice, they have become extensions of the higher levels of government that have created and controlled them, but they have increasingly concentrated on sectoral responsibilities, and, with a few exceptions, have been unable to exercise the coordinating functions.

In the search for alternatives for metropolitan decisionmaking, the experience of Calcutta's transport steering committee as a coordinating task force composed of representatives of a number of different institutions is instructive. An informal and temporary platform for a network of related agencies, it was set up to promote the pooling of knowledge and experience for the formulation and execution of metropolitan transport policies. Although subsequent long-term experience of the project has been disappointing—mainly because of the difficulties of internal management within the bus company—the committee has reflected an important structural principle for systematizing a learning process: that appropriate networks need to be created between and within existing organizations.[1] Tokyo's federal government, the city-states of Singapore and Hong Kong, and the Metropolitan Manila Management Coordination Board for investment planning and programming are also organized around this basic structural principle, although in different ways. It provides a clear alternative to the hierarchical command principle of the metropolitan development authority and points to the direction in which improvements in management and organization can be sought through appropriate elements of networking.

1. See Donald Schon, *Beyond the Stable State* (New York: Norton, 1973).

Such networking must attend to the contrasting needs and operating styles of traditional urban bureaucracies and development administrations (see chapter 4). Both types of organizations are fundamental to metropolitan management, and their differing processes can be integrated through conscious networking in which the essential components are information flows linking activity clusters.

Integrating the Planning and Administration of Development

The integration of the planning and administration of development required for metropolitan management may be illustrated in terms of clusters of activity and flows of information between them (see figure 5-1). These clusters and flows create an overall pattern that is both sequential and cyclical. It is sequential in the sense that the activity may conveniently be divided into a series of stages linked by information flows. Of these stages, the first involves research into and analysis of a given metropolitan system and its environment. The second has to do with the formulation of development policy in the light of the research and analysis completed in stage 1 and of dominant political criteria. In stage 3, the policy decided on is applied through the generation of possible development programs or projects. Stage 4 is concerned with (a) the evaluation and choice of such programs or projects in the light of the policy objectives and means available for project implementation (including, in particular, political objectives), and (b) the allocation and budgeting of resources for the implementation of the programs or projects chosen (again, including political as well as other criteria). During stage 5, projects that have been programmed and budgeted are implemented. In stage 6, performance during implementation is monitored and the results and impact evaluated so that information can be fed back to all other stages of the process.

It must be emphasized that the model is neither linear nor strictly sequential. Although it has been simplified here for purposes of illustration, the model nevertheless reflects the cyclical complexity of the activity clusters and information flows involved. For instance, there can be successive rounds of activity from stage 4 through stages 5 and 6, as information on the course of implementation continues to circulate back to the activity cluster concerned with resource allocation and budgeting. In the same way, the evaluation of the results and impact at stage 6 can directly influence the formulation of policy at stage 2, or the generation of programs and projects at stage 3. Changing inputs from international, national, or regional sources—whether political, financial, or legal—can modify the action being taken at any or all of the stages from 1 to 5. Thus the overall process is circular rather than linear.

What the model cannot reflect is that policymaking will not take place regularly and in clear-cut stages, but in fits and starts. Once begun, implementation may well be delayed by local politicking, jeopardized by admin-

Figure 5-1. Overall Metropolitan Management Process

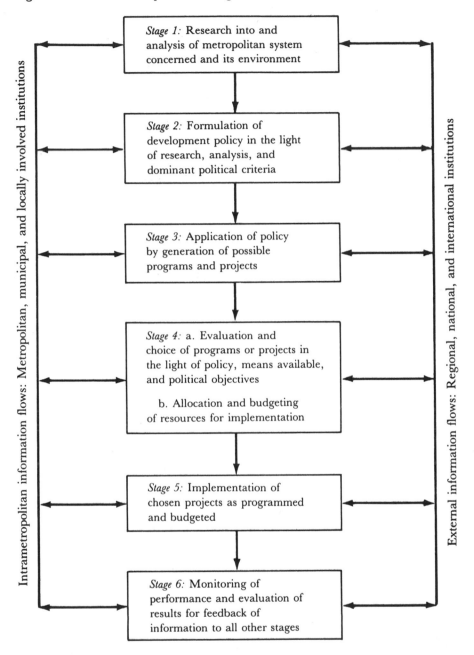

istrative bottlenecks, or halted by changes in plan priorities. Activity at one stage will affect activity at another, even though different projects are involved. The institutional environment, whether internal or external, may bring an agency to a standstill, as in the case of an internal wage dispute or external political stalemate in provincial or national governments. And different stages will undoubtedly be undertaken by different institutions, both public and private, within the same metropolitan area. According to the city profiles, their numbers in the public sector alone run into the many hundreds.

Because of this complexity, it is unlikely that the establishment of metropolitan planning and development authorities alone will achieve the integration of the planning and administration of development reflected in figure 5-1. On the contrary, organizing and coordinating the work of the activity clusters and information flows concerned requires a systematic networking of existing institutions, if it is guided by the principles embodied in the model. In stage 1 of the model, for example, research and analysis will focus on a specified system and its environment for purposes of policy preparation and adoption. The system concerned will be economic if the policy relates to goals of metropolitan economic development; it will be physical if the policy relates to goals of metropolitan land use development. Alternatively, the subject of research may be the metropolitan area's educational system, or its mass transit system, highway system, drainage system, or health services system, in whole or in part. The point is that, whatever the subject and field of research, information for the analysis will have to be gathered from many public and private sources within and outside the metropolitan area. This activity will have to be organized by an existing nodal institution (or node created by existing institutions) that can set up a network of information flows connecting the institutional sources of data, undertake the final analysis for policy information purposes, and be responsible for communicating the results to stage 2. The network will cover both the public and private sectors, and the analysis will be primarily technical.

The activity at stage 2, however—because it is involved with preparing and making decisions on metropolitan development policy—will have to be concentrated rather than dispersed, political rather than technical, and public rather than private. The institutional node here, which may be different from that of stage 1, will play a more dominant role now and the network will be less complex.

The activity of the former Calcutta Metropolitan Planning Organization (CMPO) closely followed this pattern, though in practice it extended into the model's third stage of management. The Metropolitan Basic Development Plan of 1966 included a program of projects (stage 3) to implement policy guidelines approved by the West Bengal government (stage 2) on the basis of CMPO findings and recommendations (stage 1). These findings and recommendations were the outcome of the analysis of research originally undertaken by a large number of institutions networked together by ad hoc committees set up and coordinated by CMPO. The costs of the proposed projects were sufficiently detailed to allow activity to proceed through stage 4 of the model.

The remaining problem was to institutionalize the activity to be undertaken in stages 4–6 in order to integrate the planning of development with its administration. Because the CMPO had no executive powers, the problem of institutionalization was resolved by establishing the Calcutta Metropolitan Development Authority (CMDA) in 1970. As mentioned earlier, however, serious difficulties arose during implementation (stage 5), the stage at which activity needs to be deconcentrated as far as possible and provision made for the ongoing operation, maintenance, and incremental improvement of projects once they have been completed.

An example of the successful application of the multiagency approach can be found outside the study region. Since 1979, the U.S. state of Tennessee has been coordinating the activities of federal, state, and private sector agencies in the design and creation of nature reserves.[2] The approach used there, like the one depicted in figure 5-1, is based on the following premises: the planning process is not linear but circular; administrative decisionmaking is iterative inasmuch as all options and consequences can seldom be known in advance; such planning and decisionmaking are creative activities and generate successive rounds of activity; the lack of comprehensive data need not delay implementation, provided a reasonable minimum amount is available so that the first steps can be taken; overall master plans are not indispensable and may in practice prove to be inimical to the attainment of individual agency objectives; the work of coordination can be undertaken by the agencies involved (which in practice will all be represented on an ad hoc Protection Planning Committee); cooperative participation can be encouraged and maintained through the joint use of a data source, joint development of agency agendas, and joint review of implementation; a firm, visible link between planning and administration can be provided by the participation of key agency personnel in all major phases of decisionmaking; the disproportion between resources available to each agency and the work it is expected to do can be reduced through cooperative action; and long-term continuity of funding and political leadership is essential. The Protection Planning Committee response is closely akin to the minimum organizational needs response (described in chapter 6, where specific suggestions for the institutionalization of the process are discussed).

Reconciling Development Administration and Urban Bureaucracies

As noted in chapter 4, the routine operation, maintenance, and incremental improvement of essential services, control of land uses, and similar regulatory activities have long been functions of municipal bureaucracies in South and East Asia. However, these bureaucracies have been unable to react effectively to the mounting scale of these needs. Attempts to replace or bypass municipalities with sectoral or multisectoral bodies have not solved the problem because they have failed to reconcile basic operational differences of style, procedure, and organization between the old and new systems of administration.

2. Sam Pearsall, "Multi-Agency Planning for Natural Areas in Tennessee," *Public Administration Review* 44, no. 1 (January–February 1984).

Further analysis of figure 5-1 suggests how this reconciliation can be effected. Stages 1–6 of the model portray the innovative process of development administration, including project management at stages 5 and 6; stages 4b through 6 are also concerned with routine administration covering predominantly the financing and provision of ongoing public services and controls. In practice, governments in South and East Asia have clearly been least effective in these latter stages of urban management, where confusion has been rampant. This confusion becomes resolvable in principle if the essential components of project management and ongoing administration are analyzed as shown in figures 5-2 and 5-3. Here the stages are broken down into component activity clusters and information flows and the completed development projects are shown being transferred from the project management cycle to the ongoing administration cycle for their continued operation and maintenance (including incremental improvement). The need for such a transfer has either been ignored or not fulfilled in the institution-building exercises in South and East Asia.

Figure 5-2. Project Management: Breakdown of Stages 5 and 6

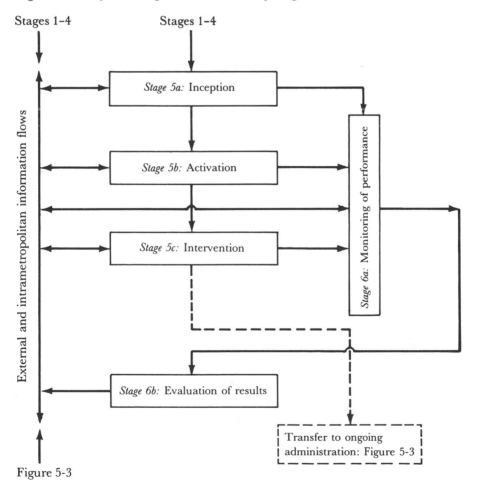

Figure 5-3. Ongoing Administration: Breakdown of Stages 4b, 5, and 6

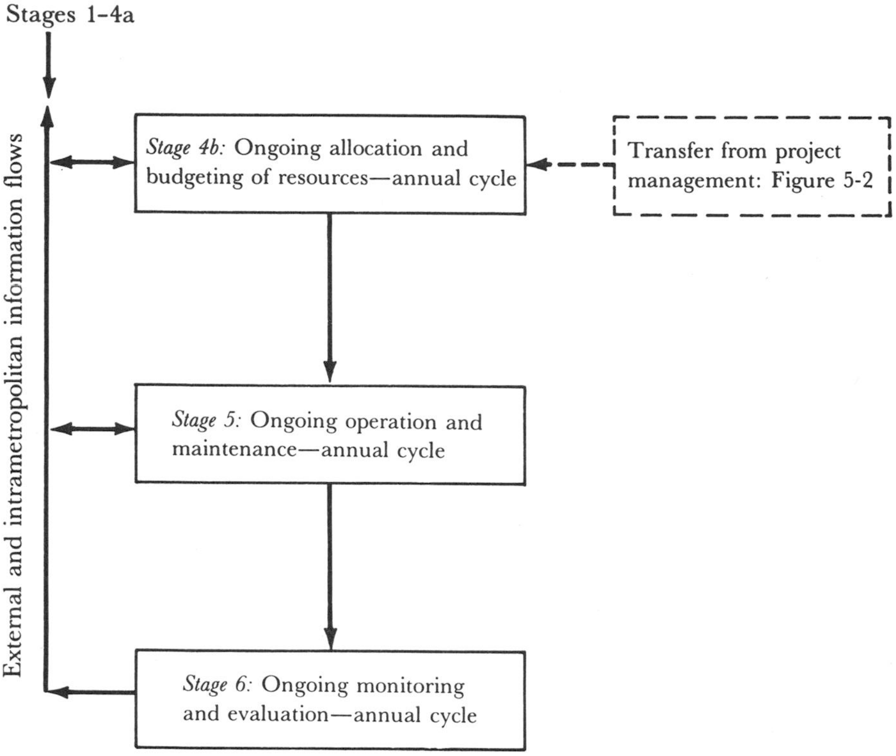

The breakdown of project management in figure 5-2 shows that project implementation (stage 5) consists of at least three clusters of activity. Stage 5a (inception) covers the action taken before implementation is set in motion; this action includes the initial updating of the project (which may need to be modified because circumstances have changed since it was finalized), drafting of enabling legislation or regulations, formulation of working procedures, bid for contracts, procurement of budgeted funds (and, where necessary, of materials and manpower), and other tooling-up activity such as setting up the machinery for monitoring in stage 6a. Stage 5b is concerned with activating the tools now assembled. Here, the necessary legislation or regulations are passed or promulgated, the circulation of procedures is authorized, timetables and work schedules are finalized, tenders or bids are evaluated, contracts are let, funds are disbursed, material and human resources are distributed, and monitoring is begun. In stage 5c, work on the site is started up by the contractor or other means; that is, the actual intervention planned, programmed, and budgeted for the project begins.

Figure 5-2 also shows that the monitoring of project performance and the evaluation of its impact and results consist of at least two clusters of activity. The first cluster—stage 6a, which has already been mentioned—has to do with monitoring performance. This activity should begin as early as possible during implementation and should continue throughout the life of the project. It will also include current evaluation of performance for the immediate use of project management. The second cluster—stage 6b—is concerned with post facto evaluations that will be fed back to earlier planning, programming, and resource allocation stages. This activity will normally follow and not precede the actual transfer of the completed project to ongoing administration for its continued operation and maintenance.[3]

Figure 5-3 shows the conventional cycle of ongoing administration (as commonly institutionalized in municipal bureaucracies) to which the project is transferred. This figure covers stages 4b–6 of figure 5-1. It reveals an annual process of financing, managing, expanding, monitoring, and evaluating the delivery of services that have already been established. Although this administrative process is cyclical, it is not closed, in that information flows back from the municipal stages of figure 5-3 to the metropolitan planning, programming, and resource allocation stages of figure 5-1, and forward again to the municipalities. This flow creates the link that should make it possible to reconcile municipal administration with metropolitan policies and priorities. Some of the information flows are external to the metropolitan complex, such as communication between national and municipal governments and departments, for example, with respect to national standards in public health and education services.

Clearly, none of these figures implies that all stages of the metropolitan management process are to be undertaken by one institution. On the contrary, different clusters of activity will normally be undertaken by different institutions within the same metropolitan complex. Furthermore, the style of administration and the professional and technical skills required will vary from cluster to cluster. And although both project management and ongoing administration are concerned with implementation, they are shown to be different processes that call for different time cycles (one cycle is determined by project exigencies and the other by the fiscal year), contrasting types of financial administration (such as planning, programming, and budgeting systems versus line-item budgeting), and contrasting personnel systems. Moreover, project management calls for interdepartmental task forces, whereas traditional administration functions through departmental units.

Responsive Networking

To institutionalize all phases and styles of metropolitan management the networks established according to the principles reflected in figures 5-1 to 5-3 must be highly flexible. The networks also need to be both horizontal

3. From a physical planning standpoint, a similar tripartite breakdown of implementation into context provision, effectuation, and execution (with two feedback information loops) has been made by R. Alterman and M. Hill, *Implementation of Urban Plans*, Working Paper CURS-WP-44 (Haifa, Israel: Center for Urban and Regional Studies, Technicon Institute for Research and Development, 1974).

and vertical if they are to respond with requisite variety to the social, economic, and physical environment of the metropolitan complex concerned, which is typically a fragmented and stratified entity. Some approaches to establishing such networks are orthodox, and rely on the integration of governmental organizations only; others are less orthodox and reach out beyond the web of government itself into the private sector.

In metropolitan Tokyo, for instance, the federal organization of its management permits the clusters of activity depicted in figure 5-3 to reside in a lower-tier network of city, town, and village bodies having local territorial jurisdiction and in special sectoral authorities with metropolitanwide jurisdictions. The top-tier metropolitan government can then focus on stages 1–4b of figure 5-1 for the city as a whole. The crucial intertier nexus is stage 4. Here, metropolitan programs or projects can be evaluated and selected for implementation in the light of overall policy and resources (see figure 5-2); their execution can be allocated to the various public and private organizations available; and resources can be budgeted accordingly. At the same time, continued operation and maintenance of many of the services and facilities thus created can become the responsibility of the lower-tier municipal and sectoral institutions concerned (see figure 5-3); if necessary, financial assistance can be provided at the metropolitan tier of government budgeted year by year, as the municipal and sectoral authorities are operating stages 4b through 6 in the annual cycle. In order to show how the conceptual principles, processes, activity stages, and information flows of the models can in fact be translated into terms of institutional functions, responsibilities, and powers in a particular, live situation, the proposals made in the 1978 plan for Greater Colombo sponsored by the United Nations Development Programme (UNDP) may be considered.[4]

At the time, the Colombo region was under the jurisdiction of two administrative districts for law enforcement, general administration, rural development, and other national activities; and under a large number of local authorities for urban services, including the Colombo and Dehiwala–Mt. Lavinia Municipal Councils, thirteen urban councils, twenty-three town councils, and fifty-five village councils. The UNDP plan proposed the creation of two new institutions by the adaptation of existing ones (each covering the urbanized area of 1.3 million people and 91 square miles) and a drastic reduction in the number of the moribund local bodies. One of the new institutions was to be a special Capital District, responsible for the planning and administration of metropolitan development (stages 1–6 of figure 5-1), including project management (figure 5-2). The other was to be a metropolitan council replacing Colombo and Dehiwala–Mt. Lavinia municipalities and fourteen other local bodies. This council was to be responsible for activating stages 4b–6 of figure 5-3, that is, the ongoing administra-

4. United Nations Development Programme, "Colombo Master Plan Project Report, Stage Two, Prague and Colombo," Project SRL/71/528, Monitoring of Housing and Local Government (Sri Lanka, Colombo, 1978).

tion of services and related facilities, together with the local planning and regulation of land use and the control of buildings, trades, traffic, and so on.

It was proposed that, as in the case of all other administrative districts in Sri Lanka, the Capital District would be headed by a district minister, but in this instance he would be assisted by a chief executive officer with the status of a secretary of a ministry. The Metropolitan Council was to be an upgraded and representative municipal authority. In effect, Colombo's status was to be raised to a level comparable to that of Jakarta and Tokyo, each of which had been made a special urban province with an administration headed by a provincial governor. But in this case an institutional distinction was to be drawn between the functions of urban planning and development on the one hand and that of ongoing administration on the other; and the division of responsibilities and powers between the Capital District and Metropolitan Council would be based on this distinction. It was thus proposed that the responsibilities of the Capital District (in consultation with an advisory council on which the Metropolitan Council would be well represented) should include the following tasks:

- Metropolitan surveys and research activities for policy planning purposes (economic, physical, and social; see stage 1, figure 5-1)
- Strategic economic planning (stage 2, figure 5-1)
- Strategic physical planning to increase housing, transport, public utilities, and facilities (stage 2, figure 5-1)
- Strategic social planning to increase the capacity to provide social services and amenities (stage 2, figure 5-1)
- Action planning (project preparation), that is, formulating for government approval proposed programs and budgets of development projects originated by the district or by any other public or private agency or firm (including the metropolitan council) and intended to realize the purposes of the plans (stage 3, figure 5-1)
- Action planning (project execution), that is, by contract or agreement allocating to public or private agencies or firms, including the metropolitan council, the execution of development projects (stage 5, figure 5-1; stages 5a–c, figure 5-2) approved by government (stage 4a, figure 5-1); budgeting for and financing in whole or in part the execution of such projects by the agencies concerned (stage 4b, figure 5-1); coordinating, supervising, and monitoring project execution (stage 6, figure 5-1; stage 6a, figure 5-2); and assessing performance and evaluating results (stage 6, figure 5-1; stage 6b, figure 5-2)
- Securing, supervising, coordinating, and, if necessary, financing the provision of essential services, by contract or agreement with the metropolitan council and other responsible bodies, including private firms (stages 4–6, figure 5-1).

Given these powers and responsibilities, the Capital District was to operate as a planning, coordinating, and controlling agency that was to create, manage, and monitor, on behalf of the national government, the

growing and changing networks of public and private bodies involved in
the preparation and implementation of projects established to realize the
district's approved development plans. To facilitate project execution, the
district was to be empowered to mobilize requisite financial and land
resources. In principle, it would thus have to be organized as outlined in
figure 5-4.

The district administration and its advisory council were to be appointed
by the national government. By contrast—as is the case in Karachi and, to
a lesser extent, Bangkok (where local elections have lapsed)—the
Metropolitan Council was to operate as a service-delivery, public works,
and regulatory agency on behalf of the metropolitan community. In this capacity, it would wield all the existing powers of the superseded Colombo
and Dehiwala–Mt. Lavinia municipalities and fourteen other local authorities, including their powers of urban taxation. It would also be empowered

Figure 5-4. Proposed Capital District Administration, Colombo

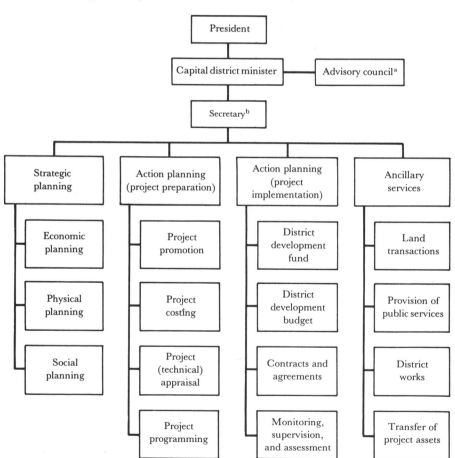

a. Including metropolitan council representatives and the private sector.

b. And secretarial and administrative services.

to prepare land use structure plans and to implement approved structure plans by means of local plans. Furthermore, it would be locally elected, employ a conventional committee structure for decisionmaking headed by a management committee, and have an executive mayor, commissioner, and appropriate departments and offices accountable to the council and its committees. At a subordinate level, the council would set up local development committees for each of the fourteen electoral districts in its area. These committees were to undertake local service and regulatory functions delegated to them. In some respects, therefore, they would parallel the barangay committees in Manila and the municipal wards of the Calcutta Corporation, being closely associated with traditional, primary social and political units, including the former municipalities. By degrees, the Metropolitan Council itself was to begin assuming overall control of the activities of a network of major utilities and transport services at present operated by independent, ad hoc statutory authorities, through their progressive attachment to the council in whole or in part as metropolitan instead of national bodies (as in Tokyo, for example). These various clusters of activity would correspond to stages 4b–6 of figure 5-3, and they would be organized institutionally as in figure 5-5.

In principle, the UNDP proposal thus sought the progressive establishment of networks focused on two nodal institutions, each maintaining the conceptual and operational distinctions between the planning and administration of urban development on the one hand and the ongoing delivery of essential services on the other. The proposal also included steps to interrelate the functions and activities of the two organizations, and to integrate the processes of metropolitan and municipal management wherever necessary, for example, for project preparation and implementation.

It was obvious from the beginning that even to initiate the preliminary steps for establishing these institutions and processes, a strong political will, clear metropolitan focus, and sophistication of a high order in organizational development were required. Subsequent events confirmed these apprehensions. By 1978, a National Housing Authority had been established with a highly publicized mandate for a massive countrywide house construction program. A Parliament complex around which a new national capital would be constructed, redevelopment of the downtown area in Colombo, and an export promotion zone near the airport were taken as priority schemes. The Urban Development Authority also established in 1978 with nationwide jurisdiction became heavily involved in these activities. Resources and attention were quickly diverted to these institutions, and the proposals for the Capital District and Metropolitan Council were quietly shelved.

Two other examples of orthodox public sector responses to metropolitan management may be cited. Both relate to Calcutta. One is the 1966 Basic Development Plan proposal for a metropolitanwide Traffic and Transportation Authority, and the other is the 1972 proposal to replace the numerous municipalities by a two-tier metropolitan council. As already indicated, for various reasons neither proposal proved to be viable politically.

Figure 5-5. Proposed Metropolitan Council, Colombo

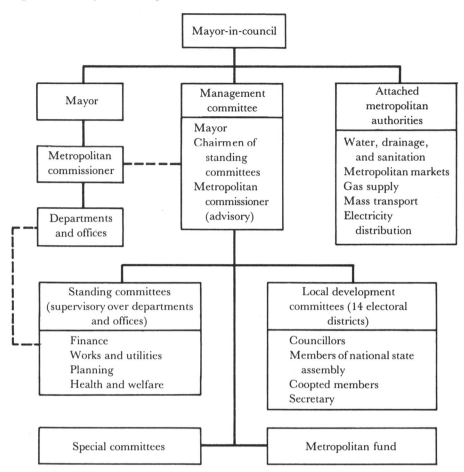

Planning, programming, and coordinating—whether at the national or city level—are unglamorous activities that seldom attract political patronage; by contrast, the amalgamation of weak and scattered municipalities can promote political strength and constitute a threat to a state government. Municipal consolidation will therefore be unwelcome in most of the cities of South and East Asia unless the consolidated municipalities are totally subordinate to the state or national government, as in Seoul, Shanghai, or Bangkok. Such consolidations are also not very useful: they fail to reflect the principles of integration discussed earlier and merely apply the command-type approach to the problems of metropolitan management.

There is thus good reason to believe that less ambitious responses than those put forward for Colombo need to be thoroughly explored, provided they conform to the basic requirements of the above models. One category of possible responses involves greater use of the private sector and private voluntary groups for project preparation and implementation and for service delivery as a means of both improving efficiency and reducing the burden placed on public systems (stage 3, figure 5-1; stages 5a–c, figure 5-2; stage 5, figure 5-3). Another category covers the minimum organizational machinery necessary at the metropolitan level for at least formulating development policy, evaluating and choosing related programs and projects, and allocating resources and budgeting for implementation (stages 2 and 4, figure 5-1). (The subject of a necessary minimum is discussed in chapter 6, the other alternatives in the following two sections.)

Using the Private Sector

The cities of South and East Asia have long used the private sector for the management, operation, and maintenance of certain public services. In many cities during the colonial era, private companies provided electricity, gas, telephone, and transport services. On independence, most were nationalized or otherwise absorbed into the public sector, but private sector utilities are still to be found in metropolitan Manila (electricity, gas, and telephone companies), Calcutta (electricity, bus, and ferry services), Bangkok (minibuses), and Karachi (gas and electricity services).

Today, the use of the private sector continues to be significant in the transport sector.[5] In Hong Kong, the use of privately operated minibuses was legalized in 1969, and franchised maxicabs with fixed routes, fares, and timetables and controlled staffing, garaging, and maintenance were introduced in 1976. In Singapore, both the main bus service company and the supplementary services are privately run at a profit. In Calcutta, as already mentioned, private buses now account for some 65 percent of all trips. Their service is supplemented by private minibuses and is controlled by voluntary route associations, which determine the fares to be charged, specify the routes to be followed, fix the timetables, and fine owners of buses not running on time. The route associations compete for routes, but all fares are collected by the owners. In Manila, 28,000 privately owned jeepneys account for some 40 percent of total public transport trips.

There is no inherent reason for limiting the use of the private sector to transport only. In many cities of South and East Asia, private sector efforts already cover a wide range of functions from health care to recreation. Hospitals and clinics are obvious examples, but in Calcutta even the expansion of primary education has been undertaken largely by the private sector. In these and similar cases, the government's essential role is not that of owner-operator or producer of the services. Indeed, in the present regional metropolitan context, it is hardly necessary to consider in depth the question of which services may best be operated by the public sector as opposed to the private sector. The scale of need is so great that, more often than not, a response from both sectors is vital. And where, as here, financial resources and skills are severely limited relative to needs, metropolitan management

5. See Gabriel Roth and George G. Wynne, *Free Enterprise Urban Transportation* (Washington, D.C.: Council for International Urban Liaison, 1982), pp. 7–9.

really has no alternative but to turn to the private sector for the delivery of a substantial range of essential services.

Using Voluntary Groups

Less common than the private sector alternative are the integrated improvement projects for the urban poor illustrated in the city profiles, such as the Kampung Improvement Program in Jakarta, Low-Income Settlement Program in Karachi, and Tondo Foreshore Urban Renewal Project in Manila.[6] Although devised to meet short-term critical situations and thus not strictly concerned with routine operation and maintenance as defined in figure 5-3, these programs and projects have included unusual methods of improving a wide range of local services and facilities for targeted urban communities. The projects have been area specific, but they have not been limited to any one sector. A wide range of activities—such as street improvements, drainage, lighting, community spaces, and schools—have been incorporated into new housing construction or rehabilitation. The voluntary groups concerned have been involved in the project cycle right from the design stage itself, as in the Tondo Foreshore Project in Manila. In Jakarta the rukun warga (RW) and rukun tetangga (RT) groups have been responsible for the upkeep and maintenance of many of the facilities in the kampungs. In Karachi the local community groups are directly involved in the improvement program for the Katchi Abadis.

The Urban Community Development Program in Hyderabad, the fifth largest city in India (population, 2.5 million), has been a model for several cities in the country. The program serves a slum population of about half a million and includes a wide range of activities from self-help housing to welfare for women and children, preschool education, income-generation activities, vocational classes, and so on. About 300 part-time volunteers help to implement the program, which is funded by the central and state governments and the municipal corporation on a 2:1:1 basis. Programs of this type indicate that an important shift is taking place toward greater local participation in the management of social services by consultative means, which differ from those of traditional representative government, and toward community self-help through volunteer task forces, as opposed to the bureaucratic delivery of services.

The barangays of metropolitan Manila (see chapter 4) illustrate a further possible stage of this evolution, in which the principles of community participation, access, and self-help are reconciled with those of orthodox municipal administration. Each barangay is organized into seventeen volunteer task forces (brigades) for the delivery of several basic services (community beautification; reduction of crime; disaster relief; information ser-

6. Also see *Integrated Improvement Program for the Urban Poor*, 2 vols. (Washington, D.C.: U.S. Agency for International Development, Office of Urban Development and Housing, September 1981).

vices; traffic control; sports and recreation; water supply; education and cultural services; personal health services; provision of shelter; food distribution; power services; environmental health; economic mobility of people, goods, and services; employment; settlement of community disputes; and promotion of clothing-oriented cottage industries). Financing is allocated by the city government from a barangay fund that receives 10 percent of real property tax collections, 20 percent of the internal revenue allotment remitted to the city by the national government, and an annual appropriation of 500 pesos for each barangay.

According to an official publication,[7] the barangay in Manila City has evolved into a

> miniature quasi-municipal corporation complete with people, territory, and government. A barangay comprises 200 families who choose a chairman and six councilmen to exercise executive and legislative powers, while judicial power is exercised by a barangay court. There are 912 barangays grouped into 100 zones of from five to ten barangays each. The 100 zones, in turn, are grouped into 20 zone groups for administrative maneuverability. This grouping ensures effective management, administrative efficiency and monitoring of activities and projects.

Roles of the Public and Private Sectors

In practice, the use of the private sector and voluntary groups will depend on the level of local capabilities and the scale of services to be decentralized. Contrary to perceptions of slum settlements as marginal and destabilizing, experience in many of the region's cities has established that it is indeed the so-called marginal communities that can best mobilize community effort and interact effectively with public agencies.[8] That experience also indicates general agreement with the principle that government need not be the owner and operator of all essential urban facilities and services, provided it can determine what needs to be done and ensure that it is done effectively and efficiently. Thus it follows that private enterprises and voluntary organizations may undoubtedly be encouraged to relieve the public sector of much of the work of project implementation and of the ongoing delivery and upkeep of at least utility services. They may also be encouraged to participate in the research and analysis for the formulation of metropolitan development plans and policies and to assist in generating potential projects for the latter's realization.

7. Manila Advisory Committee, Office of the Mayor, *Manila: Frontiers of Public Administration and the Pacific Nations* (March 23, 1982), pp. 41–42.

8. See Janice Perlman, "Urban Marginality—The State of the Art and Some Myths," Papers of World Bank Urban Poverty Task Force (Washington, D.C., October 1974); and David Collier, *Squatters and Oligarchs: Authoritarian Rule and Policy Change in Peru* (Baltimore, Md.: Johns Hopkins University Press, 1976).

This is not to argue that the public sector should divest itself of its truly metropolitan responsibilities, but that, in order to discharge these responsibilities, it should focus its efforts on those activities that the private sector cannot possibly undertake. As shown in figure 5-1, they comprise the formulation of metropolitan plans and policies, evaluation and choice of related programs and projects, allocation of resources for their implementation, and monitoring and evaluation of the performance and results of such implementation, both public and private. The public sector must also be responsible for the operation and maintenance of the information systems that are fundamental to the success of metropolitan management.

6

Manpower Needs and Development

IT IS IDLE TO TALK of effective urban management without addressing the serious manpower problems involved. The types of skills demanded in metropolitan management as distinct from those needed in traditional and routine urban management have already been discussed in chapter 4.

As the activities of government in the region's great cities have become increasingly onerous and complex and the traditional urban administration model (typified by the local municipality) has been rapidly overtaken by events, the sectoral bodies set up to undertake urgent, large scale capital works have needed additional managerial talents for project identification, preparation, and execution. The increasing size of the programs has demanded ever greater attention to technical and operational efficiency. The introduction of multisectoral authorities has added yet another dimension of organizational complexity requiring emphasis on corporate planning and management. The tasks of metropolitan management in such an environment call for both experience and experiment so that conventional, day-to-day administration of services and upkeep of assets can be carried out at the same time that creative initiatives in urban development are actively pursued.

Manpower Needs

In view of the growing need for various administrative and technical talents, the development of manpower is of utmost importance. The skills required fall into three broad categories: vocational, professional, and managerial. Although most metropolitan cities in the region have long-established facilities for training technicians and other vocational employees, the demand far exceeds the supply. In many developing countries skill shortages are exacerbated by emigration. No comprehensive estimate of the size of the brain drain from such countries is available, and most studies have focused on a single country of destination or origin and have examined gains and losses in a limited range of skills. A recent study of the Philippines, for example, estimates that if present enrollment rates continue and emigration is halted, it will take about sixteen years to produce the physicians needed nationwide; but if the present emigration rate persists, it will take some twenty-six years.

Several other countries face similar problems. The emigration of professionals and trained workers in the construction industry has been pronounced in Manila, Karachi, and Colombo. Since construction experience is more easily acquired and apt to be found in urban areas, the immediate impact of such emigration is felt in these areas. Shortages tend to be chronic and severe in local government.[1] In most cities, construction conditions are difficult and complex, particularly in projects involving slum upgrading or the provision of utilities in densely populated areas. Raw recruits are ill-suited for such projects. Not only is longer formal training necessary, but greater on-site competency is called for.

In most of the region's cities, the scale of effort and desired pace of metropolitan development have made it necessary to bring together a wide assortment of staff, both skilled and unskilled, and from varying disciplines, levels, and backgrounds. Irrigation engineers have had to become drainage specialists, civil engineers have been converted into solid waste experts, police officers into transport operators, and architects into tax collectors. Governments have had to press into use all available manpower, hoping that experience and working procedures will be built up on the job itself.[2] But that approach has to change as new directions are now required of metropolitan management, such as information exchange systems (both vertical and horizontal), urban and regional development research for policy preparation, strategic and corporate planning, and reliable long-and short-term progress-monitoring systems. Enhanced capabilities are also required in project development and evaluation, in the identification and marshaling of new sources of finance, in public information and communications, and in manpower development itself.

In sharp contrast to industry or trade, attention to manpower development and training has been conspicuously inadequate in urban management. Where training has been initiated in some of the needed disciplines or functions, it has seldom been concerned with either interdisciplinary or interagency issues. The latter are critical for metropolitan as distinct from less complex urban management and require special skills in interpersonal and interorganizational behavior. Professional and technical personnel may be reluctant to undergo general management training because of apprehensions that their advancement in technical careers may suffer. This poses

1. See World Bank, *World Development Report 1983* (New York: Oxford University Press, 1983), pp. 101–06.

2. K. C. Sivaramakrishnan, ''Training for Planning, Financing, and Managing Urban Growth,'' Economic Development Institute Bangkok Course (Washington, D.C.: World Bank, July 1984).

problems for the development of managers from internal resources. In Manila, Colombo, and Karachi the brain drain from public to private and overseas institutions during the course of advanced training is an additional problem. Only in Calcutta has any attempt been made to identify, quantify, and collate manpower needs on a metropolitanwide basis. Unfortunately, follow-up actions on the training plan have been poor. Manpower development is further complicated by the fact that the value of comprehensive training programs will greatly depend in practice on prior, or at least simultaneous, initiation of systematic career development programs. These appear to be lacking in all of the region's principal cities. Here, then, is yet another new direction to be explored by metropolitan management in seeking to respond to the continuing challenge of massive urbanization. In every metropolitan city today, a review of the broad categories of skills needed, the identification of the gaps in such skills that can be filled by training and retraining, and the formulation of training and career programs are all urgently required.

Training

In determining the training priorities, the activities concerned need to be viewed in interrelated clusters. In table 6-1, an attempt is made to identify these clusters and assess the present position of skills, training needs, and the types of training appropriate to those needs. For example, operation and maintenance, construction management, and project design are all closely related activity clusters (items 1–5). Their special needs differ markedly from those of city-level and corporate planning, as identified in item 8. It should be emphasized that the integrated application of diverse skills is itself a special need of metropolitan management. Even so, it is also important to recognize and accept the patent shortage of skills across the board in many aspects of that management. Table 6-1 furnishes an indicative rather than exhaustive list, however, and in the case of each city a special review will be necessary to assess its actual priorities.

In formulating training programs, a clear distinction needs to be drawn between "course" and "noncourse" types of training, and between course-type training that is to be undertaken locally, nationally, or internationally. Furthermore, all skill needs may not be met by training alone, and, when necessary, the programs will have to provide for, or support, more formal education in academic institutions.

A view persists that training for urban management can be imparted only by urban managers and by persons specialized in one or more of its various aspects. Although practical experience can indeed enhance the quality of instruction, it must be recognized that urban management covers a very wide field. Managers and staff have to be drawn from many different disciplines and will function at several different levels. Whether planning for a land development project or constructing a sewer network, it is the interaction between the different disciplines involved that will largely determine the

Table 6-1. Target Groups and Training Needs

Activity	Present position	Training needs	Suggested types of training and trainers
1. Operation and maintenance of daily municipal services			
Water supply distribution	Staff mostly unskilled	Large numbers involved	On-the-job and simulation
Drainage	Skills and experience acquired traditionally	Training has to be brief and replicable	Trainers with operational experiences in public utilities
Solid waste collection			
Street lights	Close contact with the people affects public image of organization	Simple in content	
Road upkeep		To impart and to update skills	
2. Operation and maintenance of central municipal facilities			
Water works and sewage treatment plants	Numbers not large, but usually understaffed	Updating of skills	On-the-job and simulation
Power plants	Staff needs not projected at design stage	Medium- to high-tech inputs for instrumentation and operating procedures	Industrial engineers
Solid waste disposal plants			
	Instrumentation, process flaws, operating procedures not fully identified	Programs needed at staff induction stage and later on	
		Replicable	
3. Construction management (traditional public works)			
Roads, buildings, water works, drainage, etc.	Conventional approaches to contract and works management	Project management, especially works, materials, and contract management	Classroom
			On-the-job attachments
	Uneven staffing		Case work
		Programs needed at induction and later on	Construction managers and professional trainers
		Replicable	
4. Construction management (new types)			
Slum upgrading, sites and services, low-cost sanitation, etc.	Staffing needs large and scattered	New and flexible standards (maintenance oriented)	On-the-job and simulation
	Small, difficult, scattered sites	Large-scale staffing	Operational staff
			Professional trainers
	Conventional skills for design and construction may not apply	Programs to be brief and replicable	

Activity	Present position	Training needs	Suggested types of training and trainers
5. Project design	Skills available for traditional public works but insufficient for new types of projects	Cost recovery and affordability as inputs to design Cost-benefit analysis Computer applications for design Programs will be varied Will address different staff levels	Classroom, case studies, and simulation Subject matter specialists Professional trainers
6. Management of taxes and charges Property rates, water charges, fees, and licenses	Problems of assessment, out-of-date information base, outmoded procedures Staff poorly paid, poorly trained Lack of incentives Process viewed as complex and mysterious by public	Analysis of tax base Data base update and control Procedure revisions Billing and accounting systems Efficiency criteria in tax collection	Classroom, case studies, simulation, and on-the-job training Financial managers Taxation specialists Management trainers
7. Personnel management In municipal councils, functional agencies, state departments of planning, urban development	Highly uneven In municipal bodies, large numbers, over- and understaffing Little or no professional inputs Lack of incentives	Personnel management Incentives system Career planning Manpower development Training program formulation and implementation	Classrooms and case studies On-the-job in certain cases Personnel managers Manpower development specialists

(Table continues on the following page.)

Table 6-1   (continued)

Activity	Present position	Training needs	Suggested types of training and trainers
8. *City-level and corporate planning*			
Municipal development programs and budgeting, corporate planning for development authorities, water boards, housing boards, etc.	Lack of staff skills to project sectoral needs, prepare multisectoral programs, and relate them to budget Capital budget in development authority and technical boards limited to compilation of schemes Multiple institutions and absence of mechanism or process for interaction Varied staff levels and skills involved	Financial and sectoral forecasting techniques Cost-benefit and other analyses for sectoral and intersectoral priorities Project and program monitoring system Medium- and long-range planning Management information system	Classroom, case studies, and simulation Interdisciplinary courses, seminars Management trainers, subject specialists, and corporate managers

quality and success of the effort. Furthermore, the number of persons with appropriate urban management experience is severely limited, and if we are to rely only on them to teach as well as to undertake the work in hand, training on any meaningful scale may be quite impossible.

In some activities, such as the operation and maintenance of municipal services, the construction management of slum upgrading, and other new types of public works projects, hands-on experience may be very useful. But in project design, works management, tax administration, and corporate planning, prior urban operational experience is not essential. The skills needed in these areas of urban management are not greatly different from those required in comparable areas of development administration in general. Indeed, it may well be important to build into programs of urban training a range of lessons from other areas of expertise. Skills in construction management, personnel administration, financial controls, and information systems are not confined to a particular service sector; they can be compared and applied effectively across several different sectors. If training for industry had depended on in-house experience alone, education in business management would not have reached its present commanding position. In corporate planning for metropolitan management, management development must receive special attention, and training for this purpose must reflect other areas of expertise, both public and private.

It is tempting to think about building up a cadre of trainers for urban management, but that may be quite unrealistic in many of the region's countries. In municipal engineering, for instance, city administrations have traditionally drawn personnel from polytechnic and engineering colleges. Overall, the supply is limited and has to be shared among many needs. Thus, despite long emphasis on and investment in engineering education, India's need for water supply and sanitation engineers during the UN-sponsored International Water Supply and Sanitation Decade may be two to three times greater than what can actually be made available during the seventh five-year plan period. This situation is probably mirrored in many other countries. Although the specific needs and work contexts of urban management are now increasingly being reflected in academic curriculums, in overall numbers the supply of personnel may still fall well short of requirements. The shortage of academic facilities and teachers will thus be felt in many sectors, and the pressures for on-the-job and in-house training will increase further.

In absolute terms, the funds required for training purposes will not be large relative to the investment in urban infrastructure or to the overall expenditure of urban organizations. Yet, experience to date indicates that the needed funds are not easy to obtain. Ironically, in some instances it has not even been possible to spend the funds allocated. Clearly, such frustrating experience highlights the need for a training plan. There is no escape from, or short-cut to, preparing such a plan. The exercise can begin most usefully at individual organizational and city levels. Training-plan exercises at regional and national levels tend to be too broad, to be couched in aggregates, and to involve a large number of agencies, none of which may be willing or available to carry the plan through from design to implementation. There may be some exceptions, particularly in city-states, but in most cases the individual agency and the city concerned should normally form the two opposing ends of the training-plan spectrum.

7

Effective Metropolitan Management

In every metropolis in South and East Asia, urban management faces a myriad of tasks. The institutional means available for dealing with these tasks are equally as numerous and varied. It is not feasible to develop a common organizational design with a jurisdiction and structure capable of encompassing this complex plurality of functions and organizations. Where a command-type, multisectoral authority has sought to accomplish many different tasks within the four walls of a single institution, its attempts have been largely unsuccessful or have led to serious interagency conflicts. Proposals for metropolitan government designed to integrate all sectors, levels, and kinds of public activity have encountered formidable practical, political, and social obstacles. The dangers in attempting a premature institutionalization of the metropolitan management process in its entirety must therefore be fully recognized.

Minimum Organizational Needs

At least initially, the focus should be on accomplishing an essential minimum. The conceptual model in figure 5-1 and the discussion of public and private sector roles in chapter 5 suggest that such a minimum will need to involve at least two main clusters of activity: one concerned with the overall decisions on metropolitan development plans and policies (stage 2), and the other with the overall choice of programs and projects to be implemented, the allocation of executive roles, and the appropriate budgeting of financial resources (stage 4a and b).

The design of a metropolitan management organization should concentrate on these minimum tasks. The powers and functions of a metropolitan management organization should be determined not by what it can do, but by what other organizations cannot do and will therefore leave undone. The metropolitan-level management tasks as discussed in chapter 5 should be specifically provided for in organizational design, and it should not be presumed that the mere creation of metropolitan development authorities will accomplish them. In India, where in the past twenty years more than two dozen development authorities have been set up in almost all of its metropolitan cities, it is now being realized that these management tasks do go by default owing to the preoccupation of the development authorities with the execution of projects. Opinion has now shifted in favor of letting the municipal bodies and sectoral agencies handle the execution and provision of services.[1] The sectoral and territorial integration of these activities is now regarded as a strategic or corporate planning task, which will be either poorly executed or wholly neglected if the development authority itself acts as a line agency.

Management Team and Investment Budget

In all of the cities surveyed, there has been a growing awareness of the need to make capital budgeting a principal activity of metropolitan management, that is, stage 4b. Manila has already established a sophisticated system for the analysis and selection of investment priorities, and metropolitan managements elsewhere are now also striving to introduce such a function. As mentioned earlier, putting together an investment budget involves a wide range of supporting activities; factual data have to be assembled, goals set, and investment options selected. In essence, the budgetary process relies on participation and moves forward by consensus rather than by command.[2]

Experience in South and East Asia strongly suggests that, to meet minimum organizational needs, emphasis should be placed on the formation of *networks* of existing institutions, in both the private and the public sectors, to channel information and policy proposals to a *metropolitan management team* for overall planning purposes, and subsequently to recommend related development projects and programs to it for metropolitan review, selection, and financing.

As the capital investment folio experience in Manila and the preparation of action programs in some other cities show, these exercises in team leadership need not be complicated and drawn out. Although they must have a metropolitan perspective, they can be informal, provided the team is given adequate power and authority to take overriding decisions on who will get what, when, and where. The political implications of these decisions cannot be ignored, however, and unless the team members bear a parallel political responsibility, they can be no more than advisors to the appropri-

1. For a detailed discussion on the subject, see David A. Grossman, *The Investment Budget: A Tool of Metropolitan Management* (New York: Nova Institute, May 1983).

2. "Report of the Task Force on Management of Urban Development" (New Delhi: Planning Commission, 1984).

ate political power center of the national or state government. Although the Madras Metropolitan Development Authority is a formal body, for example, it only advises the state finance department on the allocation of funds to implementing agencies and performs a capital budgeting and monitoring function on behalf of this department and not on its own. In these matters, the authority acts beyond its statutory powers and very much as an informal advisory management team. As long as the state is willing to support the authority's nonstatutory activities and advice, the minimum organizational requirements can thus continue to be met without legal provision, especially as the professional members of the authority represent a network of institutions.

In most cities of South and East Asia today, such an informal and advisory status is possibly all that can be expected initially for a metropolitan management team. It can at least start working on information exchange and analysis and then move on to goal-setting and identifying priorities. As it becomes more competent and its work gains professional and political acceptance, it can also begin to assume responsibility for resource allocation, and subsequently for the coordination of investment and the overall monitoring of program implementation. Here again, however, the danger of premature institutionalization needs to be stressed.

Interorganizational Relations

A team approach that emphasizes institutional networks calls for an appropriate style of metropolitan management. First, a management team needs to represent at least the main organizations and agencies—whether central, provincial, or local—that are responsible for financing and managing metropolitan investment and services. In many of the region's cities, especially in countries with a federal constitution, it has not been easy to secure the participation of central government authorities in metropolitan-level activities. In the cities of India, for example, the central government's railways and telecommunications ministries plan and implement their programs without reference to the metropolitan-level activities of other public agencies. Whether this blinkered isolation results from a reluctance to cooperate with other agencies, from total lack of a metropolitan perspective, or from the failure of the state and metropolitan-level organizations to press for such participation, the net result has been that large segments of metropolitan investment and functions are not related to overall metropolitan needs and priorities. Where the city is also the national capital, as are Jakarta and Manila, the task of promoting interagency cooperation has often been somewhat easier because the city and state administrations concerned have readier access to the national leadership. In principle, an emphasis on team work should help to improve the climate of interagency relationships.

Second, the vital role of advocacy must be considered. A management team should represent the needs of the metropolis to higher levels of government and should strive to win from them the extra resources, policy, or legal changes required to meet those needs. On behalf of the metropolis, it should also advocate that the line agencies and municipalities improve their internal efficiency and cost recovery, change their priorities, and make appropriate contributions to metropolitan programs. In this dual advocacy role, research and analysis are crucial. The collation of information about service deliveries, investment programs, and resources; the identification of inconsistencies and deficiencies; and the exploration of options and alternatives are all critical activities in securing responses and determining priorities. In this process, it is vital to strive for a consensus and to achieve changes by the exercise of collective judgment and group pressure for conformity. But informal means of achieving consensus are not enough; metropolitan management must enjoy some latent power to command loyalty, even though it may be discreet and conservative in the exercise of that power.

Such power often comes more readily from a de facto dependence on metropolitan management for needed scarce resources than from having formal control. Spatial or physical planning control is highly important, however, since it commands access to land and the permission to develop it. Command over the marginal increment of financial resources is also desirable because it enables management to exercise control over the extra uncommitted funds that may be available for new programs. Thus a metropolitan management team must be both representative of and closely associated with central or state governments, particularly with the financial and economic or development-planning corridors of power at the state level. A case in point is the newly created institutional network and reorganized Metropolitan Development Authority in Calcutta. The municipalities there can now take an active part in managing these institutions by co-opting their chairmen onto regional and local works committees. Another example is the role proposed for the Metropolitan Manila Commission as a regional directorate of the National Economic Development Authority and the advisory function it now plays by virtue of its Memorandum of Agreement with the Ministry of the Budget.

Whatever the actual situation may be, metropolitan management should, in principle, be closely associated with the major institutions involved in metropolitan development, and it should enjoy their cooperation. It can help to win and maintain this cooperation by refusing to undertake projects and provide specific services itself. Metropolitan management should in any case not become occupied with details that lie within the competence of line agencies.

Third, interorganizational relationships involve questions of local autonomy between the metropolis and regional and central governments, on the one hand, and the metropolis and local municipalities, on the other. It is clear from the city profiles, as well as from the preceding chapters, that the tasks of metropolitan management are by no means merely municipal. Even if municipal boundaries are adjusted or extended to bring the metropolitan territory within the jurisdiction of a single municipality—as was proposed for Colombo in 1978—a substantial range of managerial functions will still lie beyond municipal competence or be quite nonmunicipal in character. The Colombo proposals clearly recognized this fact. Telecommunications, nonlocal transport, higher education, environmental control, public safety, and wholesale trade are too complex for a single municipal authority to handle. They will often also be too complex for even a special sectoral authority. In transport, for example, where a variety of modes and public and private ownership are involved, it is not feasible to place a single traffic and transportation authority in charge of transit investments, tariffs, operations, traffic management, and all the other aspects of transport. Although autonomy in internal matters is essential if an agency is to perform its assigned tasks effectively within the limits of its powers and finances, autonomy cannot be an end in itself in metropolitan management. On the contrary, the cities of South and East Asia sorely need fiscal, legal, and administrative support from regional and national governments. Successful metropolitan management in these cities depends on striking a balance between, on the one hand, the responsibility of city governments and sectoral agencies to provide the services and sustain the massive investments needed to keep the metropolis functioning and, on the other, the responsibility to maintain regional and national funding support and to conform with the higher control such support must inevitably entail. In short, a practical balance has to be struck between local metropolitan autonomy and central authority in the interests of effective interorganizational cooperation and a team approach.

Management and Local Representation

In the final analysis, the legitimacy of metropolitan management derives from the public's sanction, and its effectiveness is a function of management's response to the public's expressed needs and desires. Aside from Tokyo, however, no great city in South and East Asia can claim long and well-tried experience with these political principles at the metropolitan level. (Reasons for this lack of experience have already been advanced in chapter 4.)

With some justification, it may be argued that orthodox or conventional patterns of representative government may be impossible to achieve or may be undesirable at the metropolitan level in national capitals undergoing rapid growth and change. It has often been asked how a city adding the equivalent of an Athens every year can still maintain classical forms of democracy. Yet, metropolitan policies, especially the financial aspects of those policies, need local political acceptance and support if they are to achieve their goals. In the absence of representative municipal institutions, or of more localized political units such as barangays and kampungs, metropolitan management must use other means to inform public opinion about, and obtain public support for, its courses of action. But it must also open the door to local public initiatives. The former Calcutta Metropolitan

Planning Organization, for example, established a large number of liaison committees, appointed a public relations officer, and eventually obtained considerable municipal and public support for its activities.

Even so, in the absence of any follow-up action on its plans of 1966, support for the Planning Organization rapidly dwindled. The creation of the Metropolitan Development Authority in 1970 took place in the teeth of opposition from the state government's sectoral departments and other public agencies. It is true that the authority's metropolitan development program endured over the subsequent twelve years despite considerable changes in national, state, and local political leadership, but this endurance was deceptive. Initial success was due in no small part to the bankruptcy of the municipal governments, and the authority had difficulty in establishing a strong public constituency in competition with the traditional political institutions. It eventually ran out of time. Now the municipalities have been resurrected and the sectoral agencies realigned so that they can undertake more positive initiating roles in Calcutta's metropolitan development and strengthen their capacity for ongoing service delivery.

These considerations point to the long-term need for strong representative municipal institutions that will nevertheless basically support overall metropolitan management, whether it is mainly appointed or elected, and whether concentrated in the hands of the state or devolved to a province or region. The solution to the potential problem of conflicting political interests inherent in this prescription may ultimately lie in a number of mutually supportive programs. In the long run, for example, management training and development programs that include local community leaders as well as state and municipal employees can certainly help to improve management's understanding of the interinstitutional issues involved and the need for team work. There are lessons to be learned from the Tennessee experience (see chapter 5), especially in the provision of opportunities for joint decisionmaking during the politically sensitive stages of the metropolitan management process—that is, during stages 2, 4a, and 4b of figure 5-1. The acceleration of social and economic integration should itself help strengthen the political foundations of city government. In the short run, the potential advantages of ad hoc committees, active community relations services, and similar consultative and informatory devices need to be exploited to the full.

Paradoxically, the search for alternative means of metropolitan management in the cities of South and East Asia seems to lead to a reconsideration of the potential role of municipal institutions. Development administration has brought a new, creative dimension to city management, but it has failed to build a capacity to maintain what has been created without detriment to public accountability, access, and participation. The question is whether representative municipal institutions can cooperatively provide that capacity if, as in Calcutta today, they are given the structures, powers, financial resources, and technical assistance to do so. As noted earlier, much will depend on the vitality and long-term vision of the political leadership. The countries of South and East Asia are by no means alone in tending to subordinate long-run metropolitan needs to short-run political maneuvers. This is not a problem of urban management as such, however; rather, it is one of representative government in general.

The Role of International Agencies

The growing impact of urbanization on developing countries first began to receive international attention in the late 1960s. As indicated in chapter 1, the projection of past trends then suggested that massive urban development was likely to continue well into the future, with urban populations expected to expand from 1.3 billion to 3.3 billion by the end of the century. Even in Africa, the least urbanized region in the world, the urban population was expected to quadruple between 1980 and 2000. Thus, within two generations, countries hitherto regarded as largely rural were expected to be virtually transformed. A series of studies by the United Nations and supporting university research provided these sobering demographic assessments; but they did not tell the whole story. The contribution of urban areas to national economies and the impact of infrastructure deficiencies on economic productivity and social development still needed to be investigated. In this respect, studies such as the Ford Foundation's 1972 International Urbanization Survey were of a pioneering nature. For its part, the U.N. Center for Building, Planning and Housing began to focus attention on low-income settlements in the cities, their contribution to the economy, and the need for physical and socioeconomic improvements. On a different plane, the United Nations Development Programme, the World Health Organization, and similar agencies suggested that comprehensive development plans be prepared for a number of metropolitan cities. In South and East Asia, such efforts were mounted at this time in Karachi, Calcutta, Bangkok, and Manila. As a result, in the early 1970s there was a growing awareness in the region's cities of the need for strategic policies of development and related investment plans.

The World Bank was a latecomer to this scene, but it profited from the earlier international work and experience. Its 1972 Urbanization Sector Paper reviewed recent and current national and international efforts to deal with urban problems, cautioned against ambitious and "quick-fix" solutions, and counseled selectivity in the types of projects to be assisted by the Bank through a "learning-by-doing" approach, which would lead to an expansion of assistance as it gained experience and refined its strategy. By these means, the Bank would not so much help to solve urban problems as it would "exert catalytic or dynamic influence on the pattern of growth through the project itself, or through the linkages with other sectors and the overall planning involved."[3]

3. World Bank, *Urbanization*, Sector Working Paper (Washington, D.C., June 1972); see also World Bank, *Learning by Doing: World Bank Lending for Urban Development, 1972–82* (Washington, D.C., 1983).

The Bank began its urban lending operations with a sites and services project in Senegal in June 1972. Two years later, its first involvement in a multisectoral metropolitan program began with the Calcutta project. Since then, the Bank has been involved in sixty-two urban projects. Of the total project cost of US$4,578 million, Bank lending has accounted for some US$2,018 million. Of this sum, a little more than a quarter (US$438 million) has been spent on so-called integrated projects, which are primarily citywide investment programs located in metropolitan areas.

In South and East Asia, the Bank is currently involved in all of the cities surveyed. As already mentioned, a direct and perceptible result of this involvement has been the promotion of continuity, both of the particular projects funded and of the general process of metropolitan development planning and administration. Where the Bank has financed only studies or the preparation of models and plans, as in Istanbul and Bogotá, the results have merely fueled a growing skepticism about urban economic and planning models.[4] But, generally speaking, advice on matters of planning and policy, combined with credit for specific projects, has had a significant impact. In the selection of projects, formulation of investment programs, and changes in operational policies, borrowers have increasingly been prepared to apply economic efficiency criteria. Similarly, targeting projects for low-income groups, recovering costs, and including software items such as land tenure have been receiving much more attention than in the past. Rather than seek to impart original wisdom, the Bank's approach has been to explore and learn jointly with the borrowers. The metropolitan programs it has financed have served as platforms for interagency collaboration and have helped to focus the attention of local, regional, and national governments on critical development issues. In controversial matters, Bank staff have served as listening posts rather than arbitrators, helping to develop local consensus. That it has been possible to sustain a series of three credits through different political regimes in West Bengal State, even in the politically volatile city of Calcutta, is adequate testimony to the responsiveness, sensitivity, circumspection, and, above all, realism of the Bank and borrower.

Although the Bank has only recently become involved with the urban sector, it has helped to develop a gradual convergence of views on many urban policy issues within the development assistance community. In some projects, such as those undertaken in Manila, Calcutta, and Madras, bilateral donors have financed schemes complementary to the Bank-assisted projects. In Calcutta, for example, both British and Dutch aid has been utilized in this way.

International assistance has also helped metropolitan cities to establish valuable contacts with one another and to exchange views and experiences. An entire generation of urban planners and administrators has emerged from Calcutta and Manila, two of the cities taking new planning initiatives

4. Rakesh Mohan, *Urban Economic and Planning Models: Assessing the Potential for Cities in Developing Countries* (Baltimore, Md.: Johns Hopkins University Press, 1979).

in the 1960s. Today, key officials in these and other cities, as well as in leading consultancy and international organizations, are the veterans of such early urban training grounds. Their experiences have formed the substance of training programs and seminars organized by the Bank and other agencies; indeed, the seminar organized in Manila with the Asian Development Bank in 1981 marked the starting point of this present book. A similar seminar for Latin American cities was held in Rio de Janeiro in 1983 in collaboration with the U.N. Habitat (Centre for Human Settlements; see appendix A). Workshops and training programs in metropolitan managements now form part of the urban studies curriculum in many universities, aided by the documentation produced and exchanged by international agencies. As part of its projects, the Bank has also provided for study tours and exchanges between officials of the various metropolitan cities involved.

International personalities as well as agencies have often played important roles in metropolitan development; plans, it is often said, are only as good as the people who implement them. Accounts of infrastructure projects, whether of ports or highways, dams or canals, are replete with folklore about building giants. Names such as Le Corbusier and Oscar Nemeyer are sufficient to convey the grand vision and strength of concept behind the building of a Chandigarh or Brasilia. In the great cities of the developing world, the procession of such personalities has indeed been colorful; but to assess the impact of particular individuals on particular metropolitan scenes, or on the character or style of particular metropolitan institutions, is a difficult task. Undeniably, in the context of metropolitan management the impact of personalities such as the present prime minister of Sri Lanka on Colombo, the first lady of the Philippines on Manila, and the urban minister of West Bengal on Calcutta may well have been considerable, but it has also been transient. In reality, metropolitan management is an unglamorous interagency process; its accent is on consensus rather than on command; its quality is a product of perseverance and team effort; and its success in the long run is directly dependent on the degree to which that effort can continue to be maintained in the rapidly changing kaleidoscope of metropolitan life.

PART II

City Profiles

8

Bangkok

BANGKOK HAS BEEN the capital of Thailand since 1767, when Ayuthia, the previous capital 80 kilometers to the north, was sacked by Burma. In 1782, the city's founder, King Chakri (Rama I), moved the capital, for strategic reasons, from Thonburi on the western side of the Chao Phraya River to its present site. Situated on the eastern side of a large loop in the river, the new site was better protected from military attack by a swampy plain to the east as well as by the river itself. The site also provided access to the sea and water to build a system of canals (klongs), which became Bangkok's principal means of transportation and drainage.

Growth of the City

In the 1850s during the reign of King Rama IV, the population of the city rose to about 400,000 as Bangkok became an important commercial center and point of contact with the West. The city's outward expansion along the main highways began thereafter. By the early 1950s, Bangkok's population had reached 1 million. Its importance as the headquarters of the Southeast Asia Treaty Organization and its role as a supply base during the wars in Indochina then brought a considerable investment in infrastructure, so that by 1970 the city emerged not only as Thailand's principal center of trade and industry, but also as a hub of East Asian air traffic.

Today, with a population of some 5 million, Bangkok dominates the urban sector of Thailand. It accounts for about half of the country's urban population and is forty times larger than Chiang Mai, the second city. If it continues to grow at the present rate of 4.3 percent a year, the metropolitan area's population is expected to reach 10.5 million by the end of the century. Although at present the city accounts for only 10 percent of the nation's population, it contributes one-third of the gross domestic product; has more than 18,000 industrial firms; is the country's main port, transportation hub, and commercial and financial center; and houses the regional headquarters of several international agencies and multinational companies. Like other leading cities, it serves as the nation's principal educational and cultural center—about 60 percent of all secondary schools and 85 percent of all higher educational institutions are concentrated in Bangkok.

The city has a highly competitive and dynamic private business sector that is responsive to market conditions and is characterized by small firms. Its industries are greatly diversified, but textiles and clothing account for 30 percent of employment. Unemployment rates have been low and concentrated among the young (2.5 percent in the early 1970s). Unlike many other South and East Asian cities, Bangkok has not experienced overwhelming influxes of immigrants from rural areas, mainly because rural densities are low and farmland can still be developed. It is recognized, however, that as pressures on available agricultural land increase (agriculture at present employs 70 percent of the Thai labor force), migration into urban areas, in particular Bangkok, will increase.

Metropolitan Problems

Metropolitan Bangkok covers an area of 1,600 square kilometers. About 330 square kilometers form a compact urbanized area. Part of this extends into the adjoining provinces of Nonthaburi, Samut Prakarn, and Samut Sakhon. Residential and commercial development is highly intermixed in the urban core of about 60 square kilometers, lying principally to the east of the river. Although Thonburi on the west bank has potential for growth, only three bridges connect the two sides of the river. In recent years, most development has taken place to the northeast and southeast of the metropolitan area. Much of this development has been unplanned and uncontrolled, with predictable consequences for infrastructure. The most serious problems have been poor drainage and periodic flooding.

The flatness of the land (which averages only 1 meter above mean sea level) compounded by overflows from the river, particularly during high tides, has added to Bangkok's problems. Furthermore, land subsidence is widespread owing to the excessive abstraction of groundwater. More than 1,000 square kilometers of land within and adjoining the city are settling at the rate of 100 millimeters a year or more. The Chao Phraya River drains about one-third of the area of Thailand, and Bangkok, located a bare 40 kilometers from the Gulf of Siam, is virtually at the tail end of the delta. The conservation of flood channels and outfalls is therefore particularly important. Yet, uncontrolled development of flood-prone areas and indiscriminate filling or obstruction of the klongs or drainage canals have been a pronounced feature of Bangkok's development.

About one-third of the population has no access to public water and must obtain water from vendors and other unsafe sources. The public water supply system based on Chao Phraya is being expanded, but maintenance has

Bangkok.   The Chao Phraya River serves as a port and as a transport artery for the city. Bangkok's highly mixed land use can be seen along the banks.

Map 8-1. Urbanized Areas of Bangkok-Thonburi, 1900, 1936, 1958, and 1968

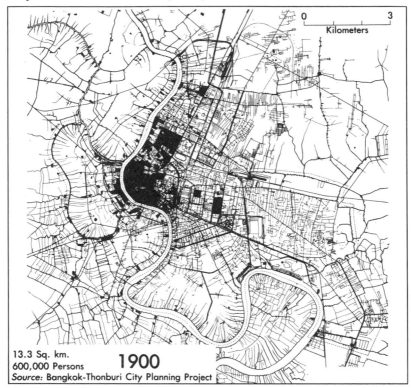

13.3 Sq. km.
600,000 Persons
Source: Bangkok-Thonburi City Planning Project

1900

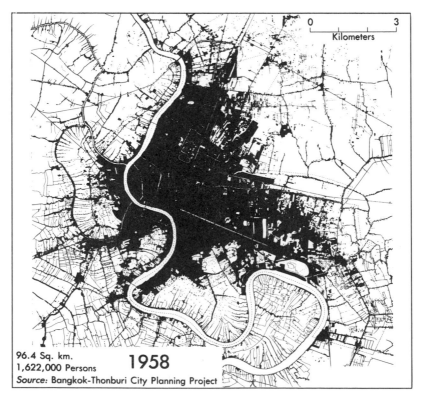

96.4 Sq. km.
1,622,000 Persons
Source: Bangkok-Thonburi City Planning Project

1958

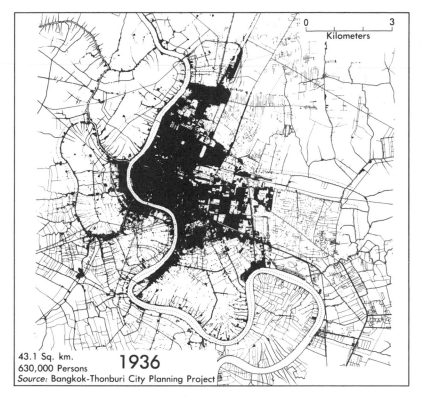

43.1 Sq. km.
630,000 Persons
1936
Source: Bangkok-Thonburi City Planning Project

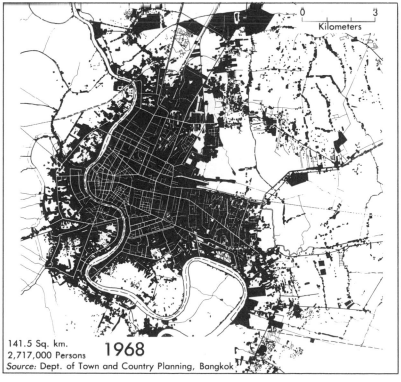

141.5 Sq. km.
2,717,000 Persons
1968
Source: Dept. of Town and Country Planning, Bangkok

Map 8-2. Boundaries of Metropolitan Bangkok, 1975

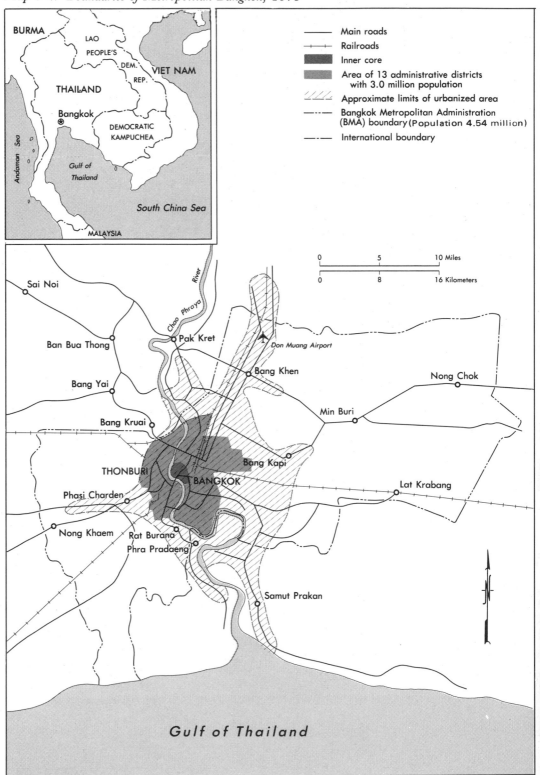

Map 8-3. Metropolitan Land Use, Bangkok, 1980

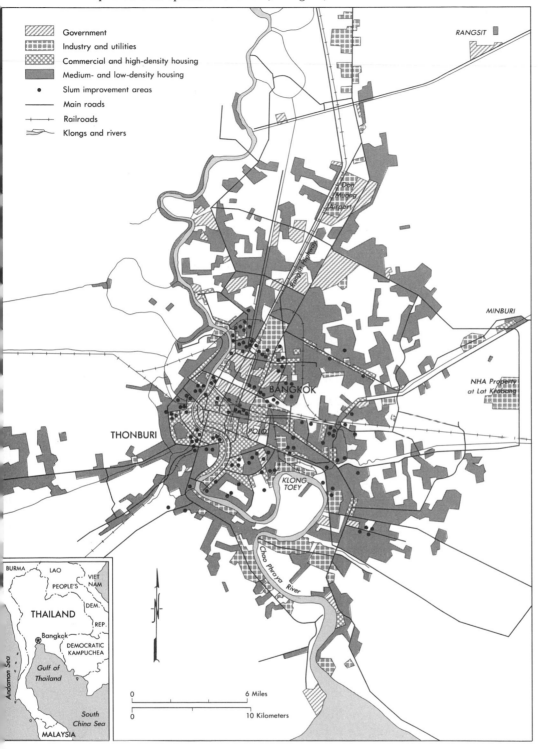

Government
Industry and utilities
Commercial and high-density housing
Medium- and low-density housing
Slum improvement areas
Main roads
Railroads
Klongs and rivers

RANGSIT

Don Muang Airport

MINBURI

NHA Property at Lat Krabang

BANGKOK

THONBURI

KLONG TOEY

Chao Phraya River

BURMA
LAO PEOPLE'S
VIET NAM
DEM. REP.
THAILAND
Bangkok
DEMOCRATIC KAMPUCHEA
Gulf of Thailand
Andaman Sea
South China Sea
MALAYSIA

0   6 Miles
0   10 Kilometers

become a serious problem because of inadequate tariffs and inefficient collection of dues.

In addition, there is no central sewerage system. Human waste is disposed of mainly through septic tanks and cesspools, and the effluents are discharged into stormwater drains or klongs. Inefficient drainage, a high water table, and periodic flooding make water pollution a health hazard; the filling up of old klongs during road construction has also contributed to the drainage problem. About half of the city's 2,500 tons of garbage finds its way into the klongs.

Traffic congestion is also serious in Bangkok. Space devoted to roadways accounts for less than 10 percent of the area of the inner core, and the road network consists of only a few main roads with a limited number of connecting links. The remainder of the network consists of a discontinuous jumble of single lanes. There is already one registered vehicle for every 2.6 kilometers of road space and the number of motor vehicles is increasing at the rate of approximately 8 percent a year. Congestion has therefore reached such high levels that no discernible peak hour can be determined. The heavy traffic is spread throughout the working day, and pollution along the few major roads is very high.

Structure of Government

The administration of the Bangkok metropolitan area cannot be understood without some knowledge of the structure of Thailand's government. The nation is governed by the Royal Thai Government (RTG) and its various ministries. At the next level are provincial and local governments of different categories. A number of national and parastatal enterprises deliver specific public services. An important characteristic of this structure is the strong concentration of power in the RTG: the other components are, in effect, instruments or agents of the central government and implement its policies.

The RTG itself has a relatively diffused organization. The responsibilities for planning, resource allocation, and fiscal management are dispersed among a number of ministries and agencies, and even within the ministries themselves individual departments enjoy significant autonomy. Programming and coordination of investment are thus complex processes. The National Economic and Social Development Board (NESDB) is responsible for appraising projects for public investment, but it does not perform a central programming or coordinating function comparable to that of other national planning agencies. Moreover, the Budget Bureau is responsible for the allocation of budgetary resources only, and these exclude several important sources of funds available to the central government, especially foreign grants and loans that are controlled by the Department of Technical and Economic Cooperation. The administration and control of foreign borrowing by all public agencies, including subnational governments and state enterprises, are the responsibility of the Foreign Loan Contracting Sub-committee of the NESDB.

Subnational administration in Thailand takes two forms: provincial administration and local government. The provincial administration, like the RTG, is highly centralized and has evolved from the territorial administrative system developed during the late nineteenth and early twentieth centuries. The provincial administration, headed by a governor appointed by the central government, is responsible for general administrative work, including budgetary control. Each province is divided into districts functioning under district administrators who are also centrally appointed.

The system of local government consists of three types of self-governing authorities, which may include elected councils. These authorities have developed since the establishment of the constitutional monarchy in 1932. They comprise municipalities, which are generally responsible for urban areas and provincial capitals; sanitary districts, which are responsible for semirural areas; and changwats, which are wholly rural administrative organizations. The range of a municipality's responsibilities depends on whether it is classified as a Nakhom (city), Muang (town), or Tambon (commune)—on the basis of its size, population density, and revenue—and whether it is a provincial capital. The services administered by a municipality generally include local roads, drainage, refuse collection and disposal, public health, and markets; but the range is limited, inasmuch as many other services—including primary education and water supply—which in other countries are provided by the local government, are operated by national public corporations or government departments in Thailand.

Although the provincial administrations and local government authorities form contrasting systems based on differing constitutional principles, the detailed control exercised by the Ministry of the Interior and the power of the provincial governors substantially negate the distinction in practice. From the standpoint of administrative and fiscal control, the local authorities remain tied to the central government. In many cases provincial governors appoint local council members, approve local budgets, and can dissolve the municipal council; and the Ministry of the Interior and its agent, the Department of Local Administration, directly control the administration of local government. The subordinate role of local authorities is also illustrated by the fact that, out of Thailand's total public outlays, local government expenditures amount to less than 5 percent. A 1973 report states, "To all intents and purposes the local authorities function as part and parcel of the national government in its local operations at the provincial, district and local levels."

This general description of local government in Thailand also applies to the Bangkok Metropolitan Administration (BMA). Created in 1972 by the merger of the former municipalities of Thonburi and Bangkok, its administrative area covers about 1,600 square kilometers and at present has a population of 5 million. Although the BMA was thus established as an autonomous metropolitan city government, it is responsible for only a limited range of services: solid waste management, construction and maintenance of local roads, sewerage and drainage, public health, and primary education. Many important services in Bangkok are in fact administered by state enterprises and other government agencies, including the Metropolitan Water Works Authority, the Telephone Organization of Thailand, the Metropolitan Police Bureau, the National Housing Authority, the Bangkok Mass Transit Authority, the Expressway and Rapid Transit Authority, the Industrial Estates Authority, the Port Authority of Thailand, the State Railway, and the Central Ministeries of Education, Health, Industry, and Communications. Even city planning is outside BMA's control and is carried out by the Town and Country Planning Department of the Interior Ministry.

Initially, the BMA Act provided for a metropolitan assembly consisting of both elected and appointed members, in roughly equal numbers. Each elected member was to represent a constituency of about 100,000 people, the equivalent of a district. Appointed members were to be selected by the Ministry of the Interior from among knowledgeable and qualified citizens. The assembly was to act mainly as a metropolitan legislative body with a four-year term, and was to pass metropolitan bylaws in keeping with national laws, rules, and regulations. The governor of the BMA, who was also to be elected for a four-year term, was to serve as the executive head of the BMA with powers and responsibilities for its operations. Since the BMA had been formed by merging Thonburi and Bangkok municipalities and some of the adjoining changwats and sanitary districts, the executive powers of these organizations as well as those of a provincial governor were vested in the governor. Because the assembly and the governor were given co-equal power, the assembly could not question or check the executive operations of the BMA for which the governor was responsible.

Compared with the traditional form of local government, which was totally subordinated to the RTG, the metropolitan administration thus proposed was a major departure. In 1978, however, the elective form of metropolitan government was abrogated by decree. The governor and assembly are now appointed by the central government. Although the assembly is largely made up of government officials, there is some representation from the city's business and professional sectors. All members are residents of Bangkok. The assembly meets infrequently, however, and it is not regarded as a policymaking body. It has a loose committee structure that holds meetings only when justified by the volume of business.

As is usual in large city administrations, the BMA is organized functionally at headquarters and territorially in the field. There are twelve departments or bureaus at the headquarters in addition to an office of Secretary to the Governor and an office of Secretary to the Metropolitan Assembly. In the field, BMA is divided into twenty-four districts responsible for various minor works and local services, including the maintenance of local roads and drains, the collection and disposal of waste, the administration of schools and health centers, and the collection of municipal taxes. In theory, the staff functions performed by the bureaus at headquarters are distinct from the line functions of the territorial districts. In practice, however, many of the bureaus exercise line functions, although the districts receive separate budget allocations.

The allocation of work among the headquarters departments is also not entirely clear. The BMA's budget, for instance, is handled by neither Finance nor Policy and Planning, but by the office of the under secretary of state for the BMA. Consequently, the under secretary is the head of the permanent government staff in the BMA and is the chief executive of the organization reporting to the governor of the BMA. But the concept is diffused in that four deputy governors look after groups of departments and report to the governor. A further complication in the design is that four under secretaries of state in the Ministry of Interior have functions similar to those of the four deputy governors. Thus it appears that most decisions in the BMA would require agreement between at least one deputy governor of BMA and one under secretary from the ministry. In some cases, that agreement must be endorsed by the governor, who enjoys the rank of a minister. The under secretary of state within the BMA may thus be performing routine and formal functions only. Being an appointee of the central government himself, the governor is responsible to the Ministry of the Interior. For all practical purposes, therefore, the BMA should be regarded as an instrument of the RTG rather than as an autonomous or semiautonomous city government.

Fiscal Situation

In Thailand, as in many other developing countries, local government authorities have limited tax resources at their disposal. By law they can levy only four taxes locally: a house and rent tax, a land development tax, a tax on signboards, and an animal slaughter tax. In addition, local authorities are authorized to add a surcharge of up to 10 percent on certain national taxes such as the business tax, nonalcoholic beverage tax, gambling tax, and entertainment duty. These taxes, together with the surcharges, are collected by local representatives of the Revenue and Excise Department of the Ministry of Finance. Certain other taxes, such as the rice export duty and the road vehicle tax, are classified as shared taxes to be levied by the Royal Thai Government, and all or a portion of their receipts are distributed to local jurisdictions. (A brief description of the different sources of taxation is contained in table 8-1.)

At present, locally levied taxes constitute some 8 percent of a local authority's income (table 8-2). The yield is relatively low, mainly because two important taxes—the house and rent tax and land development tax—suffer as a result of considerable evasion, exemptions, and deductions. In Bangkok, however, the share of these locally levied taxes is considerably higher because of its high land values. According to BMA revenue estimates, the share of total income during 1981–83 was 14–15 percent (table 8-3). Even so, when the gambling tax (which is specific to Bangkok only) is included, expected local revenues account for only 17 percent of in-

Table 8-1. Sources of Municipal Revenue, Bangkok

Type of revenue	Collecting agency	Description	Rate or revenue[a]	Distribution of revenue
House and rent tax	Municipality	Tax on annual rent for houses and buildings used for commercial purposes; owner-occupied residences exempted	Normal rate is 12.5 percent of annual rental; buildings with machinery and tools used for manufacturing and processing are taxed at one-third of normal rate	Retained by municipality
Land development tax	Municipality	Tax on assumed value of land (excluding structures and crops); partially or fully exempt are owner-occupied residential and agricultural land below specific sizes (400 square meters in the largest cities), most government land, land used for religious purposes, and land with structures subject to the house and rent tax	Rate progresses with size of holding from B0.50 to B400 per ral (1,600 square meters); for land valued at more than B10,000 per ral, the rate is regressive with respect to total land value	Retained by municipality
Slaughter tax	Municipality	Tax on slaughter of animals beyond a minimum number	B4–15 per animal, depending on type of animal	Retained by municipality
Signboard tax	Municipality	Tax on area and number of Thai or foreign-language characters on signboards	From B1 per 500 square centimeters for signs in Thai to B20 per 500 square centimeters for signs with exclusively foreign characters	Retained by municipality

Surcharge on business tax	Revenue Department, Ministry of Finance	Surcharge on businesses at points of manufacturing and import	10 percent surcharge on basic rate	Distribution to local authorities in proportion to local collection of former business tax
Surcharge on liquor and alcoholic beverages	Excise Department, Ministry of Finance	Taxes on raw and distilled liquor and fees for monopoly distribution rights	B6 per liter for raw liquor; B50 per liter for distilled liquor; B1,000 for production and up to B2,000 for sale of liquor; 10 percent surcharge on both taxes and fees	Distributed according to share of national population
Surcharge on nonalcoholic beverage tax	Excise Department, Ministry of Finance	Tax on nonalcoholic beverages	B0.20 per 440 cubic centimeters on beverages in containers; 10 percent surcharge	Distributed according to share of tax collected in jurisdiction
Surcharge on entertainment tax	Revenue Department, Ministry of Finance	Levies on viewers of movies, plays, sport matches, contests, and other gatherings for which admission is charged	Varying rates on ticket prices or gross receipts; 10 percent surcharge	Distributed according to share of tax collected in jurisdiction
Surcharge on gambling tax	Central government	Tax on betting at races	Surcharge of 10 percent on taxes on gross betting (2 percent in Bangkok-Thonburi)	Distributed according to share of tax collected in jurisdiction
Rice export tax	Customs Department	Tax on rice exports	B1 per 100 kilograms for white and parboiled rice; B0.50 per 100 kilograms for paddy rice, broken rice, and bran	Half of total tax distributed to municipalities according to population

(Table continues on the following page.)

Table 8-1 (continued)

Type of revenue	Collecting agency	Description	Rate or revenue[a]	Distribution of revenue
Motor vehicle registration fees	National Police Department	Tax on motor vehicles	Annual registration fee based on weight of vehicle	Half of tax collected in changwat distributed equally among municipalities
Fees and licenses	Municipality	Fees and licenses for activities not covered by taxes	Rates vary with activities	Retained by municipality
Revenues from properties	Municipality	Rental income from municipal properties and interest income from bank accounts	Rentals act locally	Retained by municipality
Government grants	Central government	Regular grants, generally for current expenditures, and specific grants, generally for capital expenditures, from departments	Size of grants varies with activities	Government revenues

a. Monetary units are expressed in baht (B); one baht equals about US$0.05.

come. Surcharges on taxes usually account for 15–16 percent of the total revenues of local authorities in the country, but for the BMA the share is 25 percent. Shared taxes, especially the vehicle registration tax, contribute an important revenue source for the BMA from which it derives an additional 28 percent of its income. Although grants-in-aid contribute 37 percent of the income of the local governments, they account for only 13 percent in the case of the BMA. Another 16 percent is derived from license fees, properties, and miscellaneous sources. Surcharges and assigned revenues thus account for the principal share of the BMA's revenues.

On the expenditure side, recurrent items account for about 54 percent of the total (see table 8-4). Capital expenditure on land, buildings, and construction amounts to another 21 percent. If the expenditure on education and on some other special projects is included, the BMA's annual expenditure amounts to about 93 percent of its total income. Debt servicing is negligible since the BMA seldom borrows. As in other countries in the region, the law requires the BMA to balance its budget, but the annual surpluses of 5–7 percent that the organization has been showing are due more to its conservative approaches to expenditure than to careful budgetary controls.

Moreover, a large share of the expenditure in the BMA is borne directly by the RTG through various ministries and parastatal organizations. About 40 percent of the country's expenditure on infrastructure takes place within the BMA area. As mentioned earlier, a number of organizations are responsible for the provision of services in the metropolitan area, and their capital expenditure is often relatively significant (see table 8-5, especially the expenditure of the Metropolitan Waterworks Authority). This concentration of public expenditure in Bangkok is both a measure of the city's national importance and a great problem from the standpoint of the equitable distribution of public sector outlays throughout the nation.

Response to Metropolitan Problems

Like several other Asian cities, Bangkok initially responded to its problems of rapid urbanization with physical planning. Three master plans for Bangkok have been prepared during the past twenty years, but all have suffered from a preoccupation with land use planning and control, and none has been followed consistently. The fragmented administrative structure has also resulted in much duplication of work. The 1960–90 Greater Bangkok Plan, which assumed a population of 4.5 million by the end of the period, was reviewed twice: once in 1969 by the City Planning Division of the Bangkok Municipality, and once in 1971 by the Department of Town and Country Planning, Ministry of the Interior, without much consultation between the two. Although both revisions agreed that the projected population would be reached well before 1990, neither plan came close to implementation. Planning controls have been used only recently; furthermore, they have been applied to limited areas of the city and restricted to private construction only. Under the Town Planning Act of 1976, the BMA

Table 8-2. Municipal Revenue, Bangkok, 1974–79
(amount in millions of baht)

Revenue	1974 Amount	1974 Percent	1975 Amount	1975 Percent	1976 Amount	1976 Percent	1977 Amount	1977 Percent	1978 Amount	1978 Percent	1979 Amount	1979 Percent
Taxes												
Local												
House and rent	57.3	7.0	62.9	6.2	67.6	5.3	81.4	5.7	93.0	5.7	105.0	5.6
Land development	12.1	1.5	12.0	1.2	12.3	1.0	12.5	0.9	17.0	1.0	17.1	0.9
Signboard	9.3	1.1	8.3	0.8	9.0	0.7	10.3	0.7	11.3	0.7	12.2	0.6
Slaughter	11.0	1.3	11.6	1.1	13.8	1.1	14.5	1.0	15.9	1.0	16.6	0.9
Subtotal	89.7	11.0	94.8	9.3	102.7	8.0	118.7	8.3	137.2	8.4	150.8	8.0
Surcharge												
Business	130.8	16.0	134.1	13.2	154.8	12.1	163.5	11.4	218.9	13.4	248.8	13.3
Entertainment	2.4	0.3	3.0	0.3	6.8	0.5	9.7	0.7	11.8	0.7	11.9	0.6
Gambling	0.0	0.0	n.a.	n.a.	n.a.	n.a.	0.1	0.0	n.a.	n.a.	n.a.	n.a.
Beverage	0.0	0.0	26.0	2.6	14.8	1.2	19.5	1.4	22.4	1.4	27.0	1.4
Subtotal	133.2	16.3	163.0	16.0	176.4	13.7	192.9	13.4	253.1	15.4	287.8	15.3
Shared												
Vehicle	168.6	20.6	213.3	21.0	268.1	20.9	350.9	24.5	372.6	22.7	360.6	19.2
Rice export	0.8	0.1	2.1	0.2	2.6	0.2	4.0	0.3	3.8	0.2	3.7	0.2
Subtotal	169.4	20.7	215.4	21.2	270.8	21.1	354.9	24.7	376.5	23.0	364.3	19.4
Total taxes	392.3	48.0	473.2	46.6	549.8	42.8	666.5	46.5	766.7	46.8	802.9	42.8

Local nontax revenue												
Fees and fines	36.0	4.4	37.6	3.7	43.5	3.4	51.4	3.6	61.2	3.7	68.3	3.6
Property revenues	58.6	7.2	77.9	7.7	90.6	7.1	101.8	7.1	110.6	6.7	124.4	6.6
Social services	5.3	0.6	7.4	0.7	6.9	0.5	11.5	0.8	8.0	0.5	7.9	0.4
Miscellaneous	36.9	4.5	50.1	4.9	55.7	4.3	54.2	3.8	64.9	4.0	76.2	4.1
Total local nontax	136.8	16.7	173.1	17.0	196.7	15.3	218.9	15.3	244.7	14.9	276.6	14.7
Government grants	251.2	30.7	312.1	30.7	480.0	37.4	459.2	32.0	536.2	32.7	706.4	37.6
Special revenue												
Provided funds	16.6	2.0	19.6	1.9	31.8	2.5	48.3	3.4	51.3	3.1	63.9	3.4
Loans	20.3	2.5	36.1	3.6	23.0	1.8	41.4	2.9	36.3	2.2	27.3	1.5
Other	0.0	0.0	2.4	0.2	1.9	0.1	n.a.	n.a.	3.5	0.2	n.a.	n.a.
Total special	37.0	4.5	58.1	5.7	56.7	4.4	89.7	6.3	91.0	5.6	91.2	4.9
Total	817.3	100.0	1,016.5	100.0	-,283.2	100.0	1,434.3	100.0	1,638.6	100.0	1,877.1	100.0

n.a. Not available.
Note: Columns may not add up owing to rounding.

Table 8-3. Revenue Estimates, Bangkok Metropolitan Administration, 1974–83
(baht)

Revenue	1974	1975	1976	1977
House and rent tax[a]	139,943,942	157,256,973	172,444,365	196,265,806
Land development tax[a]	35,504,082	33,370,643	33,631,389	37,606,503
Liquor tax[b]	506	42,280,418	24,625,968	30,099,417
Business tax[b]	473,701,101	517,199,074	523,933,077	639,621,475
Vehicle tax[c]	315,578,522	378,383,732	424,565,105	505,918,571
Signboard tax[a]	25,851,742	25,800,339	26,731,078	28,625,317
Gambling tax[d]	40,149,120	43,853,264	48,205,314	53,800,167
Slaughtering tax[a]	4,818,547	5,472,934	7,679,255	7,781,476
Entertainment tax[b]	10,268,717	13,201,676	16,597,960	15,931,231
Rice export tax[c]	2,392,440	2,659,720	3,793,320	3,526,739
Fees and charges for licenses	40,586,095	44,107,459	46,627,373	55,350,584
Income from properties	38,791,811	54,241,122	106,405,122	144,156,013
Miscellaneous revenue	25,264,897	44,182,922	61,000,034	112,870,263
Grants-in-aid			167,287,000	173,003,000
Total	1,152,851,522	1,362,010,276	1,663,526,361	2,004,556,567

— Less than 1 percent.
a. Locally levied taxes.
b. Surcharges on taxes.

possesses planning control powers once local or special plans have been approved, but the record of enforcement has been poor. In particular, public agencies in the city have followed plan guidelines only insofar as these have been consistent with their own intentions.

The response to some sectoral problems has been significant, however. In water supply, drainage, shelter, and transportation, Bangkok has made a considerable effort in the past decade to cope with increasing needs. The Metropolitan Water Works Authority has been successful in improving Bangkok's water supplies substantially. In 1968, the then Bangkok municipality engaged consultants to prepare a master plan for flood protection, drainage, and sewerage. The main recommendation was the "poldering" of the city into eleven self-contained drainage management areas. (Poldering is a process by which bunds are constructed around low-lying areas, water is drained out, and incursion of water into the area prevented.) Because of financial constraints, implementation did not proceed beyond creating the first polder. The BMA instituted an annual emergency protection and relief program that has been reasonably successful in the central city under average conditions. Preventing serious flooding is a major regional undertaking, however, and requires extensive improvement of the existing canal and drainage system, the construction of dikes, greatly increased pumping capacity, river training, and control of land subsidence. Initially, the problem was regarded as a local one, and efforts were limited to the BMA's Drainage Bureau. A broader, coordinated approach is now under way and is being orchestrated by the recently established National Flood Protection Committee and the NESDB. A World Bank loan of US$87 million will help implement high-priority improvements to the system, including some items identified earlier in the BMA master plan.

1978	*1979*	*1980*	*1981*	*1982*	*1983*	*Percent*
225,115,803	252,129,699	282,385,263	316,271,494	354,224,074	400,000,000	11
50,912,498	52,767,247	55,933,281	58,289,277	68,690,523	70,000,000	2
34,012,341	38,433,945	43,430,358	49,076,305	54,456,224	60,000,000	2
665,206,334	691,814,587	719,487,170	748,266,657	778,197,323	800,000,000	22
576,747,170	657,491,774	749,540,623	854,476,310	974,102,994	1,000,000,000	28
29,436,022	30,613,462	31,838,001	33,111,521	34,435,982	40,000,000	1
59,180,183	65,098,202	71,603,022	78,768,824	86,645,706	100,000,000	3
8,326,179	8,909,011	9,532,642	10,199,927	10,913,922	12,000,000	—
19,595,414	24,102,359	29,645,902	36,464,459	44,851,285	50,000,000	1
3,843,709	4,189,643	4,566,711	4,977,714	5,425,709	6,000,000	—
61,021,222	67,123,344	73,835,675	81,219,246	89,341,171	100,000,000	3
140,411,895	163,706,632	182,429,157	220,287,863	240,384,072	260,000,000	7
120,000,000	140,000,000	160,000,000	180,000,000	200,000,000	220,000,000	6
209,341,640	324,203,000	340,000,000	360,000,000	400,000,000	450,000,000	13
2,203,150,410	2,520,587,905	2,754,232,805	3,031,409,597	3,341,668,985	3,563,000,000	100

c. Shared taxes.

d. Special to Bangkok Metropolitan Administration.

Shelter

Bangkok's numerous slums, which house approximately 1 million people (or almost a quarter of its population), stand in sharp contrast to the planned development emphasized by the administration. The slums have an inadequate water supply, unsanitary conditions, and no access to public services. Structures are usually built of wood and other makeshift materials, and in the older sections of the city many families live above their small businesses. The government's initial response to these problems was to construct storied apartments, but by 1973 the output of housing units hardly exceeded 500 a year.

In 1973, four existing public agencies were amalgamated to form a National Housing Authority (NHA), which was to be a semiautonomous state enterprise under the Ministry of the Interior with a government-appointed board of directors and a management headed by a governor appointed by the RTG. By 1976, the NHA had completed a total of 6,000 units, and a further 120,000 units were scheduled for construction by 1980; but only about one-third of these were completed. For the first five years of its operation, the NHA focused on the development of heavily subsidized housing units (half of those built so far are for sale and half for rent). In the smallest and least expensive units, the NHA absorbed all the construction costs and interest greater than 6 percent of the capital, so that the rents charged reflected only estate management charges and 6 percent interest on investment costs. In the larger units, the NHA absorbed 50 percent of construction costs and interest greater than 8 percent. Households up to the sixth income decile were eligible for these highly subsidized units. Many tenants illegally sublet units (in 1973 it was estimated that 30 percent of NHA units were sublet),

Table 8-4. *Actual Revenue and Expenditure, Bangkok Metropolitan Administration, 1978–83*
(amount in millions of bhat)

Revenue and expenditure	1978		1979		1980		1981		1982		1983		Average annual percent, 1978–83
	Amount	Percent	Amount	Percent	Amount	Percent	Amount	Percent	Amount	Percent	Amount	Percent	
Revenue													
Regular													
BMA collected													
Local taxes	313.4	11	357.3	13	413.9	12	499.5	12	616.1	14	738.8	16	13
Local nontax revenue	478.3	17	564.0	19	486.3	15	508.0	13	435.4	10	519.1	12	14
Subtotal	791.7	28	921.3	32	900.2	27	1,007.5	25	1,051.5	24	1,257.9	28	27
Centrally collected shared and surcharge taxes	1,400.7	50	1,508.7	52	1,750.4	52	2,163.7	55	2,608.8	58	2,551.3	56	54
Special													
Government grants	323.4	12	463.6	16	531.3	16	626.7	16	802.0	18	750.3	16	16
Reserve fund	280.6	10	—	—	157.6	5	155.1	4	—	—	—	—	3
Total revenue	2,796.4	100	2,893.6	100	3,339.5	100	3,953.0	100	4,462.3	100	4,559.5	100	100
Expenditure													
Regular													
Recurrent	1,372.9	49	1,659.1	57	1,849.6	55	2,111.3	53	2,295.3	52	2,641.4	58	54
Capital	565.0	20	754.1	26	668.2	20	778.3	20	812.4	18	953.5	21	21
Special	604.0	22	463.6	16	688.9	21	781.8	20	802.2	18	750.3	16	19
Total expenditure	2,541.9	91	2,876.8	99	3,206.7	96	3,671.4	93	3,909.7	88	4,345.2	95	94
Annual surplus	254.5	9	16.8	1	132.8	4	281.6	7	552.6	12	214.3	5	6
Total expenditure and surplus	2,796.4	100	2,893.6	100	3,339.5	100	3,953.0	100	4,462.3	100	4,559.5	100	100

Table 8-5. Capital Expenditure Estimates, Bangkok Agencies
(millons of baht)

Agency	1978	1979	1980	1981	1982	1983
Bangkok Metropolitan Administration	1,113	1,283	1,156	1,246	1,362	1,493
Expressway and Rapid Transit Authority	286	1,314	1,224	938	555	273
Metropolitan Water Works Authority	1,472	2,685	1,371	1,548	1,677	1,524
Metropolitan Electricity Authority	648	319	n.a.	n.a.	n.a.	n.a.
National Housing Authority	n.a.	525	555	485	446	n.a.

n.a. Not available.

Note: The estimates of other agencies are not available.

often at several times the official monthly rent. By 1977, the NHA had accumulated a deficit of US$5.5 million as a result of subsidies and arrears.

The increased annual production proposed under the 1976–80 program would have considerably worsened the NHA's financial status. Thus in 1977, in an attempt to generate new revenues and recover losses, the administration developed middle-income housing schemes that the NHA hoped to sell for a profit. These schemes met with little success, however, as they competed poorly with the private sector. Growing dissatisfaction with the deficit led the government to change its housing policy drastically. For the first time, a slum upgrading program was approved. Slums located primarily on government land were selected for the first phase of development because of constraints on the NHA's power to deal with private landlords. Since then, a slum upgrading office within the NHA has been established to implement the program. The initial phase has been designed to benefit 3,500 families in five slums and will provide security of tenure, improve sanitation, and support the development of small businesses. The program is supported by World Bank financing, and capital costs will be recovered through new user charges for electricity and water and increased rents. In all, 108 slums and 38 communities have been identified for upgrading under a phased program; 12,000 families are involved.

Transportation

In transportation, as in other sectors, responsibilities are fragmented. Through its Office of Urban Transport Planning, the Ministry of the Interior has responsibility for transport planning in the city, and its Department of Highways controls some of the trunk roads. The Expressway and Rapid Transport Authority of Thailand (ERTAT) was established in 1973 to construct expressways and a rapid transit system. A fleet of 5,000 buses (among the largest in the world) is operated by the Bangkok Mass Transit Authority, and 6,000 to 9,000 private minibuses compete with it. Through its traffic engineering office and city planning and engineering department, the BMA is involved in planning, constructing, and maintaining the road network and traffic signals. The centralized traffic police force consists of 700 employees; in addition, there are 1,200 police with traffic responsibilities distributed among several precincts.

A large transportation study outlining immediate traffic management needs, short-term investments, and long-term strategy was completed in 1975 with assistance from the Federal Republic of Germany. Some of the short-term measures recommended by the team have been partly adopted, but few of the main policy recommendations have been implemented or the investments made. At present, a World Bank–funded traffic management project is implementing many of the short-term recommendations and tackling some institutional and policy issues. Already, new traffic management policies have been introduced and a Traffic Management Unit has been set up to be solely responsible for traffic engineering. It has also been proposed that a single police unit oversee all traffic control and traffic law enforcement. In addition, the BMA is implementing some road construction projects (including a large ring road and two river bridges) to improve traffic flows.

Pending Issues

In recent years, Bangkok has initiated and achieved considerable progress in selected sectoral activities such as water supply, slum upgrading, and transport. Certain basic issues on which Bangkok's viability and growth depend still require appropriate responses, however. One is the continuing in-migration from the rest of the country, which has been the main cause of the city's progressive urban dominance. The economic factors responsible for Bangkok's continued growth are unlikely to lose their force or to be altered in any significant way through state intervention, but there is much concern about the city's primacy, particularly because of the disparity in services between itself and other areas (see table 8-6). The concern about interregional equity has led some authorities to promote regional cities, and the Fourth National Economic and Social Development Plan (1977–81) has outlined an embryonic national urbanization strategy that would encourage the growth of regional urban centers in order to stem migration to, and relieve urban congestion in, Bangkok itself. The main component of this strategy is the accelerated development of nine provincial cities into the population class of 100,000–300,000. Success will clearly depend on the Thai government's ability to promote economic growth and a supporting infrastructure in them instead of in Bangkok.

Within the Bangkok metropolitan region, however, the proposed strategy could have different implications; the development of self-sufficient satellite towns, for example, has been emphasized. An industrial estate 35 kilometers east of Bangkok at Lat Krabang is already under construction, and the NHA is in charge of housing and related services. A new town, Nava Nakorn, is also being developed 50 kilometers to the north, with Commonwealth Development Corporation financing and support from Thai public and private investment. In addition, the NHA is proposing to build another new town at Bang Phli, which is 40 kilometers southeast of Bangkok. The development of satellites around Bangkok could help to alleviate the pres-

Table 8-6. Selected Indicators for Bangkok and the Regional Cities

City	Percentage of population served with piped water (1974)	Percentage of population served by electricity (1975)	Students per teacher (1973)[a]	Population per doctor (1973, in thousands)[a]	Population per hospital bed (1973, in thousands)[a]
Bangkok	73	84	24	1.9	2.3
Chiang Mai	40	80	27	5.3	12.4
Chonburi	78	65	29	8.1	8.2
Hat Yai	34	n.a.	n.a.	n.a.	n.a.
Khon Kaen	49	32	33	31.7	18.7
Korat	61	48	35	30.2	21.4
Phuket	n.a.	76	23	7.8	5.8
Phitsanulok	50	33	30	17.5	14.8
Songkhla	20	40	24	13.6	10.0
Ubon	54	54	30	27.2	34.6
Udon	49	47	35	50.7	34.8

n.a. Not available.

a. For whole province. Although provincial data that combine urban and rural areas underestimate the provision of infrastructure in the cities, they provide an approximation of the disparities.

Source: World Bank data.

sures on the central city in the short term, but there are dangers in this strategy, particularly in view of Bangkok's lack of success in the past in implementing land use controls. Ribbon development could very well take place along the main transportation links, and the satellites could eventually lose their separate identities within a single, congested conurbation.

Another important and as yet unresolved question has to do with finances. In spite of Bangkok's dominant place in the Thai economy, the financial resources available to the BMA are very limited and are more appropriate to the needs of a small municipality. For some time, the Thai government has been considering replacing the land development tax and house and rent tax with a property tax. An IMF property tax advisor has recommended switching to a dual-based system, in which land would be assessed according to its estimated market value, and improvements (that is, buildings) would be valued using factorized floor areas. Under this system, the value of a building for taxation purposes would be obtained by multiplying its floor area by the cost per square meter of similar buildings, and by applying a depreciation factor reflecting the building's remaining economic life. Although the government favors the property tax, it fears that the factorized floor area will emphasize cost of construction rather than location or use. The establishment of a central valuation authority to improve valuation practices and create a cadre of professional valuers in the public sector is also under consideration.

In the meantime, the RTG and the BMA have taken action on some fronts to improve revenues and financial management. A 1982 report has identified a number of deficiencies in the property taxation system, such as poor tax records, underassessment, indiscriminate exemptions, and unrealistic tax rate ceilings. In accepting the findings of the study, the government has agreed to set up a Central Valuation Authority and has begun to review regulations, prepare tax manuals, and train local tax officials. A complementary financial management study initiated by the BMA has led to an action plan for preparing updated tax maps, computerized tax rolls, and manuals of operation. With the improvement in the administration of collection, accumulated arrears have dropped from a peak of 15 percent in 1980 to 5 percent in 1982. A 25 percent improvement annually in the house and rent tax is envisaged up to 1987.

A 1978 study of the BMA's financial planning found no correlation between spatial or financial planning and the budget process. Furthermore, there was little coordination between capital and revenue budgets; and although capital programs were being produced by certain bureaus, they were merely lists of schemes, often limited to one year, and provided only brief statements of objectives (or none at all), no phasing of expenditures, and no analysis of revenue implications. Lack of emphasis on cash flows and performance monitoring had also contributed to consistent underspending of both capital and revenue budgets. The Bureau of Policy and Planning, the last of the bureaus to be established, began to attend to these problems. The financial management study has produced a set of procedural manuals on how to integrate the planning, budgeting, and accounting systems of the BMA and how to prepare annual income statements and balance sheets. The system is expected to be in operation by 1986.

Poor financial management, the crux of which appears to be the absence of any real authority, is only one facet of the BMA's problems. As already mentioned, the BMA functions primarily as an agency of the Ministry of the Interior rather than as an autonomous entity of the local government. The degree of control that the central government has over its activities appears to be the same as that exercised over the activities of other, much smaller local government units in Thailand, despite Bangkok's metropolitan stature. The subordinate status of its local government is also reflected in the treatment of its staff, who are considered inferior to their central government counterparts, even though they may be on the same salary scale. Although the BMA has a sizable staff, a substantial budget, and a modest range of functions, it remains a relic of the past municipal system because of these deficiencies and is not the metropolitan government it should be.

As already mentioned, many problems arise in coordinating various sectoral plans and investments in the metropolitan area. In theory, the NESDB is supposed to assemble the development plans, projects, and capital programs of all government agencies and examine them in the context of the national plan. The board examines only the timing and costs of projects, however; it does not usually evaluate the financial or economic benefits and does not assess the priorities that have been established. In practice, sectoral interests are pursued independently by interested departments and ministries up to the cabinet level. Given the degree of independence with which different ministries function and the NESDB's limited procedures, the task of allocating resources and coordinating investments at the metropolitan level is therefore an arduous one. It is clearly beyond the powers of the BMA, which depends on the Ministry of the Interior for its own internal management.

A certain amount of capital budgeting exists in many of the sectoral agencies in the metropolitan area, but no mechanism is available for relating their activities to each other. Even in specific programs, such as the upgrading of slum projects, several interagency problems have arisen during implementation. The BMA's Bureau of Public Works has perhaps been more successful than others in achieving some coordination in the repair and maintenance of roads, water, drainage, electricity, and telephones through an interagency committee it chairs. There is some degree of coordination in traffic matters, too, through the National Traffic Board created in 1978; and the Urban Planning Transport Office in the Ministry of the Interior not only acts as the secretariat to the board, but is also responsible for coordinating the implementation of a World Bank–assisted Bangkok traffic management project. But the lack of a metropolitanwide government authority continues to be felt.

Reform of the BMA has therefore been a perennial topic. From time to time there have been indications, at both the political and executive levels of government, of a willingness to devolve more functions, resources, and authority to the BMA. The most recent example was the appointment of a study group within the Prime Minister's Office to review the BMA's institutional structure and make recommendations for its improvement. One of the group's proposals envisaged the creation of a Ministry for the Capital Region headed by a minister who would be directly responsible to the prime minister. The group recommended that a Bangkok council be set up under the minister and that it be composed of representatives of the BMA and other public agencies. It was to have the power to coordinate investment planning and the operation and maintenance of services. The BMA itself would have been reorganized internally; it was recommended that the existing eleven sectoral bureaus be transferred to the central government and that the bureau directors form a senior management board (to be known as the Directorate of Policy and Planning) under the governor. The present position of the under secretary of state for Bangkok in the Ministry of the Interior (to whom bureau chiefs report) would have been abolished, and the bureau chiefs would have been given greater responsibility and authority over their bureaus.

These proposals would have brought substantial changes to the metropolitan scene, but recent political developments in the wake of an attempted coup (April 1981) have made it doubtful that any such proposal for enhancing the status and authority of the BMA will be put into effect. Though reform is still being urged, given the continued and, in fact, increasing economic and political primacy of Bangkok over the country, major steps toward autonomy—including reinstating the popular election of

BMA's executive and assembly—are unlikely to be taken. The best indications are that, in some closely related sectoral activities such as slum upgrading, water supply, and transport, interagency relations may be strengthened and the focus on improving the BMA's internal management may also be maintained. But the organization itself will continue to be a metropolitan administration in name only, awaiting a metropolitan role in reality.

9

Bombay

OFTEN DESCRIBED as the most "city-like city" of India, Metropolitan Bombay is the nation's banking and financial capital. Second only to Metropolitan Calcutta in population, Bombay has also been the country's principal center for trade and industry since the early 1970s. Originally, Bombay was made up of seven marshy, malarial islands, which became part of the dowry of Catherine of Braganza (sister of the King of Portugal), when she married Charles II of England. Five years later, in 1665, the islands were transferred to the East India Company for an annual rent of £10. During the next century, the breaches between the islands were filled and Bombay became a compact mass of land.

Growth of the City

Until late in the eighteenth century, the settlement was mainly a marine supply point; but by the 1860s, cotton-growing areas of the hinterland had been connected to Bombay by rail. With the American Civil War restricting the supply of cotton on international markets, the city's cotton prices and trade began to rise. By 1864, the city's population had expanded to some 817,000, compared with 170 in 1814 and 566 in 1845; with the opening of the Suez Canal in 1869, the city became the principal gateway to India because it was closer to Europe than was Calcutta. By 1888, Bombay had emerged as the second commercial and industrial center of India, with an area of about 70 square kilometers administered by a Municipal Corporation.

International trade largely determined Bombay's further growth. Imports rose faster than exports, and the export of raw cotton was eventually replaced by the local manufacture of cotton textiles. By 1900, Bombay's cotton and textile industry was employing 73,000 people, which was ten times the number that had been employed forty years earlier. Despite fluctuating fortunes since then, cotton has remained the city's principal employer in the industrial sector, and today cotton workers number about 250,000. Engineering and chemicals have also developed rapidly since the 1950s, with the result that the city's overall industrial sector at present accounts for about 670,000 jobs, or two-fifths of total metropolitan employment.

Trade, commerce, and services, which have also expanded considerably, account for another 700,000 jobs. In addition, the public sector is strongly established in Bombay since many offices of the national government—particularly fiscal institutions such as the Reserve Bank of India and most offices of the state government of Maharashtra—are located in the urban core. The sectoral distribution among the 1.5 million jobs in Greater Bombay indicates that economic diversity is considerable. At the same time, the annual growth rate of jobs (45,000 a year) reflects economic strength. High inmigration and rising labor participation are characteristic of Bombay's present growth. About two-thirds of the migrants originate from other states in India. The economy of Maharashtra, which itself has been expanding, outperformed the national economy in the 1970s. It follows that Bombay is by no means an economic parasite living off an impoverished hinterland; its flourishing economy is closely linked to that of an equally flourishing region, and its great and growing entrepôt function links India with the world economy at large.

Bombay occupies a narrow promontory invading the Arabian Sea. The old island city extends over 78 square kilometers in a linear strip some 24 kilometers long, which today accounts for less than 16 percent of the area of Greater Bombay but contains 51 percent of the population, 71 percent of all employment, and almost 60 percent of factory jobs. The port and two principal railway terminals are located at the southern tip of the island, and rail and road corridors connecting these terminals run along its western and eastern flanks. Suburbanization has progressively sprawled along these corridors, mainly because rapid and subsidized commuter train services are available here.

Since 1911, the suburbs and their outward extensions have been growing faster than the city proper. The 1971 census indicated a population of 5.9 million for Greater Bombay, which then covered an area of about 440 square kilometers. In 1981, an area ten times as large—known as the Bombay Metropolitan Region and including the two adjoining urban agglomerations of Thana and Kalyan together with municipal and urbanizing areas on the mainland across Thana creek—registered a population of 11.3 million. Of this massive total, the urban component, according to a 1983 estimate, is 10.5 million. If the city expands at the expected rate of 65,000–75,000 urban households per year, by 1991 it will have about 14 million people and will be the largest metropolitan area in the country.

Bombay.   Back Bay in the early stages of reclamation and development on the southern tip of the island. Reclamation of land from the sea has been the principal means of expanding the city.

Map 9-1. Bombay: The Islands in 1670

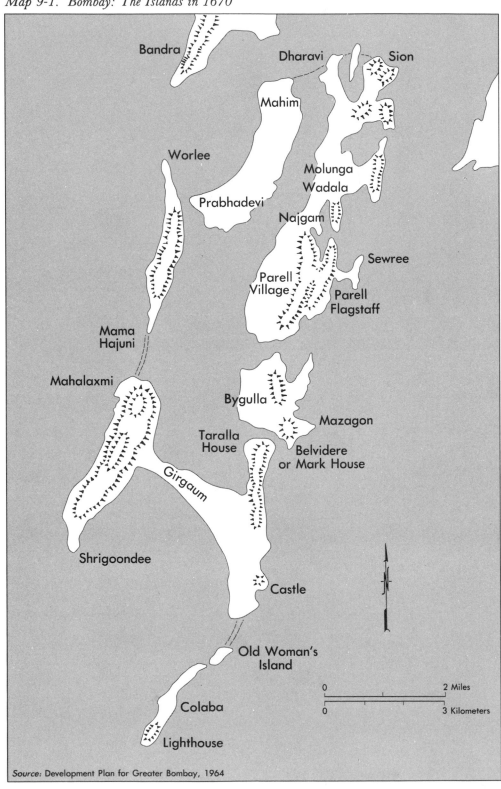

Bandra

Dharavi   Sion

Mahim

Worlee

Molunga
Wadala

Prabhadevi

Najgam

Sewree

Parell
Village

Parell
Flagstaff

Mama
Hajuni

Mahalaxmi

Bygulla

Mazagon

Taralla
House

Belvidere
or Mark House

Girgaum

Shrigoondee

Castle

Old Woman's
Island

0   2 Miles

0   3 Kilometers

Colaba

Lighthouse

Source: Development Plan for Greater Bombay, 1964

Map 9-2. Bombay, 1812–16

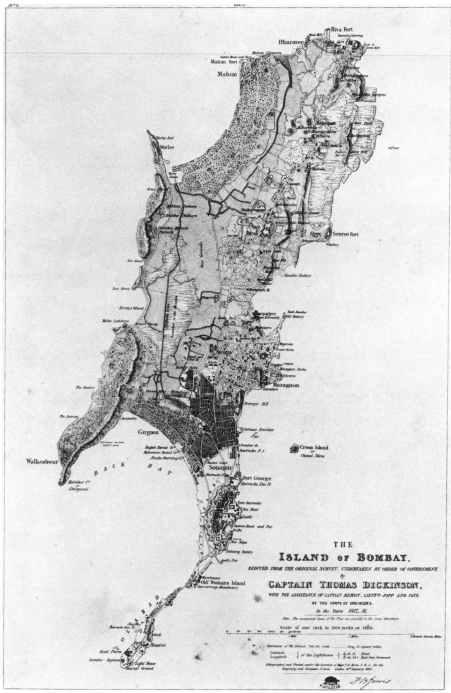

Photo: Library of Congress, Washington, D.C.

Map 9-3. Greater Bombay and Twin City Area, 1976

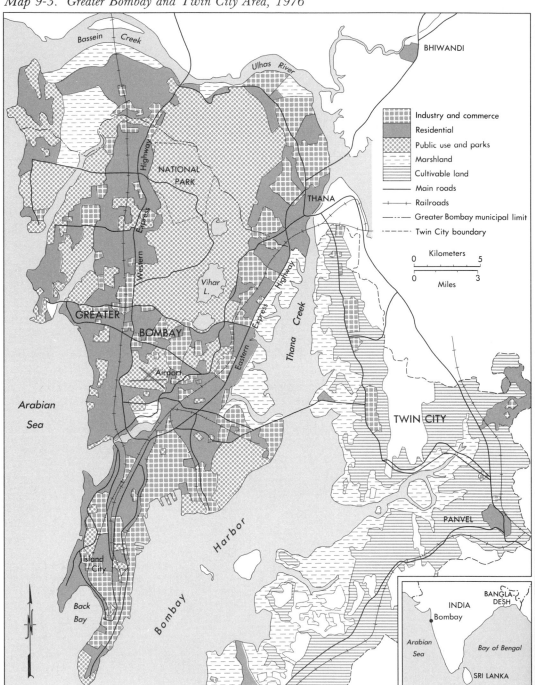

Map 9-4. Bombay Metropolitan Region, 1983

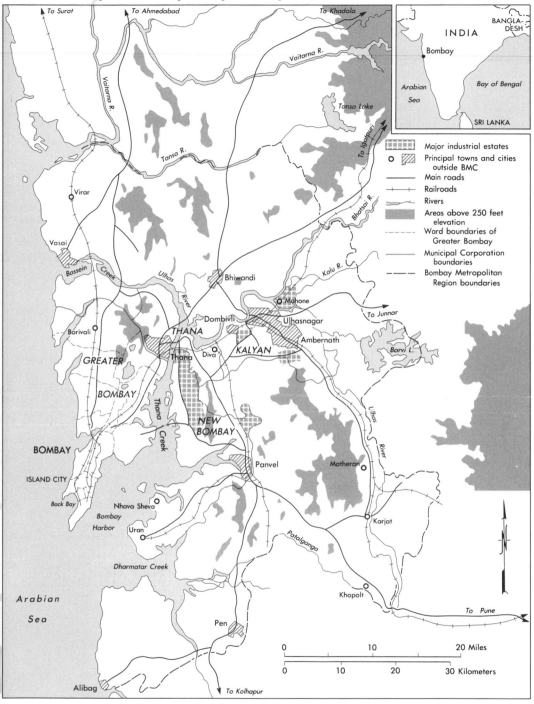

Major industrial estates

Principal towns and cities
outside BMC

Main roads

Railroads

Rivers

Areas above 250 feet
elevation

Ward boundaries of
Greater Bombay

Municipal Corporation
boundaries

Bombay Metropolitan
Region boundaries

Metropolitan Problems

Until the end of the Second World War, Bombay was considered to be one of the best served and most efficiently maintained cities of India. The island city and its immediate suburbs had a municipal water supply and sewerage network; electricity and transport services were provided by a private company; and housing (usually a single room with shared toilet and water facilities) was available for industrial workers, mainly in storied tenements that had been built by private entrepreneurs. After 1941, however, especially after partition and independence, urban growth rapidly accelerated. In the decade following 1941, Greater Bombay grew at an annual rate of 4.98 percent, mainly through the influx of refugees from Pakistan and migrants from other parts of India. Thereafter, the growth rate averaged from 3 to 4 percent a year but rose close to 8 percent in the suburbs, which were least equipped to absorb the huge increase in population.

In 1951 the city limits of Bombay were extended to include the suburbs, and again in 1958 to incorporate further suburban growth with the idea of raising the level of services in these areas. The investments made were inadequate, however, and the standards of water, sewerage, transport, and housing services declined. In the 1970s, large projects designed to expand the water and sanitation networks and bus transport systems were initiated with the assistance of the World Bank. Even so, the overall level of services continues to be poor, although considerable disparity exists between different areas of the metropolis.

A 1979 survey indicated, for example, that the water available in the Thana and Kalyan urban complexes was limited to some 25 liters a head per day, or one-fifth of the supply available in Greater Bombay, which itself had fallen short of demand. Areas outside the city had no access to a sewerage system, and those within were poorly served. Furthermore, the suburban rail system was providing 3.9 million passenger trips a day over the western and central railway lines (some 50 kilometers in length), yet neither of these lines had received any significant investment for repairs. A 1981 assessment reported the system was overloaded by at least 150 percent. The bus services operated by the Bombay Corporation's Electric Supply and Transport (BEST) undertaking were under a similar strain, with fleet renewal lagging far behind the increase in ridership, which amounted to 4 million transit trips in 1981.

Although recent projects have begun to improve the transport sector somewhat, the situation with regard to shelter has worsened. A 1976 census indicated there were 1,680 slums in Greater Bombay and that these slums contained approximately 630,000 huts, which housed more than 2.82 million people. Updated statistics from 1981 indicate that at least 3.7 million people (some 45 percent of Greater Bombay's population) are now living in slums. As for those housed in the conventional sense, 77 percent occupy one-room dwellings, and 81 percent of the households lack a separate kitchen. Even though per capita incomes in the metropolitan region (Rs13.76 a month in 1976) are the highest in the country, nearly half the population is estimated to have incomes below the poverty level. The need for 60,000 new housing units a year far exceeds the number constructed in the formal sector, which is reported to be about 20,000 units a year. Bombay's land and housing shortage is thus worse than that of other metropolitan areas in the country. A recent report cautions that, unless housing policies are changed radically, half of Bombay's households may be living in slums by 1985.

Structure of Government

The metropolitan region of Bombay today covers 4,375 square kilometers, which includes the areas of the Municipal Corporation of Greater Bombay (BMC, 440 square kilometers), thirteen municipal councils (143 square kilometers), and 1,500 semiurban and rural villages. These villages are grouped together under several panchayat samitis, or unions of villages. For purposes of land revenue and general administration Greater Bombay is regarded as one district, and the rest of the region is subdivided into three further districts: Bombay, Thana, and Kolaba. The regions delineated for planning purposes do not match the census jurisdictions. The Bombay Standard Urban Area identified by the census comprises Greater Bombay, Thana, and New Bombay. Kalyan, Ulhasnagar, and Bhiwandi are considered to be other urban agglomerations. Census returns for the rest of the region are available only as part of various revenue districts. These kinds of varying census definitions and delineations are evident throughout South and East Asia and particularly affect research for planning purposes.

Among the municipal entities, the BMC is clearly preeminent. Created by separate provincial legislation in 1888, it is the only municipal corporation in India that until recently could not be superseded by a state government. This inviolate status has been of substantial political and administrative significance; of the thirty-six municipal corporations in India, as many as thirty have been superseded at one time or another, including both Calcutta and Delhi, which continue to be administered by state-appointed officials. The unique position enjoyed by Bombay came to an end in April 1984 when the BMC was placed under an administrator through an amendment to the BMC Act by the state legislature.

The BMC's scale of investment, in addition to being the highest in the country, is the highest among the various agencies in the metropolitan region. During the fourth five-year plan (1971–72 to 1975–76), for example, Rs1,466 million of a total investment of Rs2,725 million was accounted for by the BMC and its subsidiary, BEST. Furthermore, the BMC's range of services is wider than that of any other city since it covers transportation, electricity, and hospitals, as well as the more common municipal activities. The BMC's annual budget averages some Rs2,000 million, which includes a capital account budget of Rs650–700 million. The BMC is organized in two wings—the deliberative wing, which is composed of statutory and special committees responsible for the formulation of municipal laws and policies, and the executive wing, which is headed by the municipal commissioner with statutory powers and functions for implementing and enforcing municipal regulations. With a work force of 90,000, the BMC is considered to be the largest civic body in the country.

Of the thirteen municipal councils in the region, eight were established between 1852 and 1867 to administer the early textile and industrial towns growing along the railway corridor; the others were created after independence. Their jurisdictions range in area from 6 to 60 square kilometers. Manufacturing has helped to augment all of their revenues, and on the average they spend about Rs62 a head on both revenue and capital accounts, compared with the BMC's Rs124.[1] The dozen nonmunicipal urban areas that are run as gram panchayats (village councils) together cover an area of some 92 square kilometers; they have a per capita expenditure of about Rs8. Obviously, the scope and level of services provided by these institutions vary considerably from area to area.

A large number of state government departments and agencies are involved in regulatory and investment activities in the metropolitan region. BEST provides electricity and transport services in Greater Bombay, whereas the Maharashtra State Electricity Board and State Road Transport Corporation do so in the rest of the region. The Maharashtra Water Supply and Sewerage Board handles new investments in the region outside the jurisdiction of the BMC. Shelter, a sector in which the BMC has been almost inactive, is provided by a variety of agencies that in the past operated independently, including the Maharashtra Housing Board, the Bombay Building Repairs and Construction Board, and the Bombay Slum Improvement Board. By 1977, the Housing Board, created in 1948, had constructed some 90,000 dwelling units, mostly in the Bombay-Thana belt. The Building Repair and Reconstruction Board established in 1969 (the only one of its kind in India) was responsible for structural repairs to old apartment buildings. This work was funded by a cess (tax) on old buildings and subventions from the state government. Of approximately 20,000 buildings identified as needing repair, 12,000 had been assigned priority, but by 1983 the board had completed work on only 7,275. The Slum Improvement Board was established in 1976. In the same year, however, all three bodies were merged to form a Maharashtra Housing and Area Development Authority (MHADA). The latter now consists of regional boards, one of which concentrates on the Bombay metropolitan region itself and another of which covers the Konkan region, including part of the metropolitan region.

Industrial promotion and development in the metropolitan region are the responsibility of the Maharashtra Industrial Development Corporation (MIDC), which was set up in 1962 to establish new industrial areas outside of

1. A rupee equals about US$0.80.

Bombay, particularly in the state's more backward districts. Much of the industrial development in Thana and Kalyan and along the Poona road across Thana creek is the result of the MIDC's efforts to provide industry with developed and serviced land. Another parastatal organization, the State Industrial and Investment Corporation of Maharashtra (SIICOM), has been responsible for administering a package of financial incentives to industries interested in setting up operations in these new areas. In 1970, SIICOM established the City and Industrial Development Corporation (CIDCO) as a subsidiary whose main function was to plan and build New Bombay (a twin city across Thana creek) using the MIDC-sponsored industrial development as the starting point. CIDCO is also responsible for new town development in other parts of Maharashtra, such as Nasik and Aurangabad.

Among the central government agencies that have crucial roles in the metropolitan region's development are the Posts and Telegraph Department, the Railways, and the Bombay Port Trust. The Bombay telephone system covers Greater Bombay and certain contiguous areas, and the Kalyan system covers the remainder of the metropolitan region. The former is the largest metropolitan network in India and handles the country's international communications. Its capital and operating budgets are controlled by the Posts and Telegraph Department of the Ministry of Communication.

The Bombay Port Trust, an autonomous corporation under the jurisdiction of the Ministry of Shipping, runs the country's largest port, which handles 17 million tons[2] a year, or about 26 percent of the nation's traffic. In addition, it operates its own warehousing and railway facilities, handles the marine oil terminal, and is responsible for the development of the new Nava Sheva port on the mainland. A separate Port Trust for Nava Sheva was established in 1984. The International Airports Authority, which falls under the Civil Aviation Ministry, operates the domestic and international airports at Santa Cruz, and the Ministry of Trade runs a major export promotion zone nearby.

The Western and Central Railways are two geographical divisions of the national system. Apart from connecting Bombay to the network, the suburban lines of these two railways are the principal mode of commuter traffic in the metropolitan region. Although optimization programs have been carried out in recent years, capacity has not been significantly increased, so that the commuter trains are dangerously overcrowded. The capital and operating budgets of the two railways also form part of the Railway Ministry's budget, but the revenue and expenditure accounts of the suburban facilities are not separate from those of the system as a whole. The Bombay Metropolitan Transport Organization was established in 1969 to study alternative rapid transit systems. An initial report favored the opening of additional railway corridors rather than a separate transit system. Some of these recommendations have been acted upon, but a major expansion of

---

2. Tons are metric tons throughout this volume.

Table 9-1. Public Organizations Functioning in the Bombay Metropolitan Region

Statutory bodies operating with metropolitanwide jurisdiction or a part of it
  Bombay Metropolitan Region Development Authority (BMRDA)
  Bombay Municipal Corporation
  Municipal councils of Kalyan, Thana, and New Bombay
  Zilla parishads and gram panchayats

Statutory bodies and utility undertakings that have statewide or larger jurisdiction but that
      function in the metropolitan area as well
  Maharashtra Housing and Area Development Authority
  Maharashtra Water Supply and Sewerage Board
  Maharashtra State Road Transport Corporation
  Maharashtra State Electricity Board

Institutions performing certain specific statutory planning or controlling functions for the
      metropolitan area or a sizable part of it
  Bombay Metropolitan Region Planning Board
  Regional Transport Authority
  Police Departments of Bombay and Maharashtra
  Inspectorate of Factories
  Directorate of Industries

Departments or directorates of the state and central government concerned with infra-
      structure planning or investment in the metropolitan area
  Posts and Telegraphs, Bombay Circle
  Bombay Telephones
  Western Railway
  Central Railway
  Bombay Port Trust and Nava Sheva Port Trust
  Metropolitan Transport Organization
  Public Works and Housing Department
  Inland Water Transport Department
  State Fisheries Department
  Directorate of Health Services
  City and Industrial Development Corporation of Maharashtra
  Directorate of Town Planning
  Konkon Development Corporation

the suburban network is considered a losing proposition financially and is unlikely to take place in view of the Railway Ministry's commitments to national programs of modernization. The recent decision to extend the Mankurd line to New Bombay may be the only significant exception.

In addition, a number of central government agencies and undertakings—because of their size and the nature of their work—have considerable influence on Bombay's metropolitan planning and development. They include the Oil and Natural Gas Commission, the Trombay Atomic Power Plant, the Atomic Energy Commission, the fertilizer plants in Trombay and Tal Vaishet, the Director General of Shipping, the Reserve Bank of India, and the Industrial Development Bank of India. Together, the central government and its agencies constitute the largest employer and landlord in the metropolitan region, and thus they are in a position to influence its locational and regulatory policies, although—unlike similar organizations in the private sector—they do not pay a full range of municipal taxes.

Other development and regulatory agencies such as the Regional Transport Authority, State Electricity Board, Prevention of Water Pollution Board, zilla parishads, and panchayat samitis add to the region's complex maze of institutions (see table 9-1). The Bombay Metropolitan Region Development Authority is a recent addition to the scene (its origin and present work are discussed later).

Fiscal Situation

In contrast to most other Indian cities and most of the cities being discussed here, the finances of the Greater Bombay Municipal Corporation and the other municipalities of the metropolitan region remain strong and relatively buoyant. The BMC has the largest revenue and capital budget of any city in India. In 1976–77, its revenue budget totaled Rs1,788 million, and operating expenses and debt services amounted to Rs1,544 million. Thus the city continued to maintain a nominal revenue surplus. The BMC's finances are organized around three fiscal divisions: BEST, the Water Supply and Sewerage Department, and General Services. The first two are self-contained; the third is financed principally by octroi (a tax on goods entering the Bombay municipal area), which quadrupled from Rs280 million in 1975–76 to Rs1,177 million in 1982–83. Property taxes and other sources of income have not grown in the same proportion (see table 9-2). The municipalities of Dombivli, Kalyan, Ulhasnagar, and Ambernath—which are all to be part of a proposed new Kalyan Corporation—together had revenue surpluses amounting to Rs7.4 million in 1975–76 and Rs12.8 million in 1976–77. Similarly, the municipality of Thana reported an accumulated revenue surplus of Rs10.8 million for that year. In fact, most corporations and municipalities in Maharashtra have had such surpluses as a result of their conservative financial policies.

Nevertheless, serious problems have arisen in connection with the funding of capital expenditure required to meet the growing needs of the ever expanding population. The BMC has been able to finance only 40 percent of such expenditure (mainly in the water supply, sewerage, and transport sectors) through higher tariffs. It has not been able to meet the increased demand for services in other sectors, however, especially the social services sector. The property tax and octroi, on which it relies heavily, are restricted sources of revenue. The 1947 Rent Control Act froze standard rents at that year's rental value and properties built later at their initial rental value. These controlled rents are the basis of the property taxes. Other rent control measures introduced in Bombay in 1958 have had a strong adverse effect on property taxes. Fiscal growth has been discouraged further by the restrictive national policy on industrial development in Greater Bombay, and because of rising fuel and other operating costs BEST's contributions to civic revenues have fallen into arrears.

Table 9-2. Income and Expenditure on Revenue Account, Municipal Corporation of Greater Bombay, 1975–83
(amount in 10 million rupees)

Income and expenditure	1975–76 actual		1980–81 actual		1982–83 budget	
	Amount	Percent	Amount	Percent	Amount	Percent
Income						
Octroi	28.1	36	69.1	46	117.7	52
Property tax	24.5	31	33.9	23	40.0	18
Other	26.4	33	47.1	31	68.5	30
Total	79.0	100	150.1	100	226.2	100
Expenditure						
Public health and medical services	23.8	28	40.7	28	58.7	27
Education	16.6	19	26.9	18	36.9	17
Traffic operations	9.9	12	19.8	13	30.3	14
Solid waste collection	8.8	10	17.5	12	25.8	12
Slum improvement and maintenance	7.7	9	13.1	9	17.1	8
Miscellaneous	18.5	22	29.6	20	47.5	22
Total	85.3	100	147.6	100	216.3	100
Surplus (deficit)	(6.29)		2.43		9.9	

The situation in the other municipalities of the metropolitan region is similar. For example, most of the capital expenditure for water supply and drainage in these areas is incurred by the Maharashtra Water Supply and Sewerage Board. The municipalities are expected to finance 15 percent of the regional project and on payment are to arrange to receive bulk water for local distribution. When the overall investment requirements are added to water supply and sanitation, however, they exceed the municipalities' capabilities. In practice, capital investment in the region's public facilities and services thus continues to be made principally by state and central government agencies and parastatal organizations.

The programming of these investments creates a number of problems. One is that the budgets of the central government agencies are prepared independently of each other and are not related to the state budget. Even in matters such as rail and road movements where investments have to be closely coordinated, the chances of relating the suburban railways budget to that of BEST are remote. The failure to consider a road-cum-rail bridge across the Thana creek to New Bombay is a case in point. As for the parastatal agencies, although the state government should be in a position to influence their budgets, they function under different departments, and thus their budgets are difficult to coordinate on a metropolitan, regional basis. A similar situation exists among the region's local governments, which tend to pursue their own limited interests to the detriment of policy planning and fiscal coordination on a metropolitan scale.

Response to Metropolitan Problems

The BMC has introduced a number of programs to improve services. A major effort to increase the volume of water supply and improve access to sewerage began in 1973. A second project initiated in 1978 is expected to augment the water supply from 1,600 to 2,500 million liters a day, increase storage and distribution capacities, and extend sewerage collection to 80 percent of the properties (from a base of 50 percent). Another project begun at the same time is expected to expand the bus fleet and improve traffic management. Together, these three projects cost some US$560 million, of which World Bank assistance accounts for about US$240 million. The regional water supply and sewerage scheme has already been mentioned, as have projects in housing and slum improvement. With respect to the latter efforts, the Bombay Housing Board and its successor, the MHADA, have focused mainly on the construction of walkup apartments. In 1976 the Maharashtra Slum Improvement Board launched a massive effort in slum upgrading, which was to provide water, drainage, pathways, and community latrines. So far more than 2.9 million slum residents have been covered by the program at a cost of Rs347 million. Unlike Calcutta's slums, which are long-established tenancy settlements, those in Bombay appear to lack security of tenure. This and the generally weak approaches to cost recovery account for the poor maintenance of the services.

One of the objectives of creating the Bombay Metropolitan Regional Development Authority (BMRDA) was to take up planning on a metropolitan scale. The extensions of the BMC in 1950 and 1957 had already enlarged the municipal area to 440 square kilometers, and further extension was not favored for both political and administrative reasons. The BMC's own development plan of 1964 had called for investments to sustain an infrastructure for 12 million people in Greater Bombay by 1984, but an appraisal of the plan recommended dispersing this growth as much as possible from Greater Bombay to its surrounding areas. In 1965, the Gadgil Committee endorsed this view and called for the establishment of regional planning boards for the metropolis and other regions in the state. As a result, a Regional Planning Board for Bombay was set up in 1970 under the Maharashtra Regional Town Planning Act of 1966. This board recommended that a new city be created across the harbor, that as many offices as possible be shifted to it, that the Backbay reclamation scheme be abandoned, and that no other industries be allowed to build in the Thana and Kalyan areas. CIDCO was then created, but with the slowing of investments, the waning of interest in a new Bombay, and the revival of the Backbay scheme, attention again turned to the need for a metropolitan authority with statutory powers to regulate development and coordinate investment on a metropolitan scale. Such an authority was also considered a prerequisite for the receipt of financial assistance from the central government and external sources such as the World Bank.

The 1975 act that established the BMRDA was the result of a year-long legislative battle. As in Calcutta, the concept of a metropolitan body with wide powers was resisted in Bombay as an encroachment on local self-government. Moreover, some were skeptical about the feasibility of raising the additional revenues needed, and the role of the existing parastatal organizations and their relationship to the BMRDA remained unclear. Nevertheless, with possible central government and World Bank assistance in mind, the state government pushed the legislation through. The BMRDA was to consist of forty-seven members, including eight ministers of the state government, twelve representatives of the BMC (including the mayor, municipal commissioner, and chairmen of statutory committees), seven representatives from the other local authorities in the region, eight members of the state legislature, and twelve officials. The authority was to be managed by a standing committee of nine and an executive committee of eight. In addition, three functional boards were established: one for housing, urban development, and ecology; a second for water supply and sanitation; and a third for transport and communications.

The authority's main objective is to "secure the development of the Bombay Metropolitan Region according to the Regional (Planning Board) Plan," and for this purpose it is authorized to:

- Review any physical, financial, or economic plan
- Review any proposed development project or scheme or any that may be in the course of execution
- Formulate financial programs and sanction development schemes
- Execute projects on the directions of the state government
- Coordinate execution of the projects
- Supervise or otherwise ensure adequate supervision of the planning and execution of any project or scheme, the expenses of which, in whole or in part, are to be met from the Bombay Metropolitan Region Development Fund
- Direct local and public authorities to maintain works provided by it or through its funding, and, if necessary, maintain such schemes in the event of failure to do so by the responsible authority.

A proviso to the act stipulates that the authority will not ordinarily deal with matters falling within the obligatory and discretionary duties of the BMC, except when integrated development of the region is an issue. The proviso emphasizes the metropolitan character of the authority's role and assuages the BMC's fears of possible clashes of jurisdiction.

The BMRDA is the first principally elective and federative type of metropolitan planning and development organization in India. It has been designed to encompass a variety of functions, from metropolitanwide planning, funding, and execution of sectoral programs to development control and even maintenance. As a result, it faces certain built-in conflicts, such as those arising from the sectoral nature of the authority's functional boards and its mandate to promote integrated development. Channels of communication and coordination were expected to develop rapidly, but in its early years the authority has been preoccupied with other matters.

The BMRDA became the borrower and the monitoring and supervising agency for the World Bank–sponsored urban transport project of 1976. The responsibility for the project's execution, however, was vested almost entirely in BEST and its parent, the BMC, and the latter assumed liability for the loan. The authority's role as financing agent thus appeared superfluous. Under the Bank-assisted Bombay water supply project of 1973, the authority was made responsible for undertaking a water resources allocation plan, and it was expected to have a more direct role in the subsequent second Bombay water supply project (1978) and the Maharastra water supply project (1979). This did not happen, however, and control of the projects reverted to the executing agencies, namely, the BMC and the Maharastra Water Supply and Sewerage Board. Because of the existence of the functional boards and the BMRDA's attempts to act as financing agent in sectoral projects, the sectoral agencies have come to view the authority as a competitor rather than a coordinator. Its efforts to execute the Bandra-Kurla complex land development scheme have reinforced this perception.

Because of the confusion over the BMRDA's role and the conflicts between it and other agencies, its functions became the subject of several studies, one of which was undertaken in 1977 by the BMRDA itself. This study concluded that the BMRDA's functions were to plan and coordinate development activities; formulate, promote, and monitor projects; finance development; and execute projects only when other agencies were either unavailable or unwilling to do so. Consultants who studied the organization later concurred with this view, but urged that BMRDA execute at least some projects to establish its credibility. Another view was that development financing was secondary, that it was much more important for the BMRDA to be involved directly in the allocation of financial resources in the region, and therefore that it should be a part of the state's Planning Department rather than an extension of the Urban Department. A study group of senior officials chaired by the chief secretary of the state government recommended in April 1981 that the functional boards be abolished, a single executive committee be established, and the internal organization of the authority be changed.

The BMRDA Act was finally amended in May 1983. Its membership was drastically reduced from forty-seven to seventeen. In place of eight ministers, there were now to be three; BMC representation was reduced from twelve to six, including the mayor and the municipal commissioner, and that of the state legislature from eight to three; the number of officials was reduced from twelve to five; and representation of the local authorities in the region other than the BMC was eliminated. A nine-member Executive Committee with management functions was to replace the Standing Committee and the Executive Committee. The three functional boards were abolished and subsequently their chairmen nominated to this committee. The position of the vice-chairman of the authority was also eliminated. As chief executive, the metropolitan commissioner was to be the secretary of the executive committee and was to report to the chairman. The chairman now presides over six divisions, which deal with planning, engineering, transport and communications, town and country planning, financing, and administration.

Although the authority certainly needed to be trimmed down and streamlined, the reorganized BMRDA has yet to demonstrate its effectiveness in securing a multisectoral development program in the metropolitan region. In its composition and the scope of its work the BMRDA is now more of an extension of the Urban Development Department. It has not yet been brought into the state five-year plan and annual planning process, nor is it involved in the planning and budgetary exercises of the large parastatal organizations such as CIDCO, MIDC, BEST, MHADA, and the State Electricity Board (SEB). More important, the size and phasing of the outlays of central government ministries and agencies that are critical to the region are by and large outside the purview of the BMRDA, as is illustrated by its efforts in investment programming a few years ago.

In response to a covenant in the transport project agreement with the World Bank (which envisaged the authority's role as a catalyst in reviewing and assembling a regional investment program), the BMRDA prepared a review of investment estimates for 1977–78 and 1978–79, followed by an investment plan for the sixth five-year-plan period, 1978–79 to 1982–83. The plan covered housing and urban development, industrial area development, water supply and sanitation, and transport and communications. A government of India committee set up to review metropolitan programs and projects for Calcutta, Madras, and Bombay also encouraged the BMRDA to continue with such investment programming exercises. For the sixth five-year plan, the package prepared by the BMRDA envisaged an outlay of Rs19,500 million and indicated some possible means of finance. In the absence of specific support from the state government, the exercise was not pursued further, however, and the sixth plan allocations were in fact determined as before, on the basis of separate agency and sectoral submissions.

Pending Issues

The BMRDA thus continues to have little direct involvement with investment programming. In recent years it has therefore tried to focus on developing programs for specific service sectors. In 1981, for example, it initiated an interagency exercise in the shelter sector, analyzed past performance, projected future needs, and proposed a program of 85,000 serviced sites and the upgrading of slums covering about 100,000 households. The program, which will cost about Rs2,780 million, is being considered for state government and World Bank financing. The exercise involved the MHADA, CIDCO, and BMC, and it helped the BMRDA to win some acceptance for its planning and coordinating role.

Problems remain on the financial front, however. The BMRDA expected to receive an annual contribution of Rs100 million and initial seed capital of

Rs1,000 million from the state government, but neither of these sums has been forthcoming. The state government has been either offsetting the annual payments made against routine provisions for local governments and other site-financed projects or avoiding them because of financial stringency; and the seed capital has been limited to an initial payment of Rs300 million. The BMRDA's need for capital is not acute, however. The only large scheme the BMRDA is attempting to implement is that of the Bandra-Kurla complex already mentioned, where preliminary land development and sales have so far provided it with close to Rs700 million. Because of the opposition to this effort from the sectoral agencies and other limitations, the authority is not venturing further into capital development schemes.

The principal effort in land development has been the building of New Bombay, which is part of the 1970 metropolitan regional plan to develop a growth center parallel to the old city. New Bombay is expected to have a population of 2 million by the end of the century and will encompass the existing industrial areas of Thana, Belapur, and Panvel along the mainland shore of Thana creek. The twin city's growth is heavily predicated on the shifting of office employment and wholesale trading facilities from Bombay proper. This shift has not taken place, however, mainly because of the prestigious and vast Backbay reclamation scheme undertaken at the tip of Bombay island. A highly profitable land and high-rise office and upper-income residential development involving some 250,000 jobs, the scheme has prospered despite opposition from environmentalists and other civic groups. Nevertheless, a new residential node is nearing completion at Vashi (population 20,000) on the New Bombay site, an office complex is being constructed in Belapur, a wholesale agricultural market has been established, and a wholesale steel materials market is under development. In addition, a new port is under development at Nava Sheva that will be able to handle 3.7 million tons of bulk cargo and 250,000 containers a year by 1993. CIDCO has managed to acquire large tracts of land and to provide adequate services. Its operations continue to be financially viable, but the pace of development falls far short of that needed to achieve the target population by the year 2000. In 1981, the population stood at less than 80,000.

Another reason for the slow pace of development is the poor communications link between New Bombay and the main city. A proposal to extend one of the suburban rail lines over a new bridge across Thana creek has been approved, but sufficient funds are not available. Thus, the Bandra-Kurla office complex (with its 120,000 jobs) and the rapid development of Backbay will continue to have an adverse effect on New Bombay's growth. In all probability, New Bombay will not realize its grand design, but many parts of the plan will be completed. Thus the metropolitan region's spatial pattern will most likely consist of an urban spread lacking the strong polycentric nodes envisaged by its urban planners.

The state government recently proposed to merge some of the region's municipalities to form corporations. A 1979 commission examined the financial issues that might be involved in such a move and recommended that Kalyan, Ulhasnagar, Ambernath, and Dombivli municipalities together with neighboring villages (in all, covering an area of about 93 square kilometers) should become a single corporation, and that Thana municipality and surrounding areas (in all, covering an area of 75.7 square kilometers) should be made into another corporation. The commission concluded that both corporations would have the financial capacity to meet operating costs and modest loan liabilities. It proposed that another corporation should be created for the area of New Bombay (hitherto managed by CIDCO) so that user charges and local taxes could be collected. These three new corporations came into being in October 1983. Octroi and taxes from the area's industries are to be the principal sources of revenue. In order to meet the costs of service deficiencies and proposed capital projects, however, they would need a per capita revenue of some Rs100, compared with the present revenue of Rs60.

The BMC's tax revenues have been expanding at a rate of 9 percent a year, but this increase has been barely sufficient to keep real per capita revenue constant. The national policy of decentralizing industries from Greater Bombay also affects the city's tax base. Much of the BMC's per capita revenue of Rs265 a year is spent on public health, medical relief, and education, which are all largely subsidized activities. As a result, it has to rely on borrowing to finance most capital development. Its present debt burden of some Rs300 million a year thus amounts to 11 percent of its revenues, and, although technically the corporation could incur a higher burden, its access to capital markets is strongly controlled by the state government.

In addition, in the areas of the metropolitan region outside the BMC where new capital investment is badly needed, the capacity to borrow is much more limited. Thus, for example, the regional investment program proposed by the BMRDA for the period 1978–83 envisaged an outlay of Rs19,660 million, of which Rs7,520 million (or 38 percent) would be provided from internal resources, 36 percent from long-term loans, and only the remaining 26 percent from the state and central governments. Thus far, the World Bank has been the principal source of long-term loans, with commitments of Rs3,200 million for water supply and transportation projects. Other sources of loans, such as the Housing and Urban Development Corporation, have failed to provide the needed amounts, and a large shortfall remains (Rs1,150 million in the housing sector alone). Because loan financing is needed for so large a proportion of Bombay's investment, debt servicing may later preempt much of the money required unless substantial revenues are built up in the early years of projects. Mobilization of resources thus remains one of the region's foremost problems and a central concern for the BMRDA itself, if it is to maintain a pivotal role in investment programming.

Another important and as yet unanswered question is to what extent the central government should be involved in Bombay's development. The central government and its agencies have a strong and pervasive influence as employers and landholders in Bombay, yet their investment plans remain largely outside the BMRDA's planning process. In addition, the state government has been reluctant or unwilling to provide for services such as telecommunications and railways, which it views as responsibilities of the central government. The allocation of work between, and the budgetary procedures of, central ministries permit neither a metropolitan perspective nor a metropolitan orientation. Special mechanisms thus need to be established so that regional investment projections can be periodically updated and supplemented with the details of proposed government programs. These projections can then be used to influence future decisions on investment for metropolitan development at all levels of government.

10

Calcutta

THE CALCUTTA METROPOLITAN DISTRICT (CMD) consists of a continuously built-up mass of municipal and nonmunicipal towns and a peripheral belt of densely settled rural areas. In 1965 it was statutorily defined as an area of 1,269 square kilometers that extends for more than 70 kilometers along both banks of the Hooghly River. Howrah and Calcutta, the twin cities at the core of this metropolitan region, cover an area of about 133 square kilometers. The CMD spreads outward from this core into five of the sixteen districts of the state of West Bengal to occupy all of Calcutta District and parts of Nadia, Hooghly, Howrah, and 24-Parganas.

Growth of the City

In 1961 the CMD had an estimated population of 7.5 million people. By 1971 the population had grown to 8.3 million; of this number, 516,000 lived in Howrah Municipality and 3,149,000 in Calcutta City. Density in the twin cities averaged 27,500 per square kilometer. By 1980, the CMD covered nearly 1,414 square kilometers, and the population had climbed to an estimated 10 million. Most of this growth had occurred outside the twin-city core. The growth rate in Calcutta City itself had fallen to 4.54 percent a year during 1971–81, compared with 7.57 percent and 8.48 percent in the previous two decades.

Today Calcutta City and Howrah form the nucleus of the largest economic complex in eastern India. This complex began nearly three hundred years ago as a foreign trading post on the tidal reaches of the Hooghly River. The greater part of the complex has been built on low-lying rice fields and marshes that continue to be inundated during the annual monsoons. The port itself is more than 190 kilometers inland from the Bay of Bengal. Over the years, the volume of water flowing into the Hooghly has been decreasing owing to a steady eastward shift of the mainstream of the

Ganga, of which the Hooghly is an offshoot. As a result, not only has the CMD's drainage system been silting up, but the Hooghly, which is the principal source of potable water, has become increasingly saline in its tidal reaches. The recently completed Farakka barrage on the Ganga near the Hooghly offtake point is expected to improve the flow of freshwater, but the saltwater lakes and tidal marshes that lie on Calcutta's eastern rim will continue to restrict its outward growth to a north-south alignment. Perhaps the greatest drawback of the region is its extreme heat and humidity, which moderate only in the winter months.

That metropolitan development of this scale could have occurred in such an adverse natural setting bears witness to the vital character of Calcutta's long-standing entrepôt function. By 1962–63, it was handling some 25 percent of India's total import tonnage and up to 42 percent of its exports on behalf of a vast hinterland rich in coal, iron, limestone, copper, manganese, and mica. Giant iron and steel centers had arisen at Jamshedpur, Ranchi, Rourkela, Bhilai, Asansol, and Durgapur; and greater Calcutta's manufacturers found that an internal market of more than 150 million people had been opened up by the river, rail, and road transport system. By the early 1960s, industries in the metropolis were producing 95 percent of the nation's jute, 78 percent of its railroad stock, 74 percent of its rubberized footwear, 56 percent of its electric lamps, 50 percent of its finished steel, and more than 21 percent of its paper and paperboard.

Metropolitan Problems

Today, two decades later, the contribution of the Calcutta Metropolitan District to the nation's commerce and industry is not so predominant. Its position has been challenged more and more by the metropolitan complexes of Bombay, Madras, and Delhi and their respective hinterlands, which blanket the rest of India. The CMD's traditional industries of jute, rubber, paper, and heavy engineering were already ailing in the 1960s. Since the mid-1960s, new industries have invariably set up their operations in competing centers, and the level of industrial production in Calcutta has fallen by some 10 percent, in contrast to a 52 percent rise in national production. The decline in manufacturing appears to be related to a number of factors: power shortages, labor disputes, civil disorder, influxes of refugees from Bangladesh, shortages of investment capital because of political instability, excess capacity in the older industries because of declining world markets, national price-equalization schemes in the steel industry and the freighting of coal, which offset the advantages of Calcutta's location, and a recent national ban on the construction of large and medium-scale industries in metropolitan areas. The index of industrial production (taking 1970 as the base) declined from 119.6 in 1965 to 102.5 in 1978. Only certain light engineering, craft, and service industries (for example, transport, storage, communications, and leather goods industries) have shown any appreciable growth, and this has occurred largely in small-scale and household enterprises. In the CMD as a whole, employment in 1981 was about 2.8 million, which represents only a modest increase over the 1971 figure of 2.6 million. About 1.5 million are employed in services, 1.1 million in manufacturing, and 0.2 million in agriculture and other primary sector activities. The CMD's economy is thus characterized by a dominant tertiary sector and a weak secondary sector.[1]

The district's traditional entrepôt function has also become less important. The traffic handled by the port rose from 7.1 million tons in 1948 to 11.1 million in 1964–65, but fell to 6.3 million in 1973–74. The overall share of Calcutta port in the total traffic for all Indian ports has steadily declined, from 43.3 percent in 1948 to 9 percent in 1974, even though the country's port throughput increased from 16 million to 64 million tons in the same period. The decline is the result of the opening or expansion of ports at Paradip, Vizag, Madras, Cochin, and Kandla and the region's general economic slump, which has hit its agricultural and manufacturing sector particularly hard. Problems with the river draft, technological changes in shipping, and low productivity at the port have all contributed further to the deterioration.

Thus it is not surprising that per capita income in the CMD has shown little improvement. In 1962–63, the annual net income was close to Rs5,300 million at current prices, or Rs815 (US$98) per head. Recent studies indicate that the total income for the CMD has grown only marginally since then, from Rs883 million in 1970–71 to Rs10,705 million in 1976–77 at constant prices. The overall increase in per capita income during this six-year period thus averaged only 1.5 percent a year. The pinch of a low per capita income is aggravated further by its skewed distribution. About 45 percent of the CMD households have a monthly income of less than Rs350 and are officially categorized as economically weak. About 26 percent are in the low-income category with incomes between Rs351 and Rs600. Although on the average per capita incomes in Calcutta are higher than in West Bengal or in India as a whole, in absolute numbers the concentration of low-income households is pronounced. Poverty thus underlies many of Calcutta's problems.

The population of the CMD increased rapidly from 5.4 million in 1951 to 7.5 million in 1961 and 8.3 million in 1971. About 1.1 million refugees contributed to the increase in each of these periods. Annual growth rates, which hovered around 2.4 percent during 1951–61 and 2.2 percent during 1961–71 rose to 3.3 percent between 1971 and 1981.[2] Natural increase rather than in-migration is believed to be the principal reason for this growth. Since 1981, the population has been increasing by about 200,000 persons annually. Even so, the Calcutta Metropolitan District is the slowest growing metropolis in India.

Despite the slowdown in economic development and urbanization during the past twenty years, the city has been unable to provide enough basic

1. See "Employment and Economy," papers read at the Calcutta Metropolitan Development Authority seminar held in Calcutta, February 1983.
2. Provisional population tables, 1981 Census, Commissioner of India.

Calcutta.   The Howrah Bridge, one of only two bridges to span the Hooghly River that bisects the metropolitan district. The old government and commercial center is to the right of the road and wharves are to the left.

Map 10-1. Growth and Development of Calcutta, 1690–1971

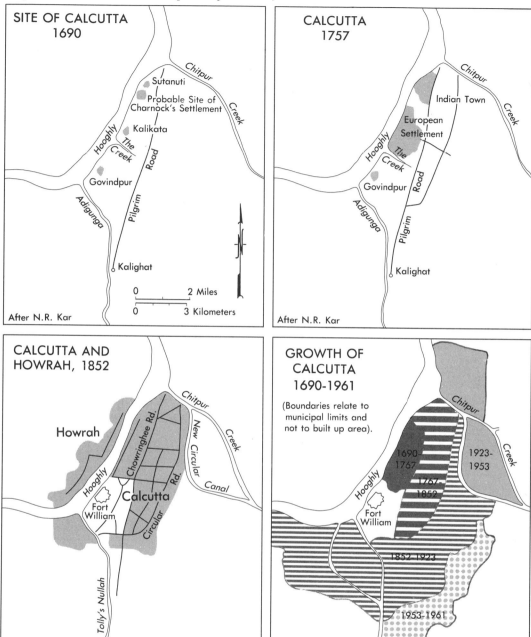

SITE OF CALCUTTA
1690

Chitpur
Creek
Sutanuti
Probable Site of
Charnock's Settlement
Kalikata
Hooghly
The Creek
Pilgrim Road
Govindpur
Adigunga
Kalighat

0   2 Miles
0   3 Kilometers

After N.R. Kar

CALCUTTA
1757

Chitpur
Creek
Indian Town
European
Settlement
Hooghly
The Creek
Pilgrim Road
Govindpur
Adigunga
Kalighat

After N.R. Kar

CALCUTTA AND
HOWRAH, 1852

Chitpur
Creek
Howrah
Chowringhee Rd.
New Circular Rd.
Canal
Hooghly
Calcutta
Fort
William
Circular Rd.
Tolly's Nullah

After N.R. Kar

GROWTH OF
CALCUTTA
1690–1961

(Boundaries relate to
municipal limits and
not to built up area).

Chitpur
Creek
1690–
1767
1923–
1953
1767–
1852
Hooghly
Fort
William
1852–1923
1953–1961

After N.R. Kar

Source: Adapted from Joseph E. Schwartzberg, ed., *A Historical Atlas of South Asia* (Chicago, Ill.: University of Chicago Press, 1978).

Map 10-2. Calcutta, 1842

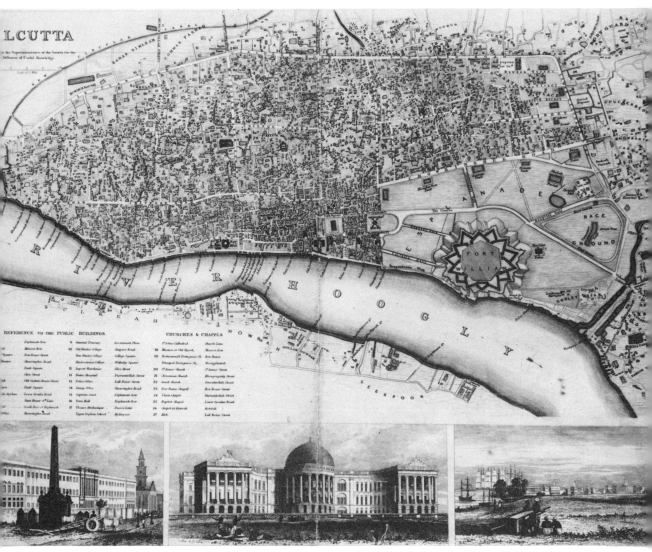

Photo: Victoria Memorial Museum, Calcutta

Map 10-3. Hinterland of Calcutta

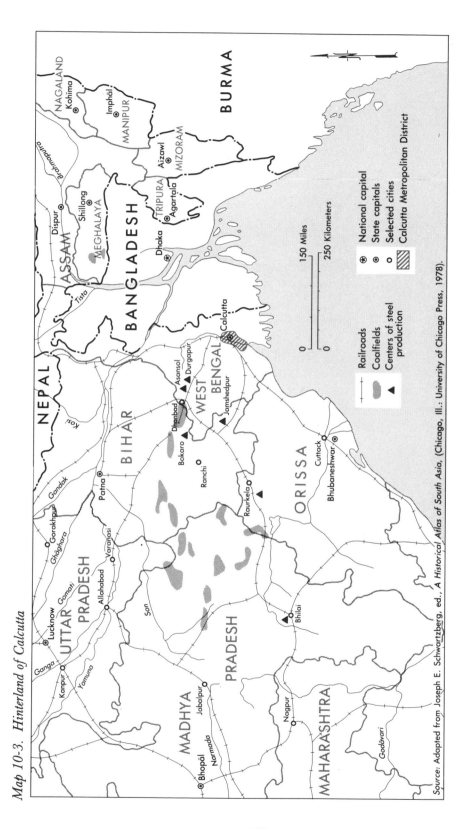

Source: Adapted from Joseph E. Schwartzberg, ed., A Historical Atlas of South Asia, (Chicago, Ill.: University of Chicago Press, 1978).

Map 10-4. Calcutta Urban Area, 1985

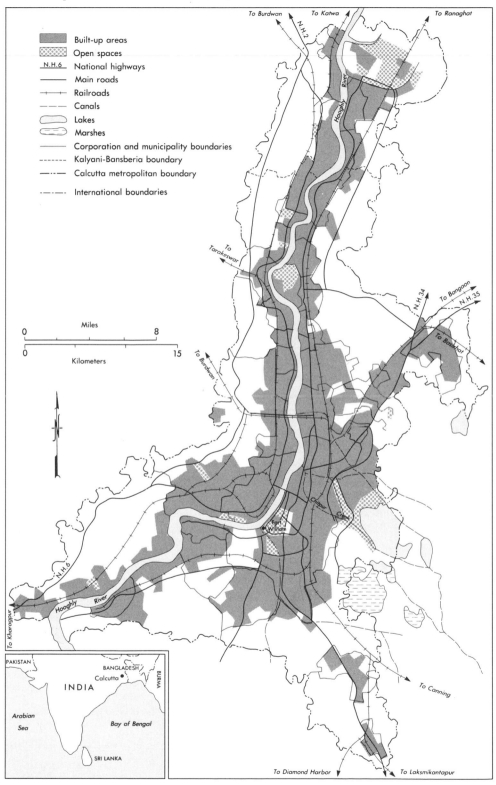

services to meet the population's needs. The supply of potable water has been grossly inadequate and piped water has been available only in Calcutta City and parts of a few other municipalities. Sewerage is limited to only a third of the area in the urban core. Poor maintenance of existing drainage facilities and periodic clogging of the system have made flooding an annual feature. Places in primary schools have been available for only two-thirds of the children, and health services have remained scanty and fragmented.

The poorer sections of the population, in particular, have been seriously affected by these deficiencies. Some 3 million people live in unserviced bustees (slum areas) and refugee settlements that lack potable water, endure serious annual flooding, and have no systematic means of disposing of refuse or human wastes. Some 2.5 million more live in similarly blighted and unserviced areas that are not officially classified as bustees because their housing is more permanent. Within the CMD the Hooghly River is spanned by only two bridges, which must meet the growing needs for communication between the east and west banks, to the detriment of general economic development and of west bank expansion in particular. Transport services in the metropolitan center are no longer able to cope with the estimated 5 million passenger trips daily.

These problems go far back in time. As early as 1914, the first chief engineer of the Calcutta Improvement Trust (CIT) catalogued many of the problems and offered four alternative plans of development "to bring Calcutta into line with even the old built-up sectors of European cities."[3] The half century of neglect that the author complained about continued for another fifty years. Indeed, inertia was the chief characteristic of the city's administration from at least the 1920s onward, although its leading citizens for a long time marched in the vanguard of the political and social development of modern India. Many were prominent in the Bengal renaissance of the nineteenth century; others were in the forefront of the nationalist movement in the twentieth; still others played important roles in the achievement of independence in 1947. Nevertheless, during these years of rapid economic, cultural, and physical change, urban management failed to keep pace. Apart from adding a drainage outfall system in 1936, the city administration was unable to discharge its most elementary housekeeping functions, let alone initiate new functions demanded by technological and political revolutions. The Second World War, during which Calcutta was used as a base for the operations in the eastern theater, also took its toll. Partition in the wake of independence brought waves of refugees into the city and its suburbs, which had been barely able to cope with their existing populations. Maintenance deficits mounted, and one service after another began to collapse. "It would be a tremendous tragedy," Prime Minister Jawaharlal Nehru pointed out in 1961, "if the country's biggest city went to pieces." Still, it took ten years before any action was taken to check the decline.

3. E. P. Richards, *Report on the Condition, Improvement, and Town Planning in the City of Calcutta* (Hertfordshire, England: Jennings and Benley, 1914).

No single public agency or class of agencies has been wholly responsible for this failure in urban management; there have been many causes—social, political, and institutional. Some problems originate in the great linguistic, religious, and cultural diversity of its large immigrant population, both Indian and foreign. In addition, family life and the social stability it fosters have both been undermined by the continuing employment of migrants in the district's manufacturing and commercial sectors. Many thousands of employees in factories, shops, and offices are single males from the rural areas of neighboring states who have no permanent stake in city life. Most treat the district as merely a place to work; many have left their wives and children behind and support them with the greater part of their earnings; many also return to their villages every year for seasonal agricultural purposes.

As a result, the district has a loosely knit society marked by tensions between noncommunicating groups. Political life reflects these social tensions and conflicts as well as the migrant employees' general lack of interest in civic betterment. These conflicts have deeply influenced the civil administration in greater Calcutta, where municipal jurisdictions and the responsibilities of the municipal governments have been geared more toward the interest of business and commercial groups than toward civic efficiency.

Structure of Government

Factionalism, fragmentation, and conflicts of interest between the provincial and local levels of administration have been a perennial feature of the CMD's politics. The Calcutta Corporation, which had campaigned so hard for the country's independence, was itself superseded in 1948 by the first elected government of the state. All the other municipalities in the district have likewise been taken over from time to time. Between 1965 and 1972, West Bengal itself went through three different coalition governments and two spells of presidential rule. (Under this arrangement, the legislative assembly and the elected Council of Ministers are either revoked or kept in abeyance; the legislative and executive process of the state is directed by the central government in the name of the president of India.) An orderly government is therefore hardly to be expected, but its fragmentation has been far greater than might have been anticipated. In 1961, the metropolitan region's public institutions constituted a veritable maze of jurisdictions and authorities that were often in conflict and in no way coordinated regionwide.[4] Thirty-six urban local authorities were responsible for 85 percent of the population and 40 percent of the area; more than 450 rural local authorities covered another 15 percent of the population and 60 percent of the area; 28 state government departments, 30 special agencies, and 20 central government ministries were also directly involved in

4. *Manual of Government in Calcutta* (New York: Institute of Public Administration, 1963).

Table 10-1. Institutions that Provide Health, Education, Welfare, Housing, and Transportation Services, Calcutta Metropolitan District, 1982

Territorial jurisdiction	Institution	Function
Local (municipal, urban, or village area)	544 gram panchayats	Village local government
	48 nonmunicipal areas	"Rurban" local government
	33 municipalities	Urban local government
	3 corporations	City local government
	1 cantonment	Urban local administration
	2 notified area committees	Urban local government
	1 development authority	Salt Lake urban development
	1 improvement trust	Urban public works, Calcutta
Submetropolitan (area of two or more local government units)	153 panchayat samitis	Block-level unions of local rural governments
	1 state transport corporation	Inner metropolitan area bus system
	1 state tramway company	Calcutta and Howrah tram systems
	1 union metropolitan transport project	Calcutta underground system
Metropolitan (Calcutta Metropolitan District)	1 metropolitan development authority	Physical development (public works)
	1 state metropolitan development department	Control over public works and urban improvement (including Calcutta Metropolitan Development Authority)
	1 state metropolitan immunization scheme	
	1 state directorate of smoke nuisance	Control of air pollution (Calcutta)

the region's public administration (see table 10-1). Together, they formed a labyrinth of 570 separate units of government having national, provincial, local, or special status, excluding territorial subdivisions such as divisional and district administrations and rural community development blocks. The laws and regulations they administered were the result of at least the last hundred years of development. Yet no single law recognized the rise of the metropolitan region, nor did any institution do so until the creation of the Calcutta Metropolitan Planning Organization (CMPO) in 1961. The CMPO was established only by a directive of the state department of health, however; it exercised no executive powers whatsoever and it possessed no independent financial resources.

Territorial jurisdiction	*Institution*	*Function*
Suprametropolitan (wider than the Calcutta Metropolitan District)	4 zilla parishads	District government (rural)
	2 state education departments	Primary, secondary, and higher education
	1 state health department	Provision of hospitals and preventive health services
	1 state valuation board	
	1 state public health engineering	Provision of environmental health infrastructure
	1 state urban and rural water supply department	
	1 state prevention and control of water pollution board	
	1 state housing board	
	1 union public works department	Construction of union government buildings
	1 state infrastructure development corporation	
	1 union controller of aerodromes	Dum Dum Airport
	1 union inland water transport corporation	
	1 port trust	Operation of Calcutta and Haldia ports
	2 union railway divisions	
	1 state directorate of local bodies	
	1 state local government and urban development department	

Fiscal Situation

For years the municipal institutions of the metropolitan district have been on the verge of bankruptcy. In 1969–70 the total revenue of the Calcutta Corporation and all the other corporations and municipalities in the CMD amounted to only Rs179 million for an area inhabited by 6.7 million people (that is, Rs27 per capita). Even this low figure masks considerable variations among municipalities. Per capita revenue ranged from Rs43 in the Calcutta Corporation to Rs13 in the other corporations and municipalities. Property taxes accounted for 58 percent of the total revenue in Calcutta and 70 percent of the revenue elsewhere. Poor tax assessment and tax collection only made matters worse. The per capita property tax revenue of Rs18.27 was well below Bombay's Rs31.53. (For more details on taxes and other revenue, see tables 10-2, 10-3.)

The largest share of expenditure was for conservancy, a general term that covers the collection and disposal of garbage and night soil and the cleaning of drains. In the Calcutta Corporation, it accounted for a quarter of the total expenditure, and in other municipalities for more than 40 percent. Conservancy staff accounted for a further 65 percent in the Corporation, and general administrative and tax collection staff for another 10 percent. About 60 percent of the resources of other municipalities were devoted to wages and salaries, more than 35 percent to maintenance, and less than 5 percent to capital outlay. This meager scale of revenue and expenditure of the municipal bodies in the country's most populous metropolis has been a determining factor in the design and administration of the urban development program that was initiated in 1970. The municipal bodies could not form a key element in the administration of the program, even though their burden in maintaining the newly created facilities increased significantly. Because of these and other circumstances, several steps were taken in the 1970s to improve municipal finances and performance (as described below).

Response to Metropolitan Problems

In a span of twenty years, Calcutta has tried to deal with its metropolitan problems in several ways. Pursuant to the recommendations of a team from

Table 10-2. *Calcutta Corporation Forecast of Revenue and Expenditure, Second Calcutta Urban Project, 1977–78 to 1981–82*
(10 million rupees)

Revenue and expenditure	1977–78	1978–79	1979–80	1980–81	1981–82
Revenue[a]					
Sources before 1976–77 reforms	12.4	13.0	13.7	14.4	15.1
Sources from 1976–77 reforms					
Surcharge on commercial properties	1.2	2.3	2.5	2.6	2.8
Surcharge on vehicles	1.4	1.5	1.6	1.7	1.8
Increased fees on taxes and professions	0.6	0.6	0.6	0.6	0.7
Octroi receipts	4.1	4.3	4.8	5.2	5.5
Total	19.7	21.7	23.2	24.5	25.9
Expenditure[b]					
Recurrent expenditures[c]	22.8	24.4	26.1	27.9	29.9
Debt service, 1976–77[d]	3.0	3.0	3.0	3.0	3.0
Operation and maintenance of new					
projects	2.2	3.5	4.7	5.2	5.6
Total	28.0	30.9	33.8	36.1	38.5

Revenue and expenditure	1977–78	1978–79	1979–80	1980–81	1981–82
Revenue deficit	8.3	9.2	10.6	11.6	12.6
Minus grants from government of West Bengal[c]	3.4	3.6	3.9	4.2	4.5
Additional government subvention required	4.9	5.6	6.7	7.4	8.1
Revenue as percentage of expenditure	70	70	69	65	67
Effect of increasing 1976–77 revenue to 73 percent of expenditure					
Percentage increase	n.a.	4	8	12	15
Revenue yield	n.a.	23.5	26.6	29.5	32.3
Percentage of expenditure	n.a.	76	79	82	84
Revised deficit	8.3	7.4	7.2	6.6	6.2
Deduct grants from government of West Bengal	3.4	3.6	3.9	4.2	4.5
Additional government subvention required	4.9	3.8	3.3	2.4	1.7
Effect of improving property tax collections[f]					
Amount of property tax included in revenue sources before 1976–77 reforms (actual recoveries in cash based on current collection of 66 percent)	9.0	9.5	9.9	10.4	10.9
Percentage increase based on government assessments	n.a.	70	80	90	90
Yield of increased property tax collections on basis of agreed recommendations	n.a.	0.5	2.1	3.8	4.0
Additional revenues required to achieve targets	n.a.	1.3	1.3	1.2	2.4
Percentage increase from accelerating improved collection performance	n.a.	77.5	85	90	90
Revised yield	n.a.	1.7	2.8	3.8	3.8
Additional revenues required to achieve agreed performance targets	n.a.	0.1	0.6	1.2	2.6

n.a. Not available.

a. Revenues representing cash receipts escalated at 5 percent a year.

b. Expenditures representing cash payments escalated at 7 percent a year.

c. The expenditures and grants do not reflect special expenditures by Calcutta Corporation on road maintenance in 1977–78 and associated grants from the government of West Bengal since these were a one-time exercise.

d. Debt service transfers to Calcutta Corporation from the Calcutta Metropolitan Development Authority began in 1982–83.

e. Government grants consist mainly of dearness allowance award repayments and have been escalated at 7 percent a year.

f. The increases in property tax collections *take no account* of possible recoveries of arrears before 1974–75. The 1977–78 collections of 9.0 crores includes normal arrears collections for the years 1975–76 and 1976–77. The arrears at the end of 1975–76 were about 12 crores (US$13 million).

Sources: Calcutta Metropolitan Planning Organization and World Bank estimates.

Table 10-3. Municipalities' Forecast of Revenue and Expenditure, Second Calcutta Urban Project, 1977–78 to 1981–82
(10 million rupees)

Revenue/expenditure	1977–78	1978–79	1979–80	1980–81	1981–82
Revenue[a]					
Sources before 1976–77 reforms	5.7	6.0	6.3	6.6	6.9
New sources from 1976–77 reforms	1.5	2.0	2.2	2.3	2.4
Octroi receipts	2.8	2.8	2.9	2.9	3.0
Total	10.0	10.8	11.4	11.8	12.3
Expenditure[b]					
Recurrent expenditures	11.2	12.0	12.8	13.7	14.6
Operation and maintenance of new assets commissioned by Calcutta Metropolitan Development Authority	1.5	1.9	2.7	2.9	3.3
Debt service	2.2	2.2	2.2	2.2	2.2
Total	14.9	16.1	17.7	18.8	20.1
Revenue deficit	4.9	5.3	6.3	7.0	7.8
Minus grants from government of West Bengal[c]	3.3	3.6	3.8	4.1	4.4
Additional government subvention required	1.6	0.7	2.5	2.9	3.4
Revenue as percentage of expenditure[d]	67	67	64	63	61
Effect of increasing 1976–77 revenue to 67 percent of expenditure[e]					
Percentage increase	—	4	8	12	15
Revenue yield	10.0	11.2	12.8	14.1	15.5
Percentage of expenditure	67	70	72	75	77
Revised deficit	4.9	4.9	4.9	4.7	4.6
Minus grants from government of West Bengal	3.3	3.6	3.8	4.1	4.4
Additional government subvention required	1.6	1.3	1.1	0.6	0.2
Effect of improving collection of holding (property) and related taxes					
Amount of holding and related taxes included in revenue sources before 1976–77 reforms, (actual recoveries in cash based on average current performance of about 55 percent)	5.1	5.4	5.7	5.9	6.2
Effect of improving collection performance by 15 percent a year					
Revised collection percentage	55	63	73	83	96
Yield of increased collections	—	0.8	1.9	3.0	4.6

— Not applicable.

a. Revenues representing cash collections are escalated at 5 percent a year.

b. Expenditures representing cash payments are escalated at 7 percent a year. However, the expenditures shown are based on past performance and, in many cases, do not represent adequate standards of maintenance.

c. Grants from the government of West Bengal consist mainly (about 90 percent) of dearness allowance awards refunded to municipalities, escalated at 7 percent a year.

d. Revenues as a percentage of expenditures represent the average of 35 municipalities. About 12 municipalities have very good performance, but about an equal number, including the largest, Howrah, have revenue yields under 50 percent of expenditures.

e. The demonstrated yields of improved cash collections are not specifically called for in assurances, but are shown as an example of a means of achieving the IDA-required targets.

Sources: Calcutta Metropolitan Planning Organization and World Bank estimates.

the World Health Organization (WHO),[5] which visited the city in the wake of the 1958 cholera epidemic, the state government set up the Calcutta Metropolitan Planning Organization (CMPO) to prepare a master plan for water supply and drainage and to recommend measures for the economic and physical regeneration of the metropolis. In its efforts, the CMPO was assisted by a team of international experts assembled by the UNDP, WHO, and the Ford Foundation.

With a staff of more than 600, CMPO was one of the largest planning organizations ever set up in a developing country. Comprehensive physical planning had already been introduced in other cities (for example, Manila, Singapore, Bangkok, and Bogotá, and subsequently in Karachi, Colombo, Nairobi, and Jakarta through international teams), but the Basic Development Plan (BDP) that the CMPO brought out in 1966 was different from conventional master plans. To begin with, it was not a typical land use plan. Within a broad spatial framework, the BDP's immediate aim was to arrest further deterioration of the physical infrastructure in the metropolis.

In the short term, the BDP was problem oriented and contained a package of specific schemes to improve water supply, drainage, traffic and transportation, and living conditions in the slums. The long-term objectives were policy oriented in that they were concerned with directing future populations to designated growth centers, developing an urban environment capable of sustaining about 12.3 million people by 1986, strengthening development planning and plan implementation, and mobilizing local finance and local government more effectively. Two sectoral plans followed the BDP; one was a master plan for water supply, sewerage, and drainage for 1966–2001, which was prepared through an engineering consortium set up by WHO; the other was a traffic and transportation plan for 1966–1986, which was prepared by the CMPO.

The BDP also proposed an elaborate reorganization of administration in the district. The preparation and enforcement of plans, capital budgeting, and project review were to be vested in a metropolitan planning authority. Autonomous functional agencies for water and sanitation, traffic and transportation, housing, river crossing, parks and recreation, and primary education were to be set up, and the existing improvement trusts in Calcutta and Howrah were to be expanded into east bank and west bank land development agencies. The many local government units were to be consolidated into ten corporations with responsibility for minor services.

The BDP reorganization proposals represented a striking example of the neatness vainly sought by metropolitan planners the world over as a solution to fragmented and inefficient administrations. The concept of functional authorities relied heavily on foreign experience. The proposal for the consolidation of municipalities reflected the noninvolvement of the CMPO, which, as an agency of the state government, had been kept out of munici-

5. Abel Wolman, Luther Gulick, Robert Pollitzer, and H. P. Cronin, "Assignment Report on Water Supply and Sewage Disposal: Greater Calcutta" (Geneva: World Health Organization, January 1960).

pal control and not allowed to become directly involved in municipal affairs. Overall, the plan was concerned more with goals than with the problems of implementation.

The first attempt to create functional agencies began with the establishment of the Calcutta Metropolitan Water and Sanitation Authority (CMWSA) set up in 1966. It was initially proposed that the authority be run by a three-member board and a thirty-member advisory council. The final decision, however, was that the board should have five members and the council fifty-two members, whose approval would be needed for any important action. Predictably, the council did not agree to give up local control of water, sanitation, and drainage to the authority, nor did it impose increased taxes and charges for services. From the outset, the CMWSA was virtually defunct; not until four years later was it activated as an implementing agency of a new metropolitan development authority.

Subsequent attempts to create other metropolitan-level functional authorities were not successful. A bill for a traffic and transportation authority was drafted but its enactment could not be pursued; proposals for a primary-education authority were resisted; and the prospects for consolidating municipalities quickly receded in the face of opposition. Furthermore, the bustee development plan and the reorganizational proposals remained blueprints until 1970.

Calcutta Metropolitan Development Authority

The establishment of the Calcutta Metropolitan Development Authority (CMDA) in 1970 was a major breakthrough. Thanks to the intervention of the central government, a program of Rs1,500 million was drawn up on the basis of projects identified in the BDP. It was to be financed partly from the fourth five-year plan and partly by a combination of loans and grants from the central and state governments. A tax on the entry of goods into the CMD (octroi tax) was introduced; half of its proceeds were to service borrowings by the CMDA, and the balance was to go toward operating the municipalities in the district. Organizationally, the CMDA embodied the metropolitan concept strongly advocated in the BDP, but its mandate combined the functions of planning, programming, financing, and implementation, with emphasis on tackling a variety of sectoral projects through the existing structure of state and local agencies.

Drafted in one week, rushed through a parliamentary consultative committee in another, and passed as an act of the president in the third week, the CMDA Act was perhaps the swiftest piece of legislation ever devised for metropolitan development.[6] It was also possible to settle on a compact seven-member board with the chief minister of the state as chairman, and three state officials and three nominated representatives of the corporation

6. See K. C. Sivaramakrishnan, *Indian Urban Scene* (Simla: Indian Institute of Advanced Study, 1978).

and municipalities as members. The composition of the authority was determined more by the immediate need to begin work on a metropolitan-level action program than by a desire to experiment with democratic forms of metropolitan administration. As a result of this compactness and the decision to use existing agencies for implementation, investments in urban infrastructure rose from Rs30 million a year in 1970 to Rs400 million in 1972.

The CMDA program incorporated most of the urban public investment in the CMD. The initial package covered several sectors such as improvements to water supply, including the construction of transmission and distribution mains, reservoirs, and booster stations; sewerage and drainage improvements such as restoration and construction of storm drains, sewers, outfall canals, and sluices; and extension and broadening of the existing roads, traffic operation measures, bus terminal constructions, and the like. In addition, the program included measures to improve living conditions in the slums and convert service privies (night soil containers that are emptied manually) into sanitary latrines. Two important infrastructure projects outside the purview of the CMDA, however, were the second bridge across the Hooghly River and the rapid rail transit system. The former was to be built by a special commission and the latter by the central government's Ministry of Railways. (A section of the subway was commissioned in October 1984).

In 1973, three years after the program had begun, the International Development Association (IDA) of the World Bank agreed to participate, picking up 44 out of the 160 or so subprojects in the program. The IDA credit of US$35 million represented about 20 percent of the total program investment and 30 percent of the selected subproject costs. A second IDA credit of US$87 million was granted in 1977, which, apart from supporting the type of subprojects selected earlier, included residential, industrial, and commercial sites and services benefiting some 45,000 people; participation in the ongoing slum improvement program; construction and extension of primary schools; rehabilitation of the city's refuse collection and disposal system; and loans to about 4,800 small-scale enterprises. The credit provided about half the project cost, but the distinction between IDA-assisted and other subprojects continued. In May 1983, the third Calcutta Urban Development Project removed this distinction. The credit of US$147 million was to be applied to the total CMDA program of US$347 million, and emphasis shifted toward project selection and programming rather than the content of individual subprojects.

In addition, a separate public transport project was initiated with World Bank assistance (US$56 million). Its overall objective was to improve the capacity and performance of the state-owned bus and tram services operating in and around Calcutta and Howrah through the revision of routes and fares, financial and operational improvements to the transit companies, and improvements in traffic engineering and management. The project was to be implemented by means of an interagency steering committee. This arrangement was an interesting institutional response to a metropolitan problem involving not only the public sector but also private companies (which, in this case, accounted for 65 percent of the road passenger services under review).

Investment in infrastructure under the IDA-assisted and other programs (excluding the second Hooghly bridge and the subway system, both under construction) amounted to about US$450 million by the end of 1983. Under the fourth five-year plan per capita investment in the metropolitan district was Rs44, but under the sixth plan it rose to Rs83.70. A brief review of the impact of these sizable investments indicates that although service delivery in all sectors has improved, some problems have persisted. To date, for example, 2 million slum dwellers have benefited from the improvements, but a group of middlemen known as the thika tenants (that is, persons who own huts in the slums, but not the land) have sought to increase rents.

Although the treated water supply has tripled (from 450 million liters a day ten years ago to 1,350 million liters a day), serious disparities persist between the core cities and other parts of the metropolitan area. Furthermore, despite considerable improvements in storm water drainage, pumping stations, and outfall capacity, maintenance of the facilities has remained poor. New sewage treatment plants, sewer networks, and large-scale conversion of service privies into sanitary latrines have contributed to better sanitation, but refuse collection and disposal have been poor despite the infusion of funds and equipment. To improve traffic and transportation, 50 kilometers of new roads have been completed and are in use, several arterial roads have been widened, principal passenger terminals improved, street lighting modernized, and several traffic management measures initiated. Nonetheless, the overall gains have been minimal, partly because of the inadequate operation and maintenance of the bus and tram fleets and the virtual closing down of the principal north-south corridor in the city during subway construction.

In summary, although the experience of the past decade has demonstrated that public authorities are able to mobilize and sustain large-scale infrastructure investment, it has also shown that the emphasis in such investment has been almost exclusively on trunk or primary facilities rather than on secondary distribution systems (such as water supply or sewerage), with the result that improvements in service delivery have been less than expected. In addition, both investment cost per capita and service delivery have varied considerably across the metropolis. About 67 percent of the investment has been concentrated in the urban core (where per capita income is 1.7 times the average for the district). Such investment concentration has adversely affected the urban poor living outside the core area. Finally, the institutional capacity of the metropolitan agencies, particularly that of the local bodies, has been unequal to the task of maintaining the assets created.

These results are not entirely unexpected. Although the efforts to improve operations, maintenance, and organizational structure did not begin at the same time as the program of works, which started in 1970, the first step, taken soon after, was to consolidate implementing responsibilities and relate them to development plans. As a result, the CMDA eventually absorbed most of the planning and implementation functions. The second step was a series of attempts to reorganize municipal jurisdictions and introduce structural changes. The third step focused on long-delayed, much-needed reforms to municipal finances. In approach and content, the fiscal and administrative changes were perhaps more significant than the improvements secured in physical infrastructure.

At the outset, as noted earlier, the CMDA functioned as a programming, funding, and coordinating agency, and the actual execution of the projects was left to a number of implementing agencies. As the program gathered momentum and the number of subprojects increased, however, the CMDA found it more and more difficult to coordinate the work of these agencies. A solution was sought in centralization (the World Bank's stipulation in the first credit that the CMDA should establish an engineering management unit was thought to support such an approach), and in 1973 the CMDA took over a number of water supply, sanitation, and road projects from agencies such as the Calcutta Corporation and the state Public Health Engineering, Public Works, and Irrigation and Waterways directorates. A year later, the CMDA also took over the management of the CMWSA and the Howrah Improvement Trust (HIT) under the provisions of an amendment to the CMDA act. A similar takeover of the Calcutta Improvement Trust was averted because of staff opposition. The CMDA's own staff increased rapidly, from about 800 in 1972 to 4,200 in 1977.

In the same year, the CMPO wound down, and metropolitanwide planning was transferred to the CMDA under the provisions of the West Bengal Town and Country Planning Act. The CMDA thus became the dominant planning and public works agency. The West Bengal chief minister remained its chairman, but the state public works minister became its vice-chairman in 1975, and a new department, Public Works (Metropolitan Development), was created to oversee the CMDA. The board's membership was broadened marginally in 1977 with the induction of two more municipal representatives. The internal organization of the CMDA was also changed to include the directorates general of planning, finance, and sectoral operations.

Municipal Reorganization

The reorganization of municipal administration was far more complex. As mentioned earlier, the Calcutta Corporation was superseded early in 1972, and many of the municipalities in the district were also taken over by the state. On the premise that a metropolitan view of things had indeed emerged from the CMDA's programs, the state Planning Board prepared a plan for a federal, two-tier form of metropolitan government. The plan provided for a top-tier metropolitan council and a series of lower-tier borough councils. The CMPO, CMDA, CMWSA, CIT, and HIT were to be attached to or merged with the metropolitan council, which was to represent the constituent borough councils, the state legislature, and the state executive; but the borough councils were to be directly elected. Although the proposal received a fair measure of support from officials, some feared that the metropolitan council would become a competing center for political power, and the proposal was not pursued. Other attempts at jurisdictional change were limited to marginal adjustments in municipal boundaries.

When a coalition of left-wing political parties regained power in 1977, municipal reform was resumed. Local government and urban and municipal development were placed under one minister who was also designated vice-chairman of the CMDA. Both the Calcutta Corporation Act of 1951 and the Bengal Municipal Act of 1932 were subjected to comprehensive review, which paved the way for the new Calcutta Municipal Corporation Act of 1980. This act ushered in India's first municipal cabinet system of government, under which a mayor-in-council elected for a five-year term would be responsible for civic management. (The 1980 act became effective in January 1984. Elections were held in June 1985, and the mayor-in-council is now in position.)

At the same time, the amended Bengal Municipal Act of 1980 sought to strengthen the financial base of the municipalities, including those within the CMD. Under this act, the state government is required to provide each municipal body with a minimum of four officers—one each for finance, health, engineering, and overall direction. In May 1981 elections were held for all the municipalities outside Calcutta and Howrah. For the first time in eighteen years, elected councils now govern all the municipalities. The Howrah Municipal Corporation Act of 1980 (which came into force in 1983) provided for a structure similar to that of the Calcutta Corporation. In May 1980 a new municipality was set up in Jadavpur, adjoining Calcutta in the south, but in December 1983 Jadavpur and two other existing municipalities were brought within the jurisdiction of the Calcutta Corporation. This enlargement of the corporation's limits for the first time in fifty years has, however, stopped short of incorporating the metropolitan core into a single municipal jurisdiction. Municipal fragmentation has thus remained, despite modest changes.

The changes accomplished in municipal finances have been far more promising. One reason for the reform was that operations and maintenance costs of the CMDA-funded projects were mounting. From time to time, studies were conducted to assess such costs. The most recent exercise in 1982 indicated that costs had risen to Rs340 million, or about 51 percent of the total revenue expenditure of the corporation and all the municipalities in the district; this figure was expected to increase to Rs390 million by 1985–86, exclusive of liabilities yet to accrue from the third urban development project. The problem of the growing shortfall between municipal revenues and escalating operation and management costs could not be avoided any longer.

In 1974, a national committee on budgetary reform in municipal administrations had stated that adequate municipal services in India as a whole required a per capita expenditure of Rs110. At that time, Calcutta Corporation was spending some Rs55 a head. Although the corporation increased its self-generated revenue by 64 percent between 1971–72 and

1975–76 and its recurrent expenditures by 87 percent, it was clearly far from solving the problem of substandard service delivery. By 1977, its annual current account deficit represented some 20 percent of current revenue. One of the main reasons for the corporation's fiscal deficits was its heavy reliance on—and poor administration of—property taxation. Property-related taxes accounted for 75 percent of its total self-generated revenue; but their yield was extremely low, mainly because property values were underassessed and the tax rates were inadequate, and partly because of inefficient tax collection, litigation, and adverse legislation.

The fiscal performance of many of the district's other municipalities was even worse. In September 1975, as part of a second World Bank urban development project, an action plan was prepared by the state government. The objective of the plan was to increase local revenues by Rs45 million a year for the corporation, and by Rs20 million for the other local authorities. The state government also established the Central Valuation Board in December 1978 in order to reform the existing system of assessing and levying property taxes throughout the Calcutta Metropolitan District and to complete the revaluation of all properties by March 1982. In addition, in an attempt to ensure long-term financial viability for the corporation's water supply and sewerage services, assurances were given that on April 1, 1978, a separate corporation fund would be established for these services, and thereafter all deficits of the fund would be met from the corporation's municipal fund. Furthermore, it was agreed that on April 1, 1981, water supply and sewerage taxes would be separated from the property tax (currently a consolidated rate), and thereafter not less than 84 percent of expenditures on these services would be met from such taxes and water supply and sewerage charges (see table 10-4). The state government also agreed to review the procedures for giving financial assistance to the district's local authorities as a whole, with a view to promoting efficiency in their financial affairs and to using grants as levers for the improvement of fiscal management.

In keeping with the plan of action, the state government set up the Municipal Finance Commission (MFC) in 1979 to inquire into revenue and expenditure performance and make recommendations. The MFC's 1982 report recommended that internal revenue generation be improved and tax sharing enlarged to fill the resource gap. The commission strongly urged the CMD municipalities to participate more directly in the development process through annual capital budgets of their own as part of the five-year plan. Maintaining its stand on municipal autonomy, the MFC also recommended that the recently created Central Valuation Authority should perform an advisory rather than executive role and should assist the municipalities in selecting assessors, issuing guidelines for property valuation, and evaluating alternative methods.

Current Initiatives

The CMDA began its work in a situation of financial and organizational bankruptcy in local government. In spite of its success in mobilizing funds

Table 10-4. Calcutta Municipal Corporation Income and Expenditure Account, Third Calcutta Urban Development Project,
March 31, 1980–88
(10 million rupees)

Income and expenditure	Actual					Projected			
	1979–80a	1980–81a	1981–82	1982–83	1983–84	1984–85	1985–86	1986–87	1987–88
Income									
Revenue account current									
Consolidated property tax	13.64	13.45	17.98	18.02	19.66	21.69	24.06	26.79	29.87
Service charge on:									
Central government properties	0.47	0.49	0.56	0.59	0.62	0.65	0.68	0.72	0.75
Surcharge on land and buildings	0.00	0.00	0.00	0.00	0.00	0.00	0.00	0.00	0.00
Tax on professions and trades	1.72	0.96	1.96	2.06	2.16	2.27	2.38	2.50	2.63
Other taxes	0.12	0.23	0.10	0.11	0.12	0.12	0.13	0.14	0.14
Subtotal	15.95	15.13	20.60	20.78	22.56	24.73	27.25	30.15	33.39
Other receipts									
License fees	0.18	0.05	0.17	0.18	0.20	0.22	0.24	0.27	0.29
Health services	0.00	0.00	0.28	0.30	0.32	0.36	0.39	0.43	0.48
Commercial services	1.09	1.42	0.67	0.73	0.81	0.89	0.98	1.07	1.18
Water supply	1.48	0.42	0.63	1.54	2.92	4.11	4.71	7.82	11.18
Solid waste	0.08	0.08	0.09	0.10	0.11	0.12	0.14	0.15	0.17
Other	1.52	1.18	3.33	3.50	3.68	3.86	4.06	4.26	4.47
Subtotal	4.35	3.15	5.17	6.35	8.04	9.56	10.52	14.00	17.77
Total own source revenue	20.30	18.28	25.77	27.13	30.60	34.29	37.77	44.15	51.16
Revenue grants									
Octroi	6.01	6.74	10.12	10.88	13.84b	15.92	18.20	21.05	24.21
Bustee services	0.00	0.00	0.00	1.00	1.00	1.00	1.00	1.00	1.00
Government of West Bengal subventions	4.48	9.76	12.96	12.38	11.20	11.59	11.25	9.34	8.34
Subtotal	10.49	16.50	23.08	24.26	26.04	28.51	30.55	31.39	33.55
Total revenue receipts	30.79	34.78	48.85	51.39	56.64	62.80	68.32	75.54	84.71

Capital receipts									
Grants, government of West Bengal	0.00	0.00	0.00	0.00	2.33	2.91	3.43	5.24	5.43
Grants, other	0.00	0.00	0.00	0.00	0.00	0.00	0.00	0.00	0.00
Loans, government of West Bengal	1.00	0.00	0.00	0.00	2.33	2.91	3.43	5.24	5.43
Loans, other	0.00	0.00	0.00	0.00	0.00	0.00	0.00	0.00	0.00
Subtotal	1.00	0.00	0.00	0.00	4.66	5.82	6.86	10.48	10.86
Total receipts	31.79	34.78	48.85	51.39	61.30	68.62	75.18	86.02	95.57
Expenditure									
Revenue account current									
Water supply	5.24	7.86	8.96	10.79	12.05[c]	13.65	13.98	14.87	15.62
Sewerage and drainage	2.25	2.09	3.32	3.49	3.66	3.84	4.04	4.84	5.81
Roads	0.92	2.26	3.30	3.63	4.00	4.40	4.84	5.32	5.85
Lighting and electricity	1.20	1.83	2.00	2.10	2.21	2.32	2.43	2.92	3.50
Solid waste	6.92	6.39	8.46	9.31	10.24[d]	11.26	12.39	13.63	15.67
Motor vehicles	0.00	0.00	1.29	1.42	1.56	1.72	1.89	2.27	2.72
Commercial services	0.77	0.90	0.73	0.80	0.89	0.98	1.07	1.18	1.30
Education services	0.00	0.00	2.42	2.66	2.92	3.22	3.54	3.89	4.28
Health services	2.04	2.03	2.37	2.61	2.87	3.15	3.47	3.82	4.20
Bustee services	0.00	0.00	0.63	0.66	1.00	1.50	2.00	2.00	2.00
Administration and support services	9.88	9.36	8.57	9.43	10.37[d]	11.41	12.55	13.81	15.88
Other	0.58	0.00	0.00	0.00	0.00	0.00	0.00	0.00	0.00
Interest	0.10	0.02	0.00	1.34	1.72	2.20	2.67	3.54	4.43
Depreciation	0.00	0.00	0.00	3.15[e]	3.15	3.15	3.45	3.45	3.45
Subtotal	29.90	32.74	42.05	51.39	56.64	62.80	68.32	75.54	84.71
Capital account current									
Development works	0.09	0.01	0.00	0.00	4.66	5.82	6.86	10.48	10.86
Other	0.00	1.24	0.00	0.00	0.00	0.00	0.00	0.00	0.00
Subtotal	0.09	1.25	0.00	0.00	4.66	5.82	6.86	10.48	10.86
Total expenditure	29.99	33.99	42.05	51.39	61.30	68.62	75.18	86.02	95.57

(Table continues on the following page.)

Table 10-4 (continued)

Income and expenditure	Actual				Projected				
	1979–80[a]	*1980–81*[a]	*1981–82*	*1982–83*	*1983–84*	*1984–85*	*1985–86*	*1986–87*	*1987–88*
Excess of income over expenditure	1.80	0.79	6.80	0.00	0.00	0.00	0.00	0.00	0.00
Transfer to municipal fund-revenue account	0.89	0.02	6.80	0.00	– 2.05	– 2.05	– 2.05	– 2.05	– 2.05
Transfer to municipal fund-capital account	0.91	n.a.	n.a.	n.a.	n.a.	n.a.	n.a.	n.a.	n.a.
Transfer to sinking fund	n.a.	0.77	n.a.	n.a.	1.67	1.67	1.67	1.67	1.67
Transfer to vehicle replacement fund	n.a.	n.a.	n.a.	n.a.	0.38	0.38	0.38	0.38	0.38
Government of West Bengal subventions as percentage of total revenue expenditure	14.98	29.81	30.82	24.09	19.77	18.46	16.47	12.36	9.85

n.a. Not available.

a. Audited.

b. Projected to increase at 15 percent a year.

c. Projected to increase at approximately 5 percent a year.

d. Projected to increase at 10 percent a year until the last year, when 15 percent is projected and the full impact of the project will occur.

e. In the absence of a fixed asset register, the depreciation quoted is the book depreciation.

Sources: Calcutta Municipal Corporation and World Bank estimates.

and speeding up the pace of project implementation, there was criticism early in the 1980s that the CMDA had become too autonomous and powerful. It was perceived as a continued superimposition on the structure of local government. The initiatives of the state government in reviewing municipal finances, reorganizing municipal administration, and holding local elections inevitably led some to question the CMDA's increasing centralization and its future role with respect to other agencies and local bodies. The findings of the Municipal Finance Commission also forced many to reconsider issues relating to the functional and spatial distribution of investment within the metropolitan area, the involvement of the municipalities in the planning and implementation process, and the allocation of operation and maintenance responsibilities. In political circles it was urged that the third Calcutta Urban Development Project (CUDP) should reflect these concerns and be formulated quite differently from the first two development projects.

As noted earlier, the third CUDP did not distinguish between the IDA-assisted and other subprojects. The investment program as a whole was prepared jointly by the CMDA and the World Bank. The CMDA's own role in the program became that of financial and policy intermediary, and the program centered on metropolitanwide planning, appraisal, monitoring, and evaluation of projects and training. The CMDA's activities as an executing agency were to be reduced, and its responsibilities for water supply, drainage, and sewerage were to be transferred to other agencies. More important, the municipalities were given an expanded role in capital budgeting and in selecting their priority schemes within broad guidelines set out by the CMDA. A third of the total investment program of US$347 million has been allocated to the Municipal Development Program (MDP); another 30 percent, to investment programs in Calcutta and Howrah. The transmunicipal infrastructure program will receive 14 percent, and the balance is to be used for metropolitanwide complementary programs (see table 10-5).

The MDP seeks to improve water supply, drainage, solid waste management, and service privy conversion in the most deprived municipal areas. Under the service delivery norms and physical design standards set by the CMDA, the municipalities will prepare schemes for its appraisal and approval. In several municipalities, improvements are also envisaged for local roads, markets, and slum areas. In a similar but more modest effort undertaken in 1972 at the inception of the CMDA program, zonal offices were set up to assist the municipalities. But in the general move toward centralization, the program languished. By 1982, less than 3 percent of the total investments were being allocated to it. With elected councils all in place, however, the share of the municipalities—which had risen tenfold under the third CUDP—could no longer remain so limited.

On the fiscal side, a major reform is the Revised Grants Structure (RGS) undertaken in April 1983. Basically, the RGS sets out current account performance targets for individual municipalities (see table 10-6). Allocations under the MDP from the second year onward depend on performance. On the revenue side, performance targets relate primarily to property tax administration and include ratable value, assessment, and minimum collec-

Table 10-5. Third Calcutta Urban Development Project: Five-Year Investment Program, 1983–84 to 1987–88

Program	10 million rupees	Millions of U.S. dollars	Percentage of total
Municipal Development Program			
Water supply	18.86		
Drainage	18.64		
Sanitation	14.48		
Bustee improvement	8.29		
Parks, playgrounds	2.02		
Crematoria	0.79		
Transportation infrastructure	22.35		
Markets and community halls	8.57		
Subtotal	94.00	98.90	33
Transmunicipal Infrastructure Program			
Water supply	23.62		
Drainage	4.97		
Sanitation	8.37		
Transportation infrastructure	.50		
Area development—Kona truck terminal	3.00		
Subtotal	40.46	42.60	14
Calcutta-Howrah Investment Programs			
Water supply	16.43		
Drainage	5.42		
Sanitation	35.09		
Bustee improvement	9.94		
Traffic and transportation	14.78		
Urban renewal and bus terminals	6.00[a]		
Subtotal	87.66	92.30	30
Calcutta Metropolitan Authority Complementary Programs			
Shelter and area development	9.00[a]		
Health	8.66		
Small-scale entrepreneur	2.50[b]		
Anchal development	11.51		
Technical assistance and training	4.21		
Subtotal	35.88	37.80	13
All programs	258.00	271.60	90
Design, supervision, and management	30.00	31.50	10
Total project cost	288.00	303.10	100
Spillover (cost and time overruns on previous program)	42.00	44.20	
Total investment program	330.00	347.30	

Note: Includes contingencies.

a. Seed capital only.

b. Establishment costs and interest rebate only. Loan funds to be provided by commercial banks.

tion for current and arrears demands. Targets have been set at 75 and 50 percent of current and arrear demands, respectively, and are to be achieved by the local bodies over varying periods, depending on their levels of efficiency. On the expenditure side, operational and maintenance expenditures have been projected by taking into account MDP liabilities and the norms set by the Municipal Service Commission. Revenue deficits based on these projections are to be met by state government grants. When deficits are less than projected, local bodies will receive additional capital funding under the MDP as an incentive. Funding will be reduced when the deficits are higher than expected.

The CMDA and the Directorate of Local Bodies in the state Department of Local Government are responsible for administering the RGS. The first-year review indicates that twenty out of thirty-six municipalities have achieved revenue increases, as projected. In all, the municipalities' finance officers and executive officers have been posted by the government as required under the 1980 Bengal Municipal Act. Although it is too early to assess how far the Revised Grants Structure will help the CMD municipalities to achieve fiscal strength, a participatory process has clearly begun to evolve in development planning, capital budgeting, and current revenue and expenditure analysis.

Pending Issues

Administrative and fiscal chaos has long been characteristic of local government in West Bengal, particularly in the CMD's municipalities. The Calcutta Corporation itself was in part responsible for the pace of deterioration, even though its function was to administer the rich core of the metropolis. As has been pointed out elsewhere, "Defective design, the gulf between the corporation and the components of the population, the adverse attitude of the state government, the poverty of finances, the splintering of government authority have all continued to conspire to bring the city's local government to a standstill."[7]

The Calcutta Municipal Corporation Act introduced in 1984 is a major reform on all fronts. This act confers considerable autonomy on the corporation, provides continuity in its administration through the mayor-in-council system, proposes a sound framework for financial management, and offers a larger and more varied tax base. The past twelve years have been the most active in Calcutta's history insofar as infrastructure and organizational developments are concerned. For most of this period, the local government of the city has been under supersession. Elections were held only recently, and the left-wing coalition came to power with a slender majority. The real test of the reform measures, particularly those concerning the Calcutta Corporation and the CMDA, is still to come.

7. Ali Ashraf, *The City Government of Calcutta* (New York: Institute of Public Administration and Asia Publishing House, 1966).

Table 10-6. *Calcutta Metropolitan District: Financial Performance Projections by Individual Local Body, 1983–84*
(100,000 rupees)

Corporation, municipality, or notified area	Revenue				Expenditure			Net revenue shortfall (7 – 4) (8)
	Property tax (1)	Other internal revenue (2)	Share of entry tax (3)	Total internal revenue (1 + 2 + 3) (4)	Commitment to CUDP-III[a] (5)	Existing expenditure commitment (6)	Total expenditure (5 + 6) (7)	
Calcutta Municipal Corp.	1,834.00	858.85	915.08	3,607.93	3.30	4,822.00	4,825.30	1,217.37
Howrah Municipal Corp.	214.16	129.51	88.20	431.87	1.75	775.04	776.79	334.92
South Suburban	52.05	26.39	33.08	111.52	1.65	114.06	115.71	4.19
Bhatpara	28.22	8.43	30.32	66.97	1.01	89.10	90.11	23.14
Jadavpur	20.47	5.11	19.95	45.53	1.03	47.90	48.93	3.40
Kamarhati	28.732	5.67	29.27	63.67	1.06	77.82	78.88	15.21
South Dum Dum	27.56	5.05	26.09	58.70	1.02	65.88	66.90	8.20
Panihati	19.96	6.44	25.58	51.98	0.95	58.30	59.25	7.25
Garden Reach	23.23	3.23	26.77	53.23	0.88	80.66	81.54	28.31
Baranagar	24.47	4.91	13.67	43.05	0.79	77.24	78.03	34.98
Bally	29.44	4.90	21.15	55.49	0.64	94.98	95.62	40.13
Hooghly-Chinsura	17.41	4.92	8.83	31.16	0.60	51.64	52.24	21.08
Serampore	20.52	14.23	20.74	55.49	0.65	64.81	65.46	9.97
Naihati	12.75	13.81	6.89	33.45	0.53	66.79	67.32	33.87
Barrackpore	17.46	3.02	9.92	10.40	0.49	40.86	41.35	10.95
Titagarh	8.44	4.90	13.23	26.57	0.48	33.66	34.14	7.57

Chandernagar Municipal Corp.	19.50	3.74	13.00	36.24	0.47	105.97	106.44	70.20
North Barrackpore	8.80	0.91	6.41	16.12	0.45	30.19	30.19	14.57
North Dum Dum	14.59	7.38	11.04	33.01	0.45	34.11	34.56	1.55
Rishra	13.60	1.51	7.17	22.28	0.45	36.71	37.16	14.88
Halisahar	6.20	6.21	8.25	20.66	0.141	40.01	40.42	19.76
Kanchrapara	4.69	1.47	6.62	12.78	0.44	26.10	26.54	13.76
Uttarpara-Kotrung	14.98	4.81	11.68	31.47	0.43	34.20	34.63	3.16
Bansberia	13.06	4.74	10.67	28.47	0.26	31.57	31.83	3.36
Champdani	14.19	2.44	4.91	21.54	0.37	32.33	32.70	11.16
Baidyabati	7.39	2.11	9.35	18.85	0.29	26.60	28.89	10.94
Budge Budge	17.49	1.49	4.23	23.21	0.30	59.96	60.26	37.05
Garulia	4.83	1.57	1.83	8.23	0.29	21.06	21.35	13.12
Barasat	3.79	2.18	3.57	9.54	0.28	10.31	10.59	1.05
Bhadreswar	7.39	1.37	7.87	16.63	0.28	31.69	31.97	15.34
New Barrackpore	2.60	5.35	4.41	12.36	0.26	13.83	14.09	1.73
Rajpur	3.22	1.22	2.88	7.32	0.20	15.64	15.84	8.52
Dum Dum	14.04	3.37	5.42	22.83	0.25	31.38	31.63	8.80
Konnagar	8.90	5.46	5.94	20.30	0.26	27.01	27.27	6.97
Khardah	6.45	3.02	4.41	13.88	0.27	30.74	31.01	17.13
Baruipur	2.34	0.47	1.72	4.53	0.26	9.75	10.01	5.48
Kalyani[b]	14.77	5.59	4.78	25.14	0.28	36.81	37.09	11.95
Gayeshpur[b]	0.61	1.55	9.12	11.28	1.19	25.50	25.69	14.41
Total	2,582.30	1,167.88	1,434.05	5,188.68	24.60	7,274.24	7,298.81	2,115.18

a. Third Calcutta Urban Development Project. No operation and maintenance costs have been assumed in the first year. Loan repayment has not been taken into account as there would be a five-year moratorium. Figures represent interest only.

b. Notified area authority.

In itself, the third Urban Development Project is not complex, but local circumstances make it so. Given the disabilities of local governments and the centralized public works approach that CMDA and other agencies have recently displayed, it will not be easy to distinguish between the different components of the program. Whether a structure is centralized or not, the task of coordinating a large multisectoral program containing numerous projects and subprojects is a highly difficult task even in the best of circumstances. That some major items of infrastructure, such as the Subway and Circular Railway System, are beyond the purview of the existing metropolitan planning and development set-up has not made that task any less difficult.

The absence of reasonably well-understood metropolitan and citywide spatial plans is another critical pending issue. The rationale of the CMPO planners in avoiding a detailed land use plan has already been mentioned. The limited improvements in infrastructure—whether in water supply, drainage, or road access—have been subjected once again to the pressures of haphazard construction with much higher densities. Most land use choices are being preempted in the process. Although the state Town and Country Planning Act made the CMDA responsible for spatial planning in 1979, thus far, it has not even published an outline of its development plans for any part of the metropolis. The new Calcutta Municipal and Bengal Municipal acts both contain some powers of land use planning. The Town and Country Planning Act also envisages the delegation of planning powers to the local authorities. Attention is only now turning to a time schedule for the preparation of plans, at least for some parts of the metropolis likely to change rapidly, and for the possible sharing of responsibilities between the CMDA and the municipal authorities.

By tradition and deed, Calcutta has been a highly politicized city. Civic institutions have tended to be political rather than administrative bodies. Ambivalence and suspicion have long characterized the attitudes of successive state governments toward municipalities. Within the corporations and the municipalities, most administrative procedures have been subject to frequent political control and adjustment. Whether in property assessment or building control, the sanction of schemes or staff development, the civic official in Calcutta has had far less autonomy than his counterpart in Bombay or Madras. Recent reforms, particularly the new Calcutta Corporation and Bengal Municipal acts and their by-laws, represent significant efforts to systematize day-to-day urban administration. Yet, the initiative for these reforms has come from political will rather than technocratic judgments. In less than a decade, Calcutta has introduced a wide array of changes in planning, funding, and operations. The success of these changes will depend principally on the continued resoluteness of the political leadership.

11

Colombo

THE COLOMBO METROPOLITAN region has never been defined in law, but regional structure plan prepared by the Colombo Master Plan Project between 1975 and 1978 identified it as an area of approximately 1,800 square kilometers and 4 million people. The urbanized core of this region covers 235 square kilometers and has a population of 1.33 million people (1971 census). At its heart lies the city of Colombo, the capital of Sri Lanka, which covers an area of 37 square kilometers and has more than 585,000 people within its municipal boundaries (1981 estimate).

Growth of the City

Colombo is located at the mouth of the Kelani, one of Sri Lanka's great rivers, which annually floods the surrounding coastal plain. In the fourteenth century, Colombo was already a flourishing port, even though it lacked a natural harbor. It was later developed by the Portuguese, Dutch, and British, in part because it afforded better access to the old capitals of Kandy and Kotte. Colombo itself eventually became the capital of Ceylon in 1815, and thereafter its growth easily outpaced all other urban centers. It was raised to municipal status in 1865, and by 1911 it had a population of 211,274, which increased to 362,074 in 1946, and to 562,420 in 1971. By then it was more than five times the size of Jaffna, the second largest city.

This growth is mainly the result of the city's entrepôt, shipping, commercial, and financial functions, which accounted for some 87 percent of all employment in 1971. In part it is also the result of Colombo's administrative role as the nation's capital. In recent years, manufacturing has steadily expanded to meet the rising local demand for consumer goods, rubber, steel, and processed foods. By 1971, Colombo district claimed 33 percent of total national employment in this sector. Even so, the district's service sector (including commercial, financial, transport, and miscellaneous services) still accounted for nearly 50 percent of all service employment in Sri Lanka and thus confirmed the city's strong commercial role. Colombo's continued dominance in public administration was reflected in the massive New Capital Project, a complex of parliament and government buildings being developed in Jayawardanapura 7 kilometers east of the town at an estimated cost of about Rs1.3 billion. One consequence of the public sector investment in and around Colombo has been a sudden property boom. In 1981 alone, the combined value of its residential and commercial land increased by an amount close to the total national income in 1977.

Metropolitan Problems

Although in-migration to Colombo has been slow compared with that in other large cities of South and East Asia, economic development and the urbanization accompanying it have promoted a growing influx, especially of young male migrants, from the rural areas surrounding the metropolitan region. By 1971, 33.4 percent of all male inhabitants of Colombo municipality were 15–29 years of age. This youthful in-migration swamped the urban job market, leaving nearly 20 percent of the male labor force unemployed, compared with 14 percent nationwide. In addition, more than 50 percent of the female labor force was unemployed, compared with the national average of 31 percent. Unemployment was particularly high among those 15–19 and 20–24 years of age; in 1971, 55 percent and 38 percent of potential male workers in these respective age groups were unemployed. Female unemployment was higher, accounting for 66 percent of the potential female workers in both groups. Despite the recent economic boom, unemployment remains one of the main challenges for urban management in metropolitan Colombo, which in 1980 reported an estimated shortfall of 310,000–321,000 jobs.

Poverty is another great concern. According to a national survey in 1975, households earning Rs400 (US$48) per month or less accounted for 67 percent of Sri Lanka's urban income. In the Colombo municipal area, this group accounted for nearly 64 percent of the urban income. Since households averaged between five and six persons each, per capita income fell below Rs800–960 (US$96–115) a year for most of the population, even in the urban core of the metropolitan region (where nearly 28 percent of the income was earned by those receiving less than Rs200, or US$24, a month). This situation has not changed. Although employment in the country as a whole improved between 1971 and 1981, the lack of new job opportunities and the low income levels of those employed remain Colombo's basic economic problems. About 45 percent of the municipal population lived in slums and shanties in 1975, and 35 percent of the male inhabitants 15–55 years of age were unemployed.

In comparison with other cities in South Asia, the delivery of urban services in Sri Lanka's cities appears to be slightly better than most. The 1981

Colombo.   Part of Beira Lake, which is still used as a waterway to transport cargo to and from Colombo harbor. The view is inland to the southeast and shows commercial and some recreational land use.

Map 11-1. Colombo, circa 1796

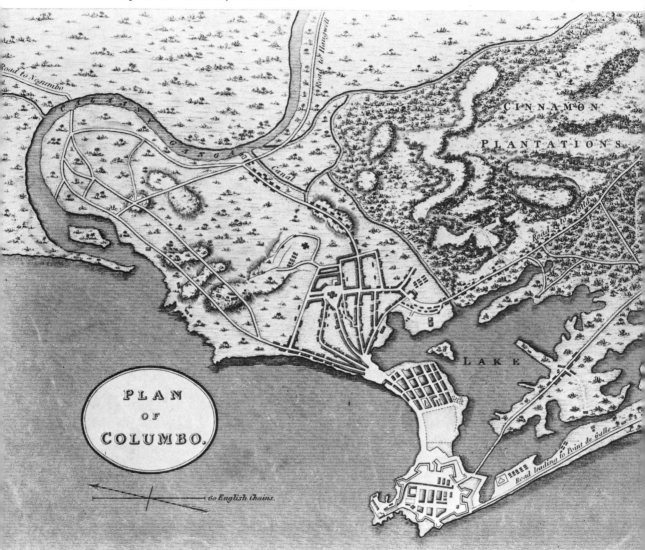

PLAN
OF
COLUMBO.

Photo: Library of Congress, Washington, D.C.

Map 11-2. Greater Colombo, 1980

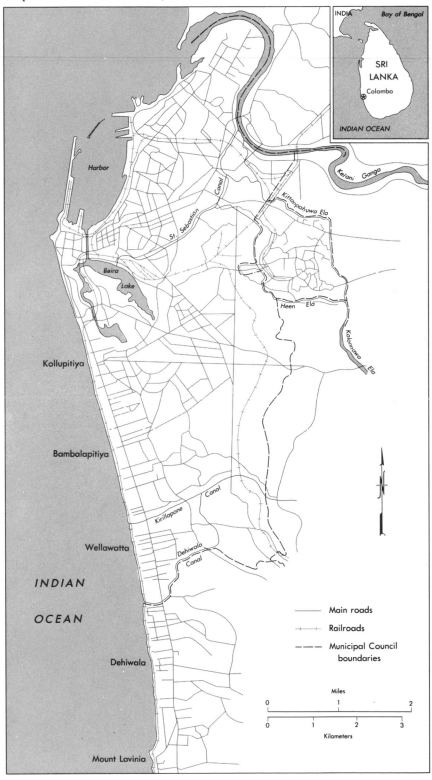

INDIA   Bay of Bengal

SRI
LANKA

⊛ Colombo

INDIAN OCEAN

Harbor

Kelani   Ganga

Canal

St. Sebastian

Kittanpahuwa Ela

Beira
Lake

Heen   Ela

Kolonnawa Ela

Kollupitiya

Bambalapitiya

Canal

Kirillapone

Wellawatta

Dehiwala
Canal

INDIAN

OCEAN

Dehiwala

Mount Lavinia

_____ Main roads

+-+-+ Railroads

— — — Municipal Council
boundaries

Miles
0   1   2

0   1   2   3
Kilometers

Map 11-3. Colombo Capital Region, 1982

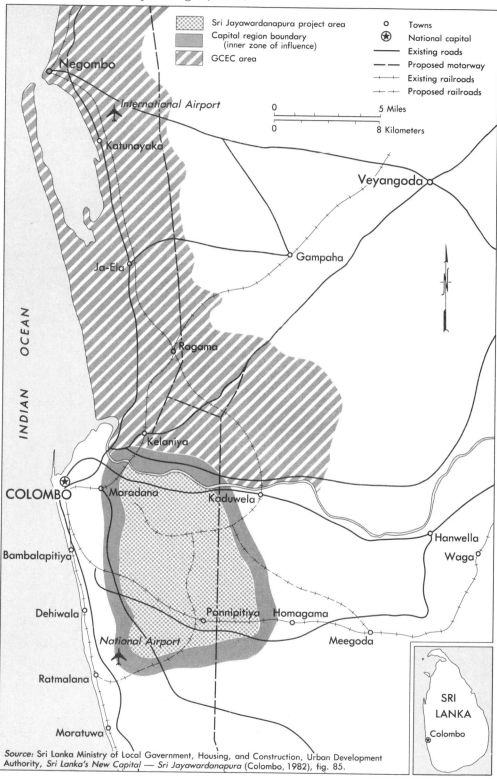

Source: Sri Lanka Ministry of Local Government, Housing, and Construction, Urban Development Authority, *Sri Lanka's New Capital — Sri Jayawardanapura* (Colombo, 1982), fig. 85.

census of population and housing estimates that about 47 percent of urban households have access to piped water and another 48 percent receive water from wells. In Colombo, about 31 percent of the houses have water piped indoors and another 20 percent have piped water outside. A waterborne sewerage system serves half the city's population. The network of roads (about 380 kilometers) in the city covers only about 7 percent of the land space, however, and thus Colombo is another road-deficient city. Within the metropolitan region, the volume of passenger traffic is estimated to be 1.5–2 million trips on a typical weekday. Of these, about 95 percent are taken on government and public buses. Overcrowding is a problem, and, as in other metropolitan cities in the region, traffic congestion has increased with the rise in car and motorcycle ownership.

Although comparatively slow rates of population growth have helped Colombo's physical structure to survive thus far, the scene is changing fast as a result of industrial development, the rapid expansion of government machinery, the growth of tourism, and other economic factors. The effects are particularly visible in Colombo's shelter sector. As of 1981, about 125,000 people in the Colombo municipal area lived in shanties. Slum growth in the fringes is considered to be greater and growing.

Under the 1972 Ceiling on Housing Property Law, the ownership of houses with a monthly rental of less than Rs25 was vested in the government. About 70 percent of the slum properties thus came under government ownership. This drastic change was intended to redistribute ownership among present occupants. A Common Amenities Board was established in 1973 to manage these properties and provide them with better services. Although the so-called tenement gardens within the city have been improved since then, the growing squatter settlements elsewhere in the metropolitan region are outside the purview of the program. A major constraint to the expansion of shelter and other infrastructure in the city is the lack of suitable land. About one-quarter of Colombo is marshy or subject to flooding. Low-density development in the past, sporadic and ad hoc reclamation of small plots, lack of clear title, rising land values fueled by government construction, remittances from abroad, and speculation have further aggravated the land problem.

In 1977 the Colombo Master Plan Project estimated that the combined public and private sector costs of servicing the Colombo metropolitan region over the next twenty-five years would amount to Rs13 billion, or US$1.56 billion (at 1976 market prices, and assuming a modest improvement in standards). Of this amount, Rs10 billion (US$1.2 billion) would be needed for capital investment in transport (7 percent), utilities (15 percent), housing (41 percent), and land (37 percent). According to these estimates, 12 percent of the total capital investment would have to be directed to slums and shanty areas in urgent need of replacement and 29 percent to new housing to accommodate the anticipated population increase. The greatest amount, however, would have to go toward planning and controlling the use of urban land.

Structure of Government

Sri Lanka has always had a highly centralized form of government. Basic urban services have been the responsibility of municipal and urban councils that have functioned with modest autonomy since the nineteenth century. The development councils in rural areas have had similar responsibilities. In the past decade, the urban institutional scene has changed somewhat. At the national level, urban development policy is determined by a cabinet subcommittee headed by the president. The Ministry of Local Government, Housing, and Construction, an amalgamation of two separate ministries, is the principal organ of the central government for the planning, control, and development of urban areas.

The ministry is composed of five departments: Local Government, Local Government Service, Town and Country Planning, National Housing, and Buildings. These departments oversee a plethora of authorities, boards, funds, and parastatal organizations:

- The Department of Local Government guides, assists, and supervises local activities. It also administers the Local Loans and Development Fund.

- The Department of Local Government Service is responsible for recruiting and appointing higher-level staff for local activities. (Sri Lanka is one of the few countries in the region having a common cadre of local government officials.) It is also in charge of the Local Government Service Advisory Board and Local Government Service Disciplinary Board.

- In the past, the Department of Town and Country Planning was responsible for physical planning for the entire country, but now its role is limited to planning for sacred areas (where Buddhist temples and other religious monuments are located) and rural and semiurban areas.

- The Department of National Housing looks after and collects the rent for approximately 6,000 government-owned apartments; it is also responsible for the administration of the Rent Control Act and enforcement of the ceiling on property under the Housing Property Act of 1973. The planning and construction of new housing has become the responsibility of the National Housing Development Authority (NHDA) established in 1979, which in 1981 also took over the administration of the National Housing Fund established some twenty years earlier.

- The Department of Buildings provides architectural, engineering, and constructional support to other ministries and local governments. The planning and construction of larger projects are left to the State Engineering Corporation. The State Building Materials Corporation regulates the price and availability of building materials.

The Urban Development Authority (UDA) established in 1978, the National Water Supply and Drainage Board formed in 1975, and the Common Amenities Board of 1973 are the important autonomous organizations under the ministry. (The role of the UDA is discussed later.)

The Colombo metropolitan region is made up of three municipal councils (Colombo, Dehiwala–Mt. Lavinia, and Galle) and thirty-six urban councils. Before 1977, there were twenty-three town councils, but these were later made into urban councils. In addition, there are fifty-five village councils in the rural fringes. The overall region falls under two administrative districts, which in turn have district development councils presided over by district ministers. In keeping with the unitary nature of the government, a variety of government departments, divisions, and public corporations are involved either directly or indirectly in the affairs of the region (see table 11-1). As many as there are, not one of these agencies reflects the metropolitan region in its organization or functions. Indeed, only the Colombo Master Plan Project, funded by the United Nations Development Programme and located in the Town and Country Planning Department of the Ministry of Local Government, has officially responded in any way to the development needs of the metropolitan region, particularly its urban hub. Among the several new organizations created after the completion of the Master Plan Project, none appears to have the mandate to undertake the integrated management of metropolitan development on the government's behalf in concert with other institutions. When two projects of high priority (the Investment Promotion Zone near the Katunayake International Airport and the National Capital Project) were initiated, their planning and construction were carried out somewhat independently of the metropolitan region's planning and development programming. Although the Urban Development Authority resembles the Calcutta Metropolitan Development Authority in structure and organization, it was endowed with a national mandate. As a result, it has been unable to respond effectively to Colombo's distinctive metropolitan needs.

During the past two decades, this maze of authorities and jurisdictions has become highly complex. Nevertheless, two important trends may be distinguished. First, a large number and wide range of parastatal industrial and commercial undertakings, initiated under the terms of the State Industrial Corporations Act of 1956, have performed noneconomic services and tasks that could have been the responsibility of urban local governments. By 1977, at least twenty of the economic and noneconomic parastatals were undertaking major operations in the urban core alone. Second, there seems to have been a definite tendency to remove responsibilities from the urban local authorities from 1965 onward, both before and after independence.

Attempts to meet the mounting challenges of urbanization were first made from within the local government system itself. For example, the number of local authorities in the urban core grew from three in 1944 to thirteen in 1965. Thereafter, only two new town councils were created; however, no elections were held after 1971, and all local authorities were

*Table 11-1. Local and Ad Hoc Corporate Authorities
in Colombo Metropolitan Region, 1980*

Territorial jurisdiction	Institutions	Functions
Local	55 village councils	Village local government
	36 urban councils	Urban local government
	3 municipal councils	Urban local government
Submetropolitan	2 district ministers and councils	Control of district development funds and activities
	Colombo District (low-lying areas) Reclamation and Development Board	Land reclamation in areas subject to flooding
	Colombo Port Commission	Operation of Colombo port
	Colombo Gas and Water Company	Public domestic gas supply in Colombo
	Port (Cargo) Corporation	Public cargo operations
	Greater Colombo Economic Commission	Management of Katunayake Investment Promotion Zone
Suprametropolitan[a]	Urban Development Authority	Physical planning and public works
	National Housing Development Authority	Planning and construction of public works
	National Water Supply and Drainage Board	Supply of water outside Colombo municipality
	State Engineering Corporation	Civil engineering construction
	State Building Materials Corporation	Supply of building materials
	Sri Lanka Electricity Board	Generation and distribution of electricity
	Industrial Development Board	Assistance to industries
	Industrial Estates Corporation	
	Sri Lanka Transport Board	Operation of public buses
	National Small Industries Corporation	Assistance to small industries
	Central Environmental Authority	Environmental control
	Sri Lanka Tourist Board	Promotion of tourism

a. Only the main agencies are listed.

eventually superseded by mid-1977, by which time they had long been in chronic financial straits. At the same time, the number of statutory bodies for urban services increased.

This increasing fragmentation of urban government has been accompanied by similar long-term changes in the system of district administration established for primarily rural affairs. Over the years, district responsibilities, authority, and control have been gradually removed from the government agent (in whom they were once concentrated) and shifted to deconcentrated, subordinate offices of central ministries and departments, each having its own, unique area of jurisdiction that differs in varying degrees

from the agent's. The introduction of the informal district political authorities in 1973, followed by the more formal district ministers in 1978, did not
reduce the growing fragmentation of public administration as a whole. As a
result, by the end of 1978 at least fifteen central ministries were operating in
the urban core in addition to the ministries operating within the system of
district administration itself.

Fiscal Situation

Undoubtedly, the most important local government authority in the
metropolitan region is the Colombo Municipal Council. Although its powers are no greater than those of other municipal councils, it is much older
(115 years), serves a much larger population (nearly 600,000), operates
over a much wider area (36 square kilometers), has been politically active
since the mid-1979 local government elections, and has a relatively large
revenue base compared with that of other municipal councils in the metropolitan region.

Measured by other standards, however, the council has little influence
over metropolitan affairs. From a financial standpoint, its activities are
greatly overshadowed by the national agencies and authorities operating in
the metropolitan region, and its sources of income have always been limited
in range. Typically, some 67 percent of the council's revenue has been derived from taxes on the rental value of land, fees, and charges; some 25 percent from central government loans and grants; and only 7 percent from all
other sources (see table 11-2). With land values rising fast (at least fivefold
between 1977 and 1979), revenues have been buoyant in recent years.
Although the annual valuation per head increased from Rs317 in 1977 to
Rs636 in 1982, the proportion of rates, taxes, and fees declined to less than
60 percent. As in Calcutta, Madras, and Bombay, property rates are
assessed on annual rental values, hypothetically fixed. Valuations on a cur-

Table 11-2. Colombo Municipal Council Revenue, Selected Years
(amount in millions of rupees)

Revenue	1975 Amount	1975 Percent	1977	1979	1982 Amount	1982 Percent
Rates and taxes	48.61	61.4	59.59	66.65	127.66	40
Fees, charges, rents	4.99	6.1	16.97	10.95	57.29	18
Revenue grants	14.42	18.2	13.77	38.39	95.08 ⎱	41
Capital grants	5.60	7.0	n.a.	5.41	35.00 ⎰	
Others	5.72	7.3	n.a.	n.a.	n.a.	n.a.
Total	79.34	100	90.33	121.40	315.03	100

n.a. Not available.

Source: W. G. Mendes, *Local Government in Sri Lanka* (Colombo: Apothecaris, 1976).

rent rental basis and periodical updating of these valuations can increase property tax yields substantially.

With respect to expenditures, in 1975 some 30 percent of the council's expenditure was taken up by health services, 20 percent by physical planning (that is, highways, land, and buildings), and 12–13 percent each by water supply, other public utility services, welfare, and general administration (see table 11-3). These proportions have changed little since then except in the category of physical planning, where expenditure on road networks and on the development of new areas has increased considerably. Colombo's water supply system was transferred to the National Water Supply and Drainage Board (WSDB) in 1981. The Municipal Council continues to manage the system on an agency basis for the WSDB, but thus far neither organization has adopted direct water charges.

In recent years, local authorities have come to depend more and more on the national government to meet current deficits, as can be seen from the steady increase in revenue grants between 1975 and 1982, from Rs14.42 million to Rs95 million (see table 11-2). Local authorities throughout the country have been unable to raise local taxes and impose adequate charges for services, in part because of the nature of the present grant system, which automatically reimburses local authorities for much of the increase in wage costs. In the case of Colombo, it was 14 percent in 1975 and 41 percent in 1982. If the trends in expenditure are ignored and taxation and service charges are not reformed, government grants to local authorities will need to be enlarged vastly (see table 11-4 for annual capital expenditure in Metropolitan Colombo by all public authorities except the Greater Colombo Economic Commission [GCEC]). Clearly, the local municipal contribution is insignificant compared with that of the NHDA or the UDA.

The two newly established central government authorities, the UDA and NHDA, alone account for more than two-thirds of current and projected capital expenditure on water supply, land, shelter, industrial and commercial infrastructure and buildings, roads and communications, sports facilities, and an integrated urban development project. This scale of expendi-

Table 11-3. *Colombo Municipal Council Expenditure, Selected Years*
(amount in millions of rupees)

| Expenditure | 1975 | | 1977 | 1979 | 1982 | | 1987 (*proposed*) |
	Amount	Percent			Amount	Percent	
General administration	10.41	13.1	9.57	32.79	44.52	17.4	80.00
Health services	23.58	29.8	27.46	39.59	84.50	32.8	109.00
Physical planning	16.13	20.3	19.01	33.39	89.16	34.7	119.00
Water sources	10.01	12.6	9.46	14.72	15.30	5.9	22.00
Public utilities	9.38	11.8	5.03	20.67	5.79	2.3	61.00
Welfare	9.81	12.4	9.35	21.09	17.72	6.9	22.00
Total	79.32	100.0	79.88	162.25	256.99	100.0	413.00

Source: W. G. Mendes, *Local Government in Sri Lanka* (Colombo: Apothecaris, 1976).

Table 11-4. Projected Annual Capital Expenditure for Colombo, 1979–81
(thousands of rupees)

Expenditure	1979	1980	1981
Water supply	114,076	262,000	482,963
Land	n.a.	164,497	n.a.
Shelter			
National Housing Development			
Authority	432,796	300,000	544,000
Urban Development Authority	335	8,175	16,162
Industrial complex	n.a.	19,000	17,000
Commercial buildings	30,200	391,800	297,000
Sports (Urban Development Authority)	n.a.	500	1,500
Roads	n.a.	26,890	n.a.
Communications	n.a.	145,170	n.a.
Integrated development project (Urban			
Development Authority)	n.a.	22,000	132,000
Administrative complex			
Department buildings	n.a.	134,000	n.a.
Urban Development Authority	100,200	577,800	462,000
Total	677,607	2,051,832	2,152,625

n.a. Not available.

Source: Budget reports of the Colombo Municipal Council.

ture—between Rs1.5 million and Rs2.0 million—is unprecedented in Colombo's history, and yet it reflects only public sector construction activities that were expected to be financed with the aid of international aid agencies and commercial banks. Part of the anticipated expenditure can be accounted for by the optimism generated by the new government that came into office in 1977. It favored private initiative, particularly among property developers. Other anticipated expenditure reflected governmental responses to the economic, social, and physical challenges of metropolitan development.

Response to Metropolitan Problems

Since the establishment of the UDA, NHDA, and GCEC, the number of ad hoc statutory authorities active in the metropolitan region has increased to at least twenty-three, and thus the responsibilities of elected local government authorities have been reduced even further. The only reform on the local government scene has been the introduction of proportional representation (for elections held in mid-1979). The creation of statutory authorities has at least stimulated interest in submetropolitan affairs and made it possible to coordinate public and private efforts in specific areas of urban development. The GCEC, for instance, now controls the tax-free Katunayake Investment Promotion Zone, which is close to the international airport on the northern side of the metropolitan region. It is responsible for providing land, constructing factory sites, installing related physical infrastructure, and supplying essential services. One hundred thirty industrial and other projects worth US$240 million have been approved and more than 60 agreements with private firms have been signed, with the expectation of creating an estimated 40,000 jobs. Now two further free-trade zones are planned. One of these, the Biyagama Investment Promotion Zone, covers 450 acres and is located 23 kilometers inland from Colombo Port along the Kelani River. It is to be financed and developed by the private sector. The NHDA was established in 1979 to construct housing, formulate and execute housing development projects, oversee the clearance and redevelopment of slums, provide land and financing for private housing, and manage housing estates. Although most of its activities were originally directed to the Colombo metropolitan region (see table 11-3), emphasis is now being placed on rural housing.

The UDA, however, may have greater impact on metropolitan affairs because it is specifically concerned with the development of urban areas (including those within the Colombo metropolitan region) that the minister of local government, housing, and construction (who is in fact the prime minister) has designated for physical and economic upgrading. The UDA is empowered to:

- Carry out integrated planning and physical development, subject to the minister's directives
- Formulate and submit development plans (including capital investment plans) to the minister for government approval
- Implement approved physical development and capital investment plans, and execute approved development projects and schemes either directly or through other agencies
- Implement related programs of development works, activities, and services
- Formulate and implement urban land use and environmental policies and schemes
- Carry out all the work required for the development of the physical infrastructure needed
- On behalf of any government agency, prepare development projects and planning schemes and supervise their execution; approve the projects and schemes prepared by any such agency and control their execution; if directed to do so, call upon a government agency to undertake development projects and schemes, and regulate the activities of that agency
- Regulate planning projects or schemes prepared by a government agency or private person and provide technical planning services
- Act as the physical planning authority for areas covered by the Town and Country Planning Ordinance, if the minister so orders.

The UDA's funds, which in 1979 increased from Rs20 million (US$2.4 million) to Rs100 million (US$12 million), are voted by the national state assembly; received through the exercise of its powers, duties, and functions; received in the form of loans, donations, gifts, or grants from any source inside or outside Sri Lanka; and borrowed by way of bank overdraft or government-guaranteed debentures. The authority is governed by a Board of Management comprising a chairman nominated by the minister (currently the secretary of the ministry of Local Government, Housing, and Construction); senior officers of the ministries of Local Government, Housing, and Construction, Finance, Lands, Industries, Transport, Health, Education, and Irrigation, Power, and Highways; the director of Town and Country Planning; the chairman of the NHDA; two members nominated by the minister to represent local government authorities; two members nominated by the minister for their special knowledge and experience with urban development; and the general manager of the UDA, who acts as the board's secretary and is also appointed by the minister. In addition, the minister may appoint a committee to advise the board whenever he considers it necessary.

Initially, the UDA was run by the staff of the Colombo Master Plan Project, who were strongly oriented toward physical planning as opposed to social and economic planning. This built-in bias may have been strengthened by the fact that the UDA is not empowered to undertake social and economic planning, and the government may well have expected it to play an aggressive, entrepreneurial role in the development of Colombo in collaboration with the private sector. No master plan has yet been approved as a basis for physical planning and land use control, however, and the UDA has been primarily concerned with initiating a series of public works projects. A three-year corporate plan for the UDA issued in December 1979 stated that "the UDA is a development agency and its activities have to be commercially and economically viable." Although the authority was created specifically to promote integrated planning and development, in practice it has been involved in a great variety of activities ranging from the acquisition, improvement, and sale of prime real estate in Colombo to the construction of a new capital in Kotte and development control in most urban areas.

Development Projects

As a result, the main projects initiated by the UDA for the period 1978–83 have not directly addressed the metropolitan problems of unemployment, the inadequate delivery of social services, and the need for augmenting shelter (except in pilot projects described below); nor has it been concerned with the planning and control of the use of urban land. The GCEC has separately sought to create new jobs in its investment promotion zones, and this effort will undoubtedly have some effect on employment, shelter, services, and land use. The UDA projects have instead focused on an urban face-lift, part of which has consisted of relocating parliamentary and other government buildings to a 13-acre island in marshlands at the old capital of Kotte outside Colombo's municipal limits, at an estimated cost of Rs350 million (US$42 million). The UDA has also embarked upon the redevelopment of Echelon Square (at an estimated cost of Rs267 million), which is a 32-acre central block at present occupied by army and police barracks, playing fields, and small government offices that will be replaced by high-rise commercial buildings and an international hotel. In addition, the UDA is committed to the downtown redevelopment of Lotus Square (which is to be the site of a national square, commercial and office space, a hotel, and a theater) and the Pettah Market complex (where it will rebuild the wholesale and retail fish markets and provide a multistoried supermarket) at an estimated total cost of Rs188 million (US$22.6 million).

Shelter

Under its mandate, the NHDA was to plan and implement an ambitious housing program. In 1979 the government launched an effort to build "100,000 houses": 50,000 rural units, 36,000 urban units, and a further 14,000 units to be financed by housing loans. Overall, about 35,000 units were completed by 1983, half of which were built in the metropolitan region. Because of the multiplicity of projects, geographic spread, inadequate time for preparation, and other problems, unit costs jumped to around Rs125,000, and the program had to be frozen. Thus the 1983–87 public sector investment program calls for a two-thirds reduction in the amount allocated for 1979–83 (which was Rs2,685 million), and the annual outlay is to be around Rs300 million. Furthermore, emphasis is to shift toward aided self-help or sites and services rather than direct construction. As a result, the housing program is unlikely to become a principal instrument of integrated urban development.

Pending Issues

Concern for overall physical, economic, and social planning in the metropolitan region is certainly not a new phenomenon in Sri Lanka. A preliminary analysis by the Master Plan Project pointed out that in 1979 "only an outline regional planning scheme originally prepared by Sir Patrick Abucrombie in 1949 and revived in [1961] was in operation." The Town and Country Planning Ordinance and the Housing and Town Improvement Ordinance had authorized the public sector to play merely a passive role in urban land use development, and resource mobilization consisted of municipal councils drawing upon the government's consolidated fund, borrowing on overdraft, and selling land. Even this was limited to a few sites. Local authorities had little power to expand infrastructure and provide economic or social facilities. The Master Plan Project was expected to address these issues, but the National Capital Development Area Plan it produced was more of an architectural plan based on the concept of a low-density garden city with a rapid transit system. Detailed technical and economic evaluations were suggested but not taken up. The institutional changes initiated after 1977 were similarly expected to devise machinery for metropolitanwide planning, investment programming, and coordination. But neither the Ministry of Local Government, Housing, and Construction nor the new UDA and NHDA have been able to tackle these critical metropolitan tasks. At the same time, however, physical planning has improved considerably since 1977.

All three new agencies have full powers to deploy the resources they mobilize, either directly or by means of contracts and agreements with both public and private sector developers. This in itself is a great improvement over the situation in 1977, although there can be no guarantee that the infrastructure and facilities installed will be adequately maintained and improved by the local government councils and statutory authorities responsible for such matters. None of the three new agencies is designed for the long-term operation of essential services that they themselves have introduced, directly or indirectly. In this respect, therefore, the situation has not changed since 1977. Service delivery remains the fragmented responsibility of local government councils and statutory authorities.

Integrated planning for urban development areas designated by the minister of local government is now made possible through the UDA. Any area falling within the jurisdiction of the GCEC in the northern sector of the metropolitan region is excluded from the latter minister's jurisdiction, however. Since the free-trade investment promotion zones are the principal public creators of industrial and commercial jobs in the metropolitan region, the planning of job creation—other than by the construction of public offices and other public works—cannot be initiated and integrated with physical and social planning by the UDA on a metropolitanwide basis.

At the same time, it has become much easier to mobilize resources. The GCEC is specifically empowered to mobilize funds, land, manpower, and materials for the development of the areas falling under its jurisdiction. The UDA is similarly empowered to mobilize resources for the projects it initiates within its own declared urban development areas; and the NHDA has been established to concentrate resources of land, finance, labor, and materials on the construction of houses and apartments. Although competition among these three powerful agencies for the relatively scarce resources available may be unavoidable, the central government should be able to resolve such conflicts through the ministries involved, especially the Ministry of Local Government, Housing, and Construction, which oversees both the UDA and the NHDA.

The important point to note about these three new agencies is that they represent short-term responses to long-term problems, and they greatly strengthen the well-established trend toward the centralization of government. They perpetuate the tradition of creating single-purpose, ad hoc statutory authorities that are responsible to the central government and give little responsibility to locally representative institutions with general powers for the ongoing discharge of a wide range of urban management functions. As a result, the machinery of urban management is becoming more and more fragmented when in fact the number of government agencies operating in metropolitan Colombo needs to be drastically reduced if local government is ever to be capable of responding to metropolitan and local aspirations and requirements. In spite of the improvements made, the machinery established since 1977 has merely exacerbated this long-standing problem. Moreover, the development program has proved to be unrealistic in its estimate of the availability of skilled manpower, financing, materials, and land.

Another problem for Sri Lanka is that alongside high unemployment it faces a shortage of construction skills because many of its carpenters, masons, and electricians, for example, have gone to work in the Middle East. Furthermore, modern technology requires nontraditional skills that have not yet been acquired by many of its people. The property boom accompanying the urban face-lift has raised construction costs and rents precipitously and created serious financial problems. Whereas income tax receipts for 1979 and 1980 amounted to Rs1,159 million (US$139 million) and Rs1,172 million (US$141 million), respectively, the expected annual expenditure on major public and private construction projects in Colombo alone is estimated to have risen to Rs4,000 million (US$480 million) a year. The massive Mahaweli irrigation project also has to be paid for. As much as 65–75 percent of the total construction costs will probably have to be financed from the private sector—including property developers, local banks, and foreign sources—if the development program is to go ahead as planned. Nevertheless, neither private sector capacity nor the probable price effects of such enormous expenditure appear to have been taken into account.

Problems with materials are also on the rise. In spite of record levels of cement production in Sri Lanka, it has become necessary to import cement. The price doubled between 1978 and 1979 alone, as did the price of timber. In addition, local construction firms have been faced with growing shortages of steel and other materials.

Yet a recent World Bank report observed that Sri Lanka's urban problems are definitely more manageable than those of some other South and East Asian countries. Birth rate and population growth are lower than in any other country in the same income class, mainly because of Sri Lanka's achievements in health, education, and welfare. Its urban population is relatively small, with 3.2 million people, and the Colombo metropolitan region has no more than 1.3 million. Although its general condition is better than that of several other cities in the region, the usual litany of underachievements is applicable to Colombo as well. This is largely due to the lack of investment planning and coordination, the fragmented sector-by-sector approach, and the failure to address city-level financial performance. The new institutions based on models borrowed from other countries have tended to embark on ambitious schemes, but several have also tended to oscillate between stop and go: after the drastic pruning of the "100,000 Houses" program, for example, there was a March 1983 announcement of a "Million Houses over the Decade" program. Thus, despite the status and power enjoyed by the new organizations, a metropolitan platform for concerted planning and action has failed to emerge. Colombo's experience so far illustrates yet again that the mere creation of institutions will not improve metropolitan government. Rather, special managerial processes and skills need to be developed for that purpose.

12

Jakarta

JAKARTA WAS FOUNDED around 1300 as a small trading port at the mouth of the Ciliwung River. Originally called Sunda Kelapa, it was renamed Jayakarta or Jakarta, "the victorious place," to commemorate a victory over the Portuguese in 1527. In 1619, the Dutch overran the city—which by then had two centers, at the old town (Kota) and the port area (Pasar Ikan)—and they renamed it Batavia. Subsequently, the city grew inland toward the south along the Ciliwung. During the eighteenth and early nineteenth centuries the old center experienced considerable flooding and recurring epidemics owing to silting up of the harbor. To escape the flooding, the Dutch located government buildings on slightly higher land to the south, an area that is now the center of the city, Merdeka Square.

The residential area known as Mentang was developed about 1 kilometer south of Merdeka Square, and the new port of Tanjung Priok was constructed to the northeast to replace the badly silted old port. A system of canals was constructed to reduce the problems of flooding and an extensive system of urban railways developed.

Growth of the City

By 1920, intercity rail lines connected Jakarta with Tangerang in the west, Serpong and the Sunda straits in the southwest, Bogor and Bandung in the south, and Bekasi and Cirebon in the east. These rail lines, and the roads parallel to them, have formed the main axes of development. By the eve of the Second World War, Batavia had grown to a city of about 500,000 people with a spacious and modern European quarter surrounded by comparatively pleasant kampungs, or traditional villages, where most of the local people lived.

Indonesia is the fifth most populous country in the world. Its urban population of 32 million accounts for about 22 percent of the country's total population of 140 million (1979 estimates). Two-thirds of its people live on the islands of Java and Madura, which have only 7 percent of the country's land area. With rural densities averaging about 700 per square kilometer and individual landholdings becoming smaller, migration to cities has become pronounced. Indonesia's urban population has been increasing at the rate of 3.7 percent a year, which exceeds that of many developed countries. Although Jakarta is not central to Java or to the many islands of the Indonesian archipelago, it has long been the commercial and administrative hub of Indonesia. Traditionally, it has been the main destination of those migrating from rural areas. Political uncertainties and large-scale construction in Jakarta have been additional causes of increased migration. According to one estimate, in 1969, the year of independence, Jakarta's population increased by half a million. Ten years later, about one million people migrated to Jakarta after rebellions in Sumatra and Sulawesi. Large-scale construction activities in and around Jakarta were a further stimulus to migration in the 1950s.

By 1961, Jakarta's population had reached 2.9 million. During the next ten years, this number rose swiftly to 4.6 million at an annual rate of 4.6 percent; migration accounted for 2.5 percent and natural increase for 2.1 percent. Although a family planning program was introduced and a closed city policy adopted in 1971, both the natural increase and migration rates have continued to rise. Under the closed city policy, migrants must show a certificate either from an employer (to indicate a job is ready for them) or from a school (to show that they have been properly enrolled). In addition, they must report the specific dwelling in which they will be staying. Finally, they must leave money for a return ticket with an official of the RT (rukun tetangga, a community of twenty to thirty families). If they do not have a job after six months, they will be returned to their home villages.

Despite these restrictions, the rate of migration to Jakarta, particularly from West Java and Central Java, remains substantial. Part of the reason is that the household income in Jakarta is much higher than it is elsewhere. If per capita income figures for 1969 are used and it is assumed that the average size of a household is five persons, the annual income for a Jakarta household may be estimated (in rupiahs) at roughly Rp197,000 (US$312.7), compared with Rp92,000 (US$146.0) in Central Java and Rp88,000 (US$139.7) in West Java. According to 1981 estimates, the population in metropolitan Jakarta and the adjoining districts of Bogor, Tangerang, and Bekasi (an area known as JABOTABEK) now totals some 10 million. The overall prospects for economic development in this region are quite favorable. Average real household incomes could show a 150 percent increase by 1993 and twice that amount by 2003. At the same time, the urban population in Java will increase by almost a million persons annually. The population of the JABOTABEK region is thus expected to double in the next twenty years.[1]

1. Indonesia Ministry of Public Works, *Jabotabek Metropolitan Development Plan: Summary Report* (June 1981).

Jakarta.   Rush hour at Djalan Djenderal Soedirman, along a major north-south axis.

Map 12-1. Batavia (Jakarta), 1757

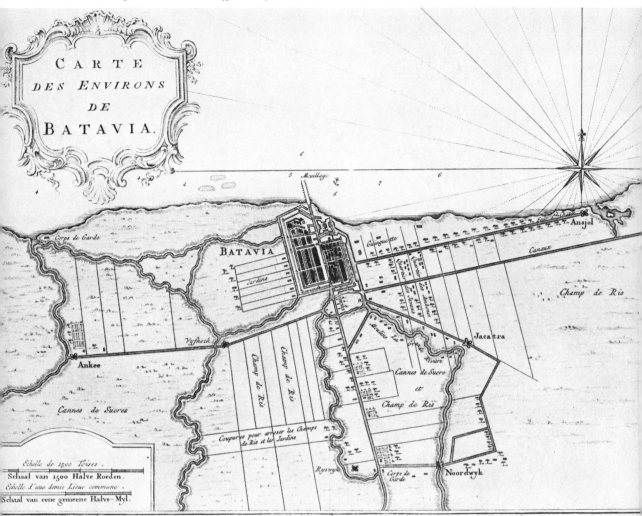

Photo: Library of Congress, Washington, D.C.

Map 12-2. Jakarta Urban Area, 1985

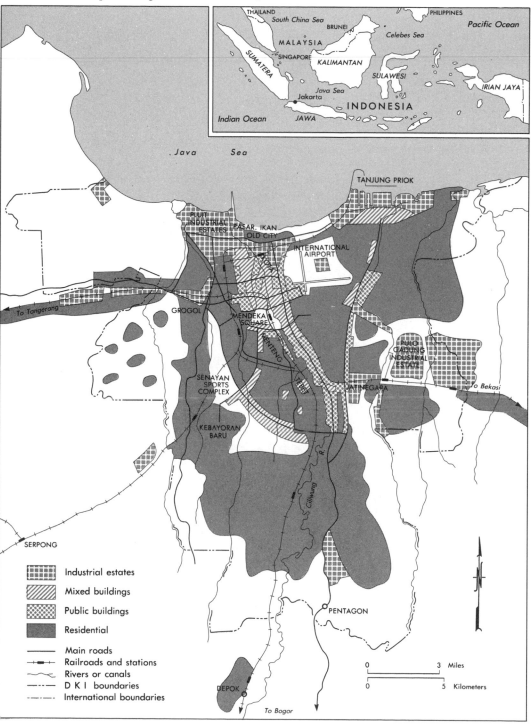

THAILAND
South China Sea
PHILIPPINES
Pacific Ocean
MALAYSIA
BRUNEI
Celebes Sea
SUMATERA
SINGAPORE
KALIMANTAN
SULAWESI
IRIAN JAYA
Java Sea
Jakarta
INDONESIA
Indian Ocean
JAWA

Java   Sea

TANJUNG PRIOK
PLUIT INDUSTRIAL ESTATES
PASAR. IKAN OLD CITY
INTERNATIONAL AIRPORT
Kota
To Tangerang
GROGOL
MENDEKA SQUARE
MENTENG
PULO GADUNG INDUSTRIAL ESTATE
To Bekasi
SENAYAN SPORTS COMPLEX
JATINEGARA
TEBET
KEBAYORAN BARU
Ciliwung R.
SERPONG

Industrial estates
Mixed buildings
Public buildings
Residential
Main roads
Railroads and stations
Rivers or canals
D K I boundaries
International boundaries

PENTAGON

0   3   Miles
0   5   Kilometers

DEPOK
To Bogor

Map 12-3. Outline Structure Plan for Metropolitan Jakarta in 1993

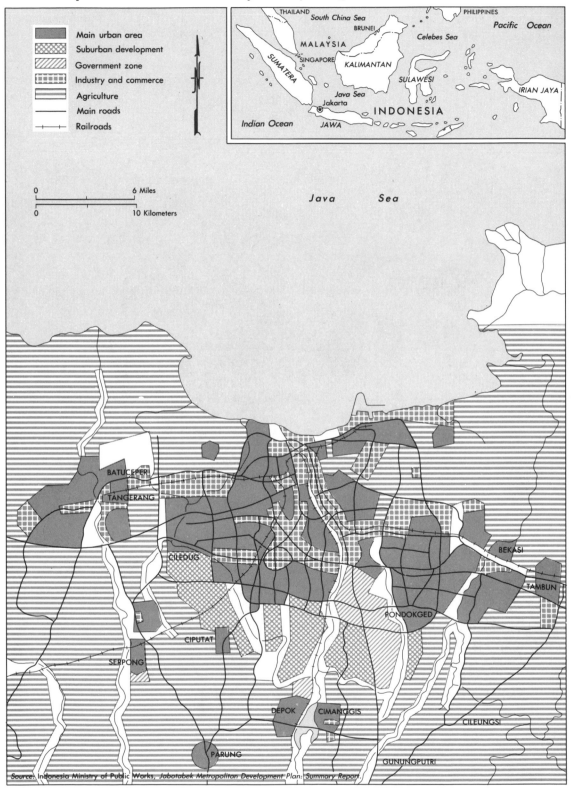

Source: Indonesia Ministry of Public Works, *Jabotabek Metropolitan Development Plan: Summary Report.*

Map 12-4. Outline Regional Structure Plan for JABOTABEK (Metropolitan Jakarta) in 2003

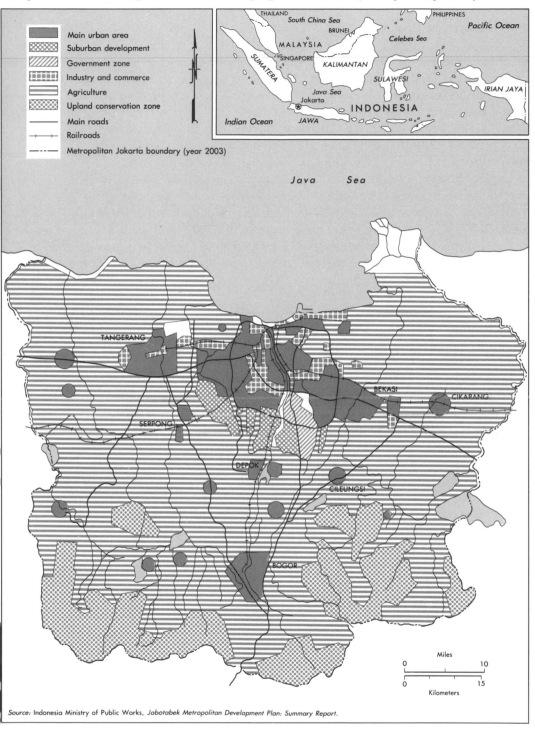

Source: Indonesia Ministry of Public Works, *Jabotabek Metropolitan Development Plan: Summary Report.*

Metropolitan Problems

During the past two decades, Jakarta City has been expanding to such an extent that it now occupies at least 560 square kilometers. The central, densely urbanized core covers some 180 square kilometers within a 7-kilometer radius of Merdeka Square and accounts for two-thirds of the city's population. During the Dutch period, new development tended to take place to the south, in the higher and cooler lands away from the coast. The subsequent pattern of development in a north-south direction was in part related to the topography of the Jakarta area, which is divided by five rivers flowing northward to the sea. After independence, this pattern continued with the construction of a large, high-income suburb at Kebayoran, which was to accommodate a population of about 175,000 in spacious, expensive dwellings. To connect Kebayoran with the old city, the avenues of Jalan Thammin and Jalan General Sudirman were widened to six-lane highways as additional north-south axes.

During the Sukarno period and in the early 1960s, construction activities included a sports complex for the Asian games, monuments, government offices, and hotels, all of which were built along these axes. Later in the same decade, however, the north-south pattern was modified when a four-lane ring road was constructed around existing development. This road provides the only rapid east-west link across the city, with the exception of the Ancol road, which is on the northern side. The ring road has opened up an opportunity for industrial development in the east and has stimulated the development of residential areas in an east-west direction between the new road and the existing city. Metropolitan Jakarta now spreads along a road to Bogor district where the Indonesian Defense Department offices are located. Some parts of the neighboring districts of Tangerang and Bekasi are by now urbanized as well.

The kampungs have been a distinctive feature of Jakarta since its early days, and as recently as 1969 they still covered about 60 percent of the inner city. As the metropolitan region has expanded, new kampungs have sprung up, but they are less dense than the old ones (310 persons per hectare compared with 515 in the inner city kampungs), and overall the kampungs now cover only about 35 percent of the urbanized area. They still account for 70 percent of the population growth, however, and remain the principal location of new households. Despite the great densities (average about 21,500 persons per square kilometer), until the 1970s most kampungs lacked basic services such as water supply, drainage, and refuse removal.

Poor urban services were not confined to kampungs, however, as was demonstrated by a 1969 survey of housing conditions in Jakarta, which found that 65 percent of all houses had no private toilet facilities, 80 percent had no electricity, and 90 percent had no piped water. Of the total housing stock, 24 percent consisted of permanent houses with solid walls, cement floors, and tiled roofs; 44 percent were temporary houses with bamboo matting walls, earthen floors, and thatched roofs; and 32 percent were semipermanent structures having some combination of temporary and permanent materials. The water supply system originally designed by the Dutch for a city of half a million has been expanded from time to time, but even now less than a quarter of the city's population have direct connections. Approximately 30 percent of the households in Jakarta still depend solely on water vendors for their supply, which costs five times more than piped water. Because of increasing population and salinity in the groundwater aquifers, the quality of raw water itself has deteriorated. In addition, the city has no waterborne sewer system. Septic tanks serve about 25 percent of the city's population; others have to use pit latrines, cesspools, and ditches along the roadside. Much of the population, however, has no alternative other than to use the drainage canals for bathing, laundering, and defecation.

Other badly neglected services include garbage collection and surface water drainage. Most of the city's uncollected garbage (estimated in a World Health Organization study to be 30 percent of the daily load) ends up in canals and rivers and along the roadside, where it clogs drainage channels and causes extensive flooding during the rainy season. Floodwaters then sweep the raw sewage and garbage out of the ditches and canals back into the kampungs. In the dry season, when there is insufficient flow to drain off wastes, they decay in exposed areas and pose a serious health hazard to the community. Surface water drainage is inadequate and large sections of the city are subject to flooding during the wet season.

As might be expected, many of those in the low-income groups with inadequate sanitation experience chronic health problems. The leading causes of death are pneumonia, child malnutrition, bronchitis, tuberculosis, rheumatic fever, and cholera. Infant mortality in the kampungs is high (160 per 1,000 live births) and approximately 50 percent of all kampung children show symptoms of malnutrition. About 80 percent of the population are chronically infected with waterborne parasites.

The Kampung Improvement Program (KIP) was among the first responses of government to these problems. During the government's first five-year development plan (1969–74), the Jakarta provincial government (DKI) began a program of upgrading the physical infrastructure of kampungs. The KIP evolved from a central government program (INPRES) supporting both rural and urban works by distributing funds on a per capita basis to local government districts for infrastructure improvements. From 1969 to 1974, DKI upgraded about 2,400 hectares, or about 10 percent of its urbanized area, at a cost of some US$6,500 per hectare. About 1.2 million residents, or 25 percent of the population, benefited directly at a per capita cost of some US$28 (at June 1974 prices). The program has drastically improved pathways, drainage, and health and school facilities in the kampungs, but citywide problems of water supply and drainage persist. One kampung improvement program has continued with World Bank assistance, and an additional 1.5 million kampung residents are expected to receive the benefits.

Structure of Government

Although DKI-Jakarta is a distinct province, a great variety of national agencies are directly responsible for providing many services. Thus it is important to know how the government is structured in urban areas, particularly in Jakarta, in order to understand how the various urban services are financed. The government of Indonesia is clearly hierarchical as it is organized into five formal levels: national, provincial, regency or district (kabupaten/kotamadya), subdistrict groups (kechamatan), and subdistricts (kelurahan). Jakarta and other large cities have, in addition, two lower levels of government: the rukun warga/kampung (RW) and rukun tetangga (RT), which are community organizations supported by the government but not part of its formal structure.

The administrative body at the national level is the people's consultative assembly (MPR), which is made up of 460 members, three-quarters of whom are elected; it is the highest authority in the country and sets the overall guidelines for development. The five-year plan, called REPELITA, is approved by the MPR and signed into law by the president, who is the highest executive authority in the country. Within the executive branch, the National Planning Agency (BAPPENAS) is a staff agency of the president. Beneath the president are the various ministries, including Interior (Dalam Negeri), Public Works, Finance, Health, Education, Industry and Cooperatives, Mining and Energy. The chairman of BAPPENAS is also the minister of economics, industry, and finance (EKUIN), and he coordinates these three areas. The Ministry of the Interior plays a very important role in urban management as the link between the national and local levels of government. Under this hierarchical system, the provincial governors, municipal mayors, and heads of other lower units are all appointed by or in consultation with the next higher authority.

Because DKI-Jakarta has special provincial status, its metropolitan government consists of a governor appointed by the president, a provincial assembly (DPRD), a provincial planning agency (BAPPEDA), and several line agencies (dinas-dinas) that report directly to the governor. At the next subordinate level, Jakarta is divided into five mayoral districts, or kotamadya, each with an average population of about 1.25 million, a mayor (walikota) appointed by the president, an assembly (DPRDK), a local planning agency (BAPPEMKO), and functional departments through which most government programs are implemented.

The next level of government in DKI-Jakarta consists of 30 kecamatans, each of which has an average population of some 220,000 and is headed by a camat appointed by the governor. The kecamatan is responsible for local security, public health, building control, and transportation; the camat issues identification cards, keeps land records, and collects statistical information. This level of administration also supervises the execution of infrastructure works.

The lowest administrative unit is known as the kelurahan. Indonesia has 227 kelurahans, with an average population of some 30,000. Each is headed by a lurah, an appointed civil servant responsible for tax collection, land transactions, statistical data, and the registration of residents and visitors. The kelurahan administers refuse collection and community health services and supervises the two informal levels of government, the RW and RT community groups. Each RW (about 150 families) and RT (about 30 families) is headed by a volunteer member. They organize cooperative community efforts in local road building, refuse disposal, security, festivals, and the dissemination of government information. The lurahs, their staff, and RW and RT heads also form kampung committees to assess local development priorities, organize self-help labor, and collect funds for special kampung programs.

The DKI and the kotamadyas have been given revenues of their own, including a share of the property tax, a motor vehicle tax, entertainment taxes, and taxes on foreigners. Other levels of government are administrative units only, but subsidies from the central government are allocated to all levels.

In addition to this elaborate hierarchy, the several central government ministries have established provincial or district branches. These units, called kanwils, form part of their ministries for technical administrative purposes, but since the governor, or bupati (walikota in the case of Jakarta), is also the representative of the central government, he has the power to supervise the working of these branch units. Perhaps the most important organization for urban services is the Directorate General of Housing, Building, Planning, and Urban Development (CIPTA KARYA) in the Ministry of Public Works; its range of functions includes water supply and sanitation. The Directorate General of Public Administration and Regional Autonomy in the Ministry of the Interior, which supervises the administration of local governments and controls the appointment of its heads, is another important government organ.

Apart from the ministries and their branches, a number of central parastatal corporations discharge important responsibilities in Jakarta and several other urban areas. The National Urban Development Corporation (NUDC, or PERUMNAS) is empowered to develop and resell urban land for specified residential, industrial, and commercial uses and to provide housing either by means of sites and services schemes or low-cost housing projects. The National Mortgage Bank, or Bank Tebungan Negara, was restructured in 1975 to finance relatively large-scale, low-cost housing projects. In addition, the central government agencies of Binamarga and Jassamarga oversee the construction and operation of main roads and toll highways. Bus operations are handled by another government enterprise. The provincial government has its own parastatal agency for water supply, the Perusahan Air Minum.

Fiscal Situation

As in many other countries, the national government in Indonesia appropriates the principal share of public revenues, which derive mainly from corporate income tax on oil (44 percent), indirect taxes (20 percent), and other sources. Borrowings represent another 20 percent of the national resources. In Jakarta, the main sources of revenue available to the DKI are a share of the ipeda, or property tax, taxes on motor vehicle transfers and registrations, development taxes, and taxes on tourists. Although the property tax is the most important local source of revenue in many cities in developing countries, in Jakarta it accounts for only about 4 percent of the total. Inadequate cadastral surveys, poor assessments, low tax rates, and weak enforcement all contribute to this shortfall. By aggressively pursuing the remaining tax sources, however, DKI-Jakarta has been able to achieve considerable increases in taxes and charges, including revenues from enterprises. Since 1974, the city's own revenues have been increasing at a rate of 5.3 percent a year. In addition, Jakarta has been looking for revenues from gambling and entertainment taxes, which have recently been taken over by the central government. Jakarta has been able to increase its borrowings steadily. In contrast to many of the other cities in the region, the DKI has been able to cover all of its revenue expenditures in recent years and is likely to continue to do so, at least in the near future (see tables 12-1 and 12-2).

Capital development and the provision for expansion of services, however, are heavily dependent on central government allocations and direct

Table 12.1. DKI-Jakarta Revenue, 1974–75 to 1980–81
(millions of rupiahs, 1981 prices)

Source	1974–75	1975–76	1976–77	1977–78	1978–79	1979–80	1980–81	Growth rate 1974–80
Own revenue								
Taxes	40,305	42,075	45,180	44,713	51,665	51,509	65,790	8.5
Gambling	19,632	18,411	18,366	17,621	15,509	11,460	9,017	– 12.2
Charges	9,107	11,171	10,943	12,853	13,519	12,492	15,583	9.4
Ipeda[a]	4,555	4,515	4,463	4,402	5,359	5,122	5,425	3.0
Enterprises	646	764	862	1,023	1,957	1,556	2,051	21.2
Other	7,599	10,314	11,390	12,047	10,872	12,015	13,750	10.4
Subtotal	81,844	87,250	91,204	92,659	98,881	94,154	11,616	5.3
Grants	27,608	38,309	46,682	50,672	50,038	49,128	57,135	12.9
Loans	1,928	4,984	9,727	11,321	9,439	7,465	8,489	28.0
Total	111,380	130,543	147,613	154,652	158,358	150,747	77,240	8.1

Note: Figures up to 1979–80 are actual and those for 1980–81 are estimated.

a. Property tax.

Source: JABOTABEK Implementation Advisory Team, *Jakarta Finance and Implementation Report* no. I/8 (June 1981).

Table 12-2. DKI-Jakarta Expenditure, 1974–75 to 1980–81
(millions of rupiahs, 1981 prices)

Expenditure	1974–75	1975–76	1976–77	1977–78	1978–79	1979–80	1980–81
Routine expenditure							
Staff	20,335	25,000	32,045	32,564	34,542	36,916	39,533
Equipment and							
maintenance	7,809	11,758	16,636	18,042	25,228	26,995	29,138
Other	8,382	14,538	17,993	18,572	10,838	9,223	9,926
Subtotal	36,526	51,296	66,674	69,178	70,608	73,134	78,597
Balance	74,854	79,327	80,939	85,474	87,750	77,612	98,703
Non-JMDP[a]							
expenditure	42,138	41,474	41,016	42,660	38,805	41,724	49,776
JMDP[a] expenditure	40,221	34,825	43,858	35,713	36,919	27,029	23,690
Total	82,359	76,299	84,874	78,373	75,724	68,753	73,466
Selected items of JMDP[a]							
Water	296	654	269	326	n.a.	329	633
Drainage	2,191	2,255	2,305	4,306	3,474	2,678	2,421
Sanitation	128	49	0	0	53	84	301
Solid wastes	333	20	171	717	787	733	738
Kampung							
Improvement							
Program	14,823	20,033	23,786	14,704	19,812	9,558	7,470
Traffic	23	1,037	1,377	1,318	1,176	1,653	862
Roads	22,040	10,640	15,691	14,138	11,324	11,674	8,757
Small industry	177	138	259	205	294	321	400

n.a. Not available.

Note: 1980–81 figures are estimated, the others actual.

a. JABOTABEK Metropolitan Development Plan.

Source: JABOTABEK Implementation Advisory Team, *Jakarta Finance and Implementation Report* no. I/8 (June 1981).

spending through its branches and agencies. Since 1977–78, these allocations together with expenditures in Jakarta have been rising steadily, and this trend is likely to continue. The JABOTABEK planning team, for example, has already recommended that investment in various sectors be substantially increased. In water resource development, flood control and drainage, transport, and small industry, the central government is expected to finance the outlay almost entirely (see table 12-2); and, it is estimated that some 60 percent of all urban service investments in Jakarta will be funded by the central government under REPELITA III and IV, that is, up to 1988–89.

Response to Metropolitan Problems

Jakarta's initial response to the problems of rapid urban growth was through major programs in water supply, drainage, and road development. Physical planning and land use controls were also emphasized. In

1967 a master plan for the period 1965–68 was introduced to deal with problems within a 15-kilometer radius of the city's center, which was expected to have a population of 6.5 million by 1985. By the early 1970s, however, it was already clear that the population of the DKI and its adjoining areas would soon be much greater (close to 25 million by the end of the century) and that the city's economy was fast expanding beyond its established administrative boundaries. The master plan that had been based on the old Dutch system of rigid planning regulations, with inappropriate standards and inadequate analysis of the city and its surrounding regions, was no longer viable. Thus, in 1974, the concept of a physical and economic development plan was introduced for the JABOTABEK region. As a first step, the two governors of Jakarta and West Java provinces in 1975 set up a coordination board (BKSP) consisting of the heads of the two provincial planning bodies (BAPPEDA) and other functional officials. This board was empowered to coordinate services and projects and to control development.

A more elaborate intergovernmental planning arrangement was initiated through Presidential Instruction no. 13 of 1976, under which the minister for economics, industry, and finance (who is also the chairman of BAPPENAS, the national planning body) chaired a group (consisting of the minister of industries, minister of public works, and the governors of Jakarta and West Java) that was charged with revising the development planning of the JABOTABEK region. The planning team itself consisted of the deputy minister in charge of regional and local development in BAPPENAS (chairman), director general of administration and autonomy in the Interior Ministry (director general, PUOD), director general of housing, building, and planning in the public works ministry (director general, CIPTA KARYA), the chairman of BAPPEDA, Jakarta, and the chairman of BAPPEDA, West Java. This team is also to review the development plan prepared by DKI-Jakarta and West Java.

Assisted by the national government and the World Bank, the JABOTABEK planning team has undertaken comprehensive studies to help the government:

- Formulate alternative development strategies and select spatial plans and a preferred plan
- Determine the resources to be committed to REPELITA III and IV, their sources, and their allocation among jurisdictions, levels of government, and sectors
- Identify projects that would require immediate action in any development strategy within REPELITA III
- Reappraise standards, development processes, and programs in each sector and prepare revised sectoral plans that are in accordance with the strategy selected and the resources available
- Identify the implementation mechanisms, organizational structure, and manpower required to carry out the plan, and assist the government in undertaking the initial actions required to implement it.

The team completed the JABOTABEK Development Plan in June 1981. The plan considered two alternative strategies within the time frame of 2001. One, a concentrated strategy, sought a considerably higher GDP and emphasized large-scale manufacturing, construction, transport, business, and financial services in DKI-Jakarta. The other, a distributive strategy, focused on the rapid expansion of public services, faster rate of income growth in BOTABEK (the partly urbanized hinterland of the DKI), increased agricultural and service employment in the region, and the expansion of small businesses. The distributive strategy was preferred since it was more in line with national aspirations and promoted intraregional equity. The team defined metropolitan Jakarta as the area made up of greater Jakarta and Bekasi and Tangerang urban centers to the east and west. Greater Jakarta was defined as the DKI and its immediate outgrowths. The team estimated that metropolitan Jakarta would have a population of about 13.6 million by 2003. The structural plan for the area favors expansion to the east and west along the national provincial road and rail corridors. Urban growth is to be restricted in the coastal plains to the north and in the uplands in the south. The plan recognizes that the metropolitan area is highly sensitive to a complex environmental cycle of water supply and disposal. It recommends a series of sectoral programs that would provide storage reservoirs to supplement groundwater reserves and dry season river flows; protect upstream rivers and drains from pollution; intercept sewer and flood drains in the lower reaches; build strong road connections between Jakarta and the subcenters of Bekasi, Tangerang, and Bogor; improve regional road networks, tollways, and intraregional rail movements; restrict passenger cars in the central area; guide land development in the growth areas; and provide many other services.

The total estimated cost of these programs under REPELITA III and IV is Rp1,508 billion. The tollways will cost an additional Rp408 billion (see table 12-3 for the sources of funds and agency responsibilities). Of the total projected investment of Rp1,916 billion, the DKI is to provide 29 percent, which includes its own share of loans and central government grants. Bank loans, donor loans, and private capital will account for 59 percent. The central government's equity will account for 9 percent, and Perusahan Air Minum water supply company cash surplus and funds from the sale or rent of industrial sites will provide a further 3 percent.

The development plan regards the present staff and management of agencies required to implement the plan as highly inadequate, particularly in the BOTABEK area (Bekasi, Tangerang, and Bogor). Two of the principal measures proposed in the plan are the development of a mortgage system for middle-income housing and the establishment of a water resources coordination organization to integrate watershed management, water resources, sewage disposal, and pollution control. The development plan also envisages yearly and five-year program budgets for capital improvements, mandatory review after five years, and revision after ten years. A separate transport subcommittee of the planning team has also been established to

Table 12-3. Financing Proposals for the JMDP Sectors in Jakarta,
1981–82 to 1988–89

Program	Total cost (billions of rupiahs)	Source of funds	Cost recovery
Water resources			
West Tarum Canal doubling	31.3	Central government DIPS plus loan to Jatiluhur Water Authority	From PAM (economic price for raw water) and from DKI (for flushing water)
Organization/study	0.4	Central government DIPS	None
Subtotal	31.7		
Water suppy			
Jakarta water supply project	64.1	Donor and government loans to PAM plus small amount of central government equity	PAM tariffs
Urgent rehabilitation (raw water improvements, leakage, survey, management improvements)	17.5	Donor and government loans to PAM	PAM tariffs
Urban betterment (standpipes, etc.)	27.7	Grants (50 percent central government, 50 percent DKI)	Only for operational costs, via standpipe tariff
Pipeline rehabilitation	14.1	PAM cash surplus	PAM tariffs (increased)
Distribution expansion	57.3	PAM cash surplus plus loans to PAM	PAM tariffs (increased)
Major expansion of water supply capacity	62.4	Loans to PAM (could be on commercial terms)	PAM tariffs (increased)
Subtotal	243.1		
Flood control and drainage			
Microdrainage	24.3	DKI	No direct cost recovery
Urban betterment, guided land development, and SILD (off-site costs)	39.2	DKI	No direct cost recovery
Macrodrainage: regular rehabilitation program	42.3	Central government DIPS initially; DKI, 50 percent of costs in 1981–82, 100 percent by 1984–85	No direct cost recovery
Macrodrainage: major improvements (ongoing programs)	70.4	Land costs, DKI; other costs, central government DIPS (grants) and donor loans	No direct cost recovery
Depok Dam	16.8	Central government DIPS (grants)	No direct cost recovery
Subtotal	193.0		

Program	Total cost (billions of rupiahs)	Source of funds	Cost recovery
Sanitation			
Pilot JSSP project	19.6	Donor loan/central government DIPS	No direct cost recovery
Urban betterment	17.0	DKI (possibly with donor loan)	No direct cost recovery
Sewerage program (Stage I, phase I)	22.0	DKI (possibly with loans)	As much as possible from beneficiaries via surcharge on water bill
Subtotal	58.6		
Solid waste			
All projects	76.0	DKI	Only where costs of local house-to-house collections are recovered by local RW/RT charges
Urban betterment (UB)			
All projects	25.7[a]	DKI via new UB implementing agency, possibly with donor loan	All or part of cost recovered through Pajak Khusus only for certain components
Guided land development (GLD)			
On-site costs	15.0	DKI via new GLD implementing agency, possibly with donor loan	Pajak Khusus to recover 60 or 100 percent of on-site costs
Off-site costs	—[b]	DKI	None
Land for community facilities	9.0	DKI	Revolving fund recovered from agency or department requiring the land
Subtotal	24.0		
Transport			
Roads	232.6	National roads, central government DIPS; all other roads, DKI	No direct cost recovery
Traffic engineering	52.2	DKI, possibly with loan for bus priority schemes	No direct cost recovery
Bus fleet	75.2	Donor and central government loans to bus companies	Fares set so as to cover operating costs; loan repayments covered either from fares or from DKI subsidy to bus companies

(Table continues on the following page.)

Table 12-3   (continued)

Program	Total cost (billions of rupiahs)	Source of funds	Cost recovery
Transport (continued)			
Bus facilities (terminals, bus-rail interchanges)	25.0	Loans to DKI or to bus and rail companies	Terminal fees; possible subsidy from DKI
Railways	212.5	Donor and central government loans to PJKA	From fares; no subsidy if possible
Tollways	407.6	Donor loans plus private capital (bonds or overseas loans)	From tolls; no subsidy
Subtotal	1,005.1		
Small-scale industry			
BIPIK (including service centers)	13.1	Central government DIPS	Credit programs should recover costs, but otherwise no cost recovery
Governor's fund	2.9	DKI	As above
Industrial estates and land development	37.7	DKI with loans from central government or donor	Rents and sales should recover costs as far as possible
KIK/KMKP programs	205.4	Commercial banks	Repayments should fully cover costs including economic rate of interest
Subtotal	259.0		

Note: JMDP = JABOTABEK Metropolitan Development Plan; DKI = Jakarta provincial government; PAM = Perusahan Air Minum water company; RW/RT = rukun warga and rukun tetangga, community organizations; SILD = staged industrial land development; BIPIK, KIK, and KMKP are acronyms for government programs to promote industry; and PJKA is the acronym for the railway organization.

a. An additional Rp112 billion for urban betterment is included under other sectors.

b. Listed under other sectors.

coordinate transport-related functions and programs. In the planning team's view, the hierarchy for planning must be closely linked with the administrative hierarchy of the JABOTABEK region. Thus it has recommended that the administrative boundaries of Tangerang and Bekasi be made contiguous with those of DKI-Jakarta. A permanent JABOTABEK metropolitan planning institution is another recommendation.

Pending Issues

Although the development plan has an extensive analytical base and contains a framework for future involvement, several important issues remain unresolved. Principal among these is the level of public investment in the

JABOTABEK region compared with the rest of the country. Excluding INPRES, which is a countrywide form of revenue sharing, central government expenditures in DKI-Jakarta have averaged 20 percent of its total development outlay even though Jakarta has only 4 percent of the country's population. Public expenditures in Jakarta—which are three to four times higher than the national average—amount to 31 percent of GDP per capita and are thus prominent in the city's economic growth. The DKI has considerable resources of its own and its per capita resources of Rp17,500 are much higher than those for other cities in the country. Yet it is becoming more and more dependent on the central government: grants to the DKI have increased from less than 25 percent of the total DKI budget in 1974–75 to more than 32 percent in 1980–81. Moreover, when all central government assistance to Jakarta is taken into account, the city's per capita share of grants is Rp13,500 compared with Rp12,000 nationally. A strong case has thus been building up for Jakarta to decrease its dependence on central funds, in part by substantially increasing its own resources.

A related issue is the considerable discrepancy between expenditures in the BOTABEK area (Rp2,000, or US$3, per capita annually) and those in the DKI (Rp10,000, or US$16, per year). The BOTABEK area has a low tax base, as do many other rural provinces, but it has been able to increase its local tax revenues faster than the DKI. Some have argued that the province with the strongest revenue base should not continue to depend on central government subsidies. Others note the problem of parity in revenue generation and expenditure within different parts of the metropolitan region.

Indonesia's official policy is to prevent or at least slow down the concentration of growth in Java in general and Jakarta in particular. Despite the attempt to guide growth farther away to the east, west, and south, large industries and upper-income housing continue to locate on the immediate periphery of the DKI. The population of the JABOTABEK region is expected to reach 20–26 million in the next twenty years. Most of the growth (which will amount to about 10–16 million persons) will be outside DKI boundaries, that is, in the BOTABEK area, but at least a quarter of a million will be added annually at the periphery of the DKI itself.

As in many other developing countries, technical skills are scarce and poorly distributed in Indonesia. In urban areas and in local governments, the distribution of the limited technical skills is a matter of concern. The DKI, for instance, has three times as many staff (of all categories) per capita as the BOTABEK area, and technical staff is in short supply in local governments. Existing staff within the JABOTABEK region therefore needs to be decentralized and better used.

Among the financial concerns is the question of what proportion of the projected increases in the central government's petroleum revenues should be made available for urban development. Sectors and agencies that have some experience in using large capital resources will be able to absorb the funds faster than sectors and agencies with services that may have a higher social priority but are less able to obtain and spend the funds. Growth and income distribution could then become more unbalanced.

If Jakarta's growth is to be sustained efficiently and equitably, priorities, planning, and the budgeting of investment must be constantly reviewed and development projects coordinated. Apart from the permanent metropolitan planning team and special intersectoral coordination bodies recommended in the JABOTABEK plan, stronger forms of metropolitan government to absorb or replace DKI-Jakarta and the BOTABEK area have also been proposed. Political and social as well as technical and administrative considerations should be taken into account in any such reorganization. The following are some of the options:

- The DKI-Jakarta boundaries could be progressively extended to incorporate the entire JABOTABEK metropolitan region as outside areas become urbanized.
- An interprovincial development authority with representation from DKI-Jakarta and West Java province could be established to handle overall planning and administration of industrial, commercial, and residential development and to provide basic infrastructure.
- A metropolitan council with representation from DKI-Jakarta, West Java province, the kabupatens of BOTABEK, and the kotamadya of Bogor could be empowered to vote funds from member governments, receive central government funds, and finance intergovernmental projects to be implemented by existing agencies.
- A special metropolitan government could be created.
- The metropolitan region could be converted into a special territory of the central government.

As in other metropolitan cities of South and East Asia, the choice between these options is likely to be determined by political rather than planning considerations.

13

Karachi

KARACHI HAS A LONG recorded history of settlement, but its rapid growth has been recent and came only after Pakistan was partitioned from India in 1947. By 1843 it was still a small town of some 14,000 people that had been developed as a port by the British for exporting the products of the Punjab. A hundred years later, the population was on the rise and approaching half a million mainly as a result of the influx brought on by the Second World War, during which Karachi was a major air base. Upon partition and independence, Karachi became Pakistan's new capital. It was also the principal destination of refugees from India.

Growth of the City

By 1951, Karachi's population had reached about 1.13 million, which represented an increase of 160 percent over the 1941 census. Pakistan's development strategy, much like that of its neighbor India, emphasized industrialization and import substitution and thus it generated high rates of rural-to-metropolitan migration. Although migration was moderated by the "green revolution" of the 1960s, together with natural growth it kept Karachi's population increasing at a rate of 4.78 percent a year between 1971 and 1981. If this trend continues, metropolitan Karachi could have close to 13 million inhabitants by the end of the century, which is more than twice the 1987 estimated population of 6 million.

Although Karachi has only 6 percent of the country's population, it plays an important role in the economy of Pakistan. It accounts for one-sixth of the country's gross domestic product, one-half of its bank deposits, and one-quarter of the federal reserves. Furthermore, it is Pakistan's only seaport; the new port of Bunder Qasim will also fall within the metropolitan area and thus will add to Karachi's national stature as the principal commercial and industrial center. It already accounts for more than 10 percent of the country's mining and manufacturing employment; 12 percent of the employment in trade, commerce, and banking; 35 percent of its large-scale manufacturing in terms of gross value added; 50 percent of its bank deposits; and 72 percent of its issued capital.

The Development Plan Report of 1974 defined metropolitan Karachi as an area covering some 349 square kilometers. Today it is ten times larger and stretches from the Dhabeji Water Works in the east to Baldia and the port in the west. This vast stretch of land along the Arabian Sea includes Pakistan's first integrated iron and steel plant at Bin Qasim, the industrial and commercial estates in Landhi and Korangi, the existing port and the new port at Bunder Qasim, the city center, and North Karachi.

Despite official attempts to contain Karachi's growth and disperse development to secondary cities, economic activities in the metropolis have been expanding steadily. Tax incentives and import duty reliefs designed to develop other centers have in fact prompted industries to set up operations at the edge of the Karachi administrative district in areas such as Hub Chowki in Baluchistan, just 24 kilometers from Karachi's center, and Dader in Sind, 80 kilometers along the Karachi-Hyderabad highway. Thus the metropolitan area now covers 3,530 square kilometers. Close to 30 percent of the population in Sind province lives in the metropolitan area in about a million holdings and some 33,000 households are added to the area annually.

Metropolitan Problems

Although close to 45 percent of all employment is concentrated in four areas—the Sind and Landhi industrial trading estates, the port, and the city center—the adjoining areas are not highly populated. In fact, more than one-quarter of the built-up area has been preempted for defense purposes and developed under cantonment boards at very low densities. About 5 square kilometers of fully or partly serviced land lies unused in the heart of the city, and infrastructure has been extended into outlying areas at great expense in response to private speculation. Labor outflows to the Middle East and remittances from the 1.25 million emigrant workers there (said to average Rs30,000 a year per worker) have been largely responsible for the speculation in land and housing. The 1970s witnessed a building boom and soaring house prices along with an increase in underpriced housing. Although approximately 80 percent of the land in the metropolitan area is publicly owned and a planning study was undertaken between 1968 and 1973 to deal with land use, Karachi has been unable to control the development of its urban land.

A large part of Karachi's housing is now situated on the periphery of the city, in sprawling informal settlements that exhibit little planning and nominal infrastructure. To add to its problems, Karachi has by far the largest squatter settlements in the province. Referred to as katchi abadis, these house about one-third of Karachi's population (about 257,000 households) in generally unsanitary conditions. In addition, the city suffers from other

Karachi.   One of the oldest settlements at the center of Karachi, the "native town" grew up near the harbor and is now the Lyari slum.

Map 13-1. Karachi Tramways, 1885

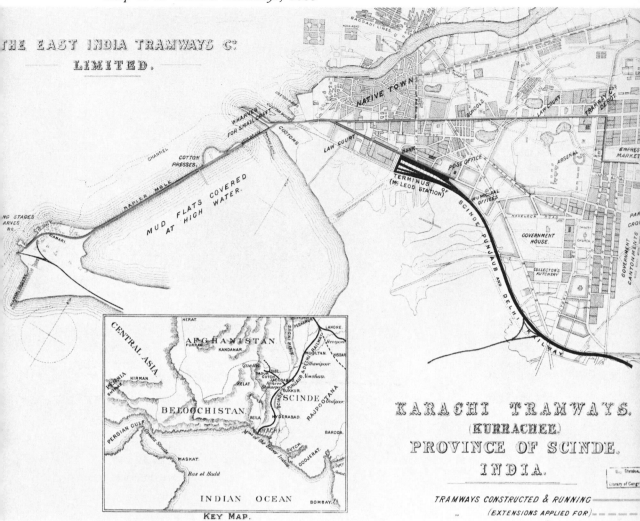

Photo: Library of Congress, Washington, D.C.

Map 13-2. Bird's-Eye View of Greater Karachi, 1951

W OF GREATER KARACHI

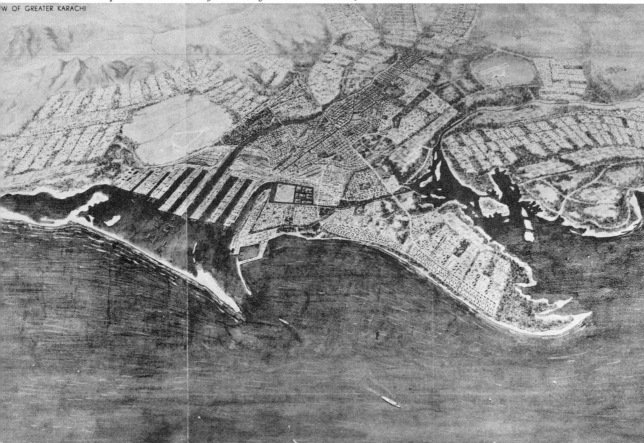

Photo by Ceyhan, courtesy of Town and Country Planning Department Library, Calcutta; from Merz Rendel Vatten
(Pakistan) Consulting and Designing Engineers, ''Report on Greater Karachi Plan''
(Stockholm, Sweden, April 1952; processed).

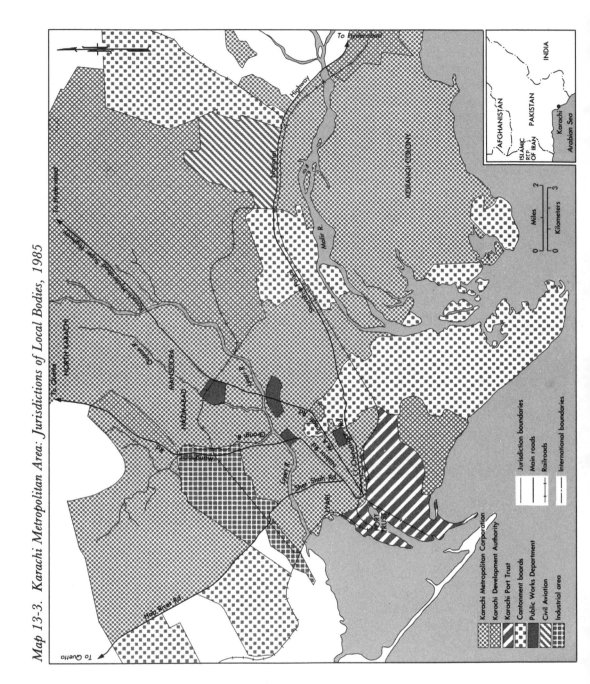

Map 13-3. Karachi Metropolitan Area: Jurisdictions of Local Bodies, 1985

common metropolitan problems. Potable water has to be brought more than 160 kilometers from the Indus and thus is available for only a few hours a day in most areas, only one-third of the households have piped water connections, and most slum-dwellers and squatters must either use public standposts or buy water from vendors at inflated prices. Nevertheless, Karachi receives more water per capita (37 gallons a day) than Hyderabad (25 gallons a day) or other towns in Sind. About 30 percent of the city proper is connected to the main sewerage system, and most of Karachi's sewerage, which is untreated, finds its way into watercourses, such as the Lyari River, which have become the repository of industrial wastes as well. With the methods used at present, only about one-third of the 4,500 tons of solid waste generated daily can be removed properly. In the area of education, only 59 percent of the population is literate, there are primary school places for only 70 percent of the eligible children, and only one-third of the secondary-school age group can be accommodated.

Structure of Government

Karachi's urban management operates through national, provincial, and local institutions. Some, such as the cantonment boards, are relatively old; others, such as the Karachi Metropolitan Corporation, are new. All bear the imprint of an eventful political history that began in 1947, when Pakistan was created through the amalgamation of several ethnic groups and regions having a shared common faith. Although religion has remained a powerful unifying force, it has not prevented deep social conflicts, the hiving off of Bangladesh, and far-reaching constitutional changes. Organs of central government were established by the First Constitution of 1956, which provided for a national assembly and two provincial assemblies (in West and East Pakistan), both elected. Under the Second Constitution of 1962, which incorporated the Basic Democracies Order of 1959 and the Municipal Administration Order of 1960, the central government retained jurisdiction over such matters as national security, planning, and economic development, but the provinces were allowed to function in fields not reserved for the central government. Furthermore, local governments were to be established to provide, administer, and maintain the basic amenities. The powers and functions of the Karachi Municipal Corporation, which had been established in 1852, were retained and amplified and its jurisdiction marginally enlarged. The Karachi Development Authority (KDA) was also established in 1962 to oversee development planning and major land and infrastructure projects.

According to the terms of its charter, the KDA was to function as an autonomous public corporation under the supervision and control of the Sind provincial government. The KDA was to provide an outline, perspective, and master plans for urban physical development; plan and install major capital works to be maintained by the Karachi Municipal Corporation; construct main highways; build new houses, urban settlements, and sites and services schemes; provide the water supply, including headworks and the primary distribution system; and control land use and building. Its governing board consists of six members headed by the divisional commissioner for Karachi and includes a director general, two full-time and two part-time members, all appointed by the provincial government.

In the wake of the political changes after the loss of East Pakistan, the Basic Democracies system was replaced by a new system of Peoples Local Governments. The constitution of 1973 officially established the provinces of the Sind, Baluchistan, North West Frontier, and the Punjab to accommodate regional demands. Although the constitution did not specify what structure local government was to have, both central and provincial governments were empowered to delegate powers and functions to subordinate authorities. Under the Sind People's Ordinance of 1972 (amended in 1976), provision was made for the establishment of the Karachi Metropolitan Corporation (KMC), which was to have an elected mayor and corporation members and was to integrate the functions of the Karachi Municipal Corporation and the Karachi Development Authority. Local elections did not take place until 1979, however, and the Metropolitan Corporation came into existence a year later with 167 elected councillors and a mayor. Its jurisdiction included most of the built-up parts of the metropolitan area, but the promised integration with the KDA did not occur.

A few years earlier, the Karachi Development Authority had been entrusted with the implementation and operation of a large water supply project based on the Indus river. Although the KDA was responsible for production and delivery in bulk, the municipality was responsible for distribution and cost recovery from the consumers. With a monopoly on the sale of bulk water supplies, the KDA had little incentive to reduce costs, and the municipality had little incentive to improve the service or recover costs. Disputes between the two organizations became frequent, and in 1981 the Karachi Water Management Board (KWMB) was created to handle distribution throughout the entire metropolitan area and to recover costs. Although the tariff structure and the distribution networks were subsequently improved somewhat, the KWMB still could not meet the dues of the KDA and had to rely on the KMC for support. A new authority, the Karachi Water Supply and Sewerage Board (KWSB) was thus established in February 1983 under a revision of the Sind Local Government Ordinance of 1979. The KWSB, organized to manage water affairs from source to tap, is now responsible for production, distribution, operation, and cost recovery. With the mayor of the KMC as its chairman, the deputy mayor, two councillors, a government of Sind appointee, and a managing director as chief executive, the KWSB is an autonomous subsidiary of the KMC.

The KMC, as a metropolitan and local agency, has replaced the former municipalities, but six cantonment boards still continue to exercise local government powers within their respective boundaries. The KDA has remained a separate public corporation under provincial control. In addition, a number of federal and provincial committees, departments, and organizations are responsible for a variety of planning, regulatory, construction, and operational functions. There are more than fifty such committees (see table 13-1) that relate directly to matters of urban planning and development. Of these, some thirty-five have suprametropolitan status, six metropolitan status, and the remainder submetropolitan or local territorial status. The situation is actually less complicated than in the other profile cities, mainly because Karachi has very few organs of local government.

No single organization is responsible for budgeting capital investment in the metropolitan area. Despite its metropolitanwide jurisdiction, the Karachi Metropolitan Corporation cannot exercise authority over the expenditures of the KDA or the many provincial and central government departments operating in the area. Nor have any formal links been forged between the investment activities of Sind and Baluchistan provinces, although the district of Lasbela in metropolitan Karachi falls under the latter's jurisdiction. There has also been no institutional means for coordinat-

Table 13-1. Main Governmental Institutions Involved in Urban Planning in Metropolitan Karachi, 1981

Status	Institution	Function
Federal	Ministry of Local Government and Rural Development	Annual perspective and development plans
	Planning Division (Physical Planning and Housing Section)	National housing policy and technical assistance for physical planning
	National Finance Commission	Intertier revenue sharing
	National Economic Council	Approves large-scale projects and grants
	Central Development Working Party	Approves medium-scale projects
	National Credit Consultative Council	Intersectoral credit allocations and loans
	House Building Finance Corporation	Small-scale soft loans to housing cooperatives
	Civil Aviation Authority	Karachi airport
	Pakistan Railways	Karachi rail system
	Ministry of Housing and Works	Federal buildings and residential estates for government servants
		Supervision of implementation of Karachi master plan
	Ministry of Defense	Jurisdiction over cantonment boards
	Karachi Electricity Supply and similar corporations	Electric supply, gas, telephones, air transport, shipping
	Water and Power Development Authority	National water and power policy
	Karachi Transport Corporation	Public sector bus company
	Karachi Port Trust	Management of port and shipping facilities

(Table continues on the following page.)

Table 13-1   (continued)

Status	Institution	Function
Provincial (Sind)	Department of Town Planning, Housing, Local Government, and Rural Development	Supervises local councils, including KMC and KDA
	Planning and Development Department	Provincial annual development programs; approves all major investment decisions and allocates intersectoral resources
	Regional Planning Organization	Provincial master plan
	Department of Public Health Engineering	Plans water, sewerage, and drainage systems outside Karachi
	Department of Industry, Transport, Mineral Development, Excise, and Taxation	Assists industrial development and provides infrastructure and services to industrial areas
	Sind Industrial Facilities Board	Coordinates facilities for industrial development
	Department of Transport and Communications	Provincial policy on transport and communications
	Sind Regional Transport Operation	Public sector transport outside Karachi
	Karachi Regional Transport Authority	Sets fares, issues licences, grants routes
	Sind Small Industries and Handicraft Development Corporation	For areas outside Karachi
	Sind State Bank	Loans to small businesses
Local	Karachi Metropolitan Corporation	Major municipal services except water
	Karachi Development Authority	Karachi planning authority; water production and treatment; sewerage and drainage infrastructure; land use development controls
	Karachi Water Supply and Sewerage Board[a]	Production, distribution, and operation of water supply
	560 cooperative housing societies	Housing projects for members
	6 cantonment boards	Local services in defense areas
	7 residential estates for government employees	Public Works Department responsible for municipal services
	2 industrial trading estates	Sind Industrial Trading Estate and Landhi Industrial Trading Estate offices

Note: Some of the provincial functions in Sind are performed by divisions (Karachi, Southern Sind, and Northern Sind), which are subunits of the province, headed by divisional commissioners.

a. Established in 1983 to replace the Karachi Water Management Board.

ing the land development activities of public agencies, although 80 percent of the land in the metropolitan area is in public ownership. The development decisions of the Metropolitan Corporation and Development Authority have been guided largely by the Karachi Metropolitan Development Plan, 1974–85, but its guidelines have not been formally accepted by the government, and no institutional arrangement has been made to ensure that other agencies conform to these guidelines.

Similar problems exist in the regulation of land use and the control of buildings. The KDA enforces zoning regulations only on a scheme-by-scheme basis, and it has been unable to prevent commercial or other nonconforming uses of land in areas zoned for residential purposes. In addition, there has been no consistency in the control exercised in areas under the jurisdiction of different public agencies. Under the Sind People's Ordinance of 1972, no clear distinction was made between the building control powers of the municipality and the KDA. In practice, the Karachi Metropolitan Corporation has accepted and administered building regulations issued by the KDA in areas that have subsequently come under the corporation's jurisdiction for operation and maintenance, whereas the KDA has continued to administer its own regulations within the areas specified in its development scheme.

Fiscal Situation

As in India, the federal government has the first call on taxable resources in Karachi, although the other two levels of government are also able to raise taxes and revenues. At the same time, the federal government is by far the largest spender at the provincial and local levels; in Karachi, for example, it is estimated to account for more than half the total public expenditure there. Moreover, federal government expenditure in Karachi increased from 49 percent to 57 percent of total public sector outlays between 1970–71 and 1977–78, whereas Sind provincial expenditure (including the expenditure of the Karachi Development Authority, which is a provincial agency) remained at 32–33 percent, and the expenditure of the Karachi Metropolitan Corporation even decreased, from 18 percent to only 11 percent (see table 13-2). In addition, financial transfers from the federal government to Sind province (mainly in the form of grants and loans) rose from 49 percent to more than 67 percent of provincial expenditure between 1970–71 and 1978–79 (table 13-3), and the province's current account deficit has grown steadily during the same decade (table 13-4). Thus, Karachi's dependence on central funding has increased even more rapidly than some figures suggest.

Several factors account for this situation. For one thing, it has been difficult to expand provincial revenue because of the narrow tax base at that level; the federal government abolished land taxes in 1979, and various tax revenues have been lost through progressive Islamization of the economy. For another, the share of property taxes devolving to local governments has

Table 13-2. Estimated Per Capita Government Expenditure in Karachi, 1970–71 and 1977–78
(rupees)

Level of government	1970–71		1977–78		Annual growth rate (percent)
	Amount	Percent	Amount	Percent	
Federal	94.1	48.9	412.9	56.7	23.5
Sind	53.3	27.7	149.1	20.5	15.8
Local					
Karachi Metropolitan Corporation	33.9	17.6	80.1	11.0	13.1
Karachi Development Authority	11.0	5.7	85.7	11.8	34.5
Total	192.3	100.0	727.8	100.0	19.6

Note: Federal estimates exclude transfers to lower levels. Local bodies in Karachi other than the Karachi Metropolitan Corporation and the Karachi Development Authority are excluded.
Source: World Bank data.

increased. Until recently, 50 percent of the property tax receipts were taken by the provincial government, but the proportion has now been reduced to 15 percent. Water rates and a number of other charges are linked to the property tax, and since property tax has not been reassessed for many years, the revenues are extremely low.

The corporation is obliged to balance its annual budget and receives no financial aid from either the federal or provincial governments. In 1978–79, more than 54 percent of its current revenues were derived from the octroi (a sales tax on goods entering Karachi), and only 8 percent from the general property tax, to which the water, conservancy, and fire taxes were linked (see table 13-5). The share from octroi rose to 56 percent in 1981–82. Maritime imports account for most of the proceeds. Although considered regressive, damaging to trade, and prone to corruption and inefficiency in collection, the octroi has been a buoyant revenue resource for many South Asian cities. Karachi is no exception.

Some 60 percent of current expenditure and 80 percent of development expenditure go into the operation, maintenance, and extension of water supply, sewerage, drainage, conservancy, fire, road, and park and recreational services. Education and health services account for 40 percent and 20 percent, respectively. In general, current expenditure has been rising much faster than development expenditure because the labor force has been expanding and unit costs increasing. Increases in service charges have lagged behind, however, and service costs have not been covered. The resulting operating deficits in water, sewerage, conservancy, and fire services have been met from general revenues instead of from designated sources (that is, linked taxes). The water account in particular has deteriorated because tariffs have not been raised since 1942, meters have been poorly maintained, and meter coverage has been inadequate. All told, these operating deficits now absorb nearly half of total revenues.

*Table 13-3. Financial Transfers from Federal Government
to Sind Provincial Goverment, 1970–71 and 1978–79*
(millions of rupees)

Type of transfer	1970–71	1978–79
Shared taxes	210.9	799.1
Current grants	2.0	320.0
Development grants	16.7	210.6
Loans	86.9	619.4
Total	645.5	1,929.1
Percentage of Sind expenditure	49.0	67.5

Source: World Bank data.

Table 13-4. Sind Government Revenue and Expenditure, 1978–79
(millions of rupees)

Revenue and expenditure	Amount	Percent
Current revenue		
Own tax	569.8	29.1
Own nontax	260.3	13.3
Shared tax	806.5	41.2
Federal grants	320.0	16.4
Total	1,956.6	100.0
Current expenditure	2,036.4	
Development expenditure	830.0	

Source: World Bank data.

*Table 13-5. Karachi Metropolitan Corporation Revenue and Expenditure,
1978–79 and 1981–82 Budgets*

Revenue and expenditure	Millions of rupees		Percent	
	1978–79	1981–82	1978–79	1981–82
Current revenue				
Octroi	200.0	410.00	54	56
General property tax	30.0	75.00	8	10
Water tax[a]	32.4	94.23	9	13
Conservancy tax[a]	20.0	28.36	5	4
Fire tax[a]	6.0	8.44	2	1
Other taxes	4.1	39.41	1	6
Nontax	76.8	75.68	21	10
Total	369.3	731.12	100	100
Current expenditure	320.5	491.80		
Development expenditure	120.8	414.05		

a. Linked to general property tax.
Source: World Bank data.

The corporation's financial difficulties can be attributed to other factors as well. Property tax assessments, for example, are based on rental values, but most rental properties are subject to rent controls; there have been no reassessments since 1969, and for a variety of reasons many properties are excluded. As a result, property tax revenue and the related water, conservancy, and fire taxes have been rising at a rate of only 9.5 percent a year, whereas the rate of inflation is up to 16 percent. Although the corporation's share of property tax revenue was increased to 85 percent in 1979–80, it still accounts for no more than 10 percent of total current revenue (as of 1981– 82). Thus, real revenue has been increasing at a rate of only 2 percent a year during the past decade. Since most of this increase has been absorbed by current expenditure, very little has been left for development works.

The Karachi Development Authority has also been experiencing financial problems, with deficits of more than Rs300 million in 1977–78 and 1978–79. These problems have been particularly severe in the area of water supply, where current expenditure exceeded current revenue by more than Rs93 million in 1978–79 and development costs amounted to a further Rs170 million (table 13-6). Arrears in receipts of water charges, which have also been rising, reached Rs244 million in June 1978. The newly created Karachi Water Supply and Sewerage Board will eventually alleviate these problems, but it, too, will face financial difficulties in connection with land development. The KDA is required to undertake such development on a break-even basis, scheme by scheme, but at the same time it must address the needs of the low-income groups. It has been unable to take advantage of rising land values and heavy demand, although it has made some small overall profits from selling plots for commercial schemes. As a result, the authority has been forced not only to underexploit one of its major assets, but also to borrow in order to finance its land development schemes. In servicing these debts, the KDA has had to divert funds from land development activities and to delay payments to creditors, such as the Sind

Table 13-6. Karachi Development Authority Revenue and Expenditure, 1978–79

Revenue and expenditure	Millions of rupees	Percent
Current revenue	255.6	100.0
Sale of water	124.0	48.6
Sale of plots	97.8	38.2
Other	33.9	13.2
Current expenditure	242.7	100.0
Water supply	92.8	38.2
Water debt servicing	124.5	51.3
Other	25.4	10.5
Development expenditure	270.8	100.0
Land development	100.5	37.1
Water capital works	170.3	62.9

Source: World Bank data.

government. The net effect has been to encourage large-scale land speculation and to deprive both local and provincial governments of an important potential source of revenue.

Response to Metropolitan Problems

In the past ten years, Karachi has endeavored to organize and reorganize its institutions in order to improve urban management. In some fields, such as water supply and sewerage, sectoral objectives have been accepted and the institutional mechanisms needed to achieve them have been established. In others, such as land and shelter, solutions have been difficult to find.

As noted earlier, since about 80 percent of the land is government owned, Karachi's position is somewhat different from that of other Asian cities. When the Karachi Improvement Trust (established in 1950) prepared plans for the redevelopment of Lyari and other slum settlements, the unprecedented scale of refugee immigration rendered these plans inappropriate and the focus shifted to developing new housing on the fringes. The KDA, which began its operations in the early 1960s, proceeded to build completed housing units. Later, it began to develop serviced sites near employment centers such as Baldia and the Korangi Industrial Estate. Between 1968 and 1974, the KDA, assisted by the UNDP, was involved in a comprehensive planning exercise, the outcome of which was the 1974–85 Karachi Development Plan. The Metroville Program was a significant component of this development plan. Introducing the new concept of utility walls for water, sewerage, and electricity connections, the plan envisaged the provision of 182,360 plots by 1985. Metroville I, which called for 4,131 plots, was implemented by 1976 at an excellent location near the Sind Industrial Trading Estate. The plots were rapidly sold, but because of delays in allocating plots, most of the allottees have held on to the land for speculation. Very few plots have been occupied and Metroville I is still an open space lying in a prime location. The experience with serviced plots in Metroville II has been similar. The 1974 plan recommended that about 150,000 such plots be developed by 1985, but about 80,000 are still unoccupied.

Unrealistically high standards have weakened Karachi's land development strategy. The minimum size of low-income plots was initially fixed at 67 square meters, but this has since been reduced to 50 square meters under the Sind Disposal of Plots Ordinance, 1970. The ordinance also laid down the procedure for allotting plots through computer ballot. Although simple and fair, it appears to put low-income families at a disadvantage because of the need for written announcements and applications and the randomness of the selection (which disregards social and ethnic mix, for example). Thus, the KDA is now operating under new concepts such as incremental land development and the redevelopment of previous army lines, established when plot sizes and standards were still lower.

In dealing with katchi abadis, Karachi, like some other Asian cities, has abandoned the demolition of these slums and instead favors their upgrading. Under Martial Law Order (MLO) 110 of 1979 (amended in 1982), the regularization (that is, the provision of a 99-year lease to squatters) and the upgrading of katchi abadis occupied before January 1978 are entrusted to local councils, which must prepare and implement schemes. The order also provides for the recovery of lease money and development charges and for the setting up of a revolving fund. A 1978 estimate indicated that about 4,000 hectares consisted of katchi abadis with a population of 1.65 million. Lyari, near the city center, was the oldest and the most populous (717,000 people) of these slum areas. An upgrading scheme for Lyari with World Bank assistance was proposed in 1976 but never signed because of cost recovery problems. In accordance with MLO 110, the KMC is now upgrading and regularizing about 10,000 katchi abadis households annually. These settlements are said to be spreading at the rate of about 120 hectares annually and the population increasing by about 200,000 persons a year. At this rate, Karachi's entire population growth is being accommodated by katchi abadis.

About 80 percent of all motor vehicles registered in Sind are in the Karachi district. Of the 209,000 motorized vehicles (as of 1981), nearly half are motorcycles and 83,000 are private cars, both of which have been increasing by 25 percent a year. As in Calcutta, private buses (about 2,100 in number) provide most of the transportation. There are also 800 state-owned buses, about 2,000 minibuses, and about 20,000 taxis and autorickshaws. Unlike Bombay, Calcutta, or Madras, Karachi does not rely on its railways for extensive public transport. The regulation of public transport and its integration with traffic and transportation development are handled by a number of agencies. The state-owned buses, for example, are run by a corporation, fares and route permits are determined by the Regional Transport Authority, and the construction of new roads has been handled largely by the KDA as part of its development scheme in the city's outskirts. It is also engaged in long-term transportation planning within the framework of the 1974 master plan. A traffic engineering bureau was set up in 1981, but the KMC retains traffic engineering responsibilities. Furthermore the Transport Commission created in late 1982 has indicated the need for a metropolitan transport authority.

Pending Issues

In March 1980, after meeting with the Karachi Metropolitan Corporation and the Karachi District Council, the president directed the Ministry of Housing and Works to explore ways of making Karachi's administration more effective. A subcommittee of experts assessed Karachi's urban problems and concluded that at least seven of these needed close attention: the deficiencies in the provision of urban services (for example, only 30 percent of the katchi abadis population and 40 percent of the remaining urban population have a direct supply of water); socioeconomic and territorial inequalities in the distribution of urban services (for example, a concentration of deficiencies in the katchi abadis); inefficiencies within local government organizations; too narrow a tax base and unfair incidence of taxation (especially the property tax); lack of machinery to implement the Karachi master plan and to enforce development standards and controls; lack of co-ordination among federal and provincial government departments, civic agencies, and autonomous authorities; and constitutional, financial, and administrative weakness in local government, which lacks constitutional support and adequate sources of revenue.

The subcommittee proposed the following responses to these problems: a massive financial investment in infrastructure and social services; a more logical and equitable allocation of functions and resources between provincial and local government; the integration of major sectoral functions at the metropolitan level and decentralization of minor functions to the submetropolitan or local levels; and changes in the systems and procedures of civic organizations.

Accordingly, the following institutional changes were proposed:

- Karachi Metropolitan Corporation's jurisdiction should be extended to the entire metropolitan area; the Karachi Development Authority and Water Management Board should function as subsidiaries of the KMC. According to the subcommittee, this would effectively integrate metropolitan development planning and implementation, on the one hand, and operation, maintenance, and control, on the other.
- Eight zonal municipalities should be established with elected committees, and chairmen who are ex officio members of the corporation. They should be made responsible for local urban services, such as public health, and should enjoy certain local taxing powers; disparities in per capita revenues could be offset by equalization grants.
- The corporation should become the metropolitan planning authority for the cantonment board areas by virtue of its control over the Karachi Development Authority, and should become responsible for the collection of the octroi.
- Proper accounting procedures, improved working terms and conditions, effective staff training, and reform of organizational and departmental procedures should be introduced.
- The corporation should prepare five-year development plans for the metropolitan area, and the zonal municipalities should do the same for each of their submetropolitan areas.

In addition, the subcommittee proposed that the federal government should provide a mass transit system; provide the corporation with financial aid for the improvement of katchi abadis, and low-cost resettlement schemes; and finance, by means of grants, water supply and sewerage development projects and thereby permit service charges to reflect only the costs of operation and maintenance. At the same time, the Sind provincial government would transfer the administration and financing of all primary education to the corporation; would also transfer the entire property, betterment, capital gains, motor vehicle, and profession taxes to the corporation; and would strengthen the legal foundations of local government. To coordinate the activities of all three levels of government in the metropolitan area it was also recommended that an intergovernmental coordination council be established, with the governor or chief minister of Sind as president and the mayor as deputy president.

Part of the proposal dealing with water supply and sewerage has been implemented with the establishment of the Karachi Water and Sewerage Board as a subsidiary of the KMC, but the recommendation that the KDA be subordinated to the KMC is still under consideration. Although the proposal endorsed by the World Bank is intended to integrate metropolitan development planning, control, and implementation with maintenance functions under one authority, it appears to continue to rely on a simplistic command-type approach to institution building. The creation of the KDA itself was a hybrid attempt to unify the functions of metropolitan planning, implementation, and regulatory control, with almost exclusive emphasis on the physical aspects of development. At the same time, it was made responsible for the bulk supply of water. These incompatible functions in fact demanded contrasting clusters of activities, organizations, personnel, and procedures. Apparently it is now being recommended that the Karachi Metropolitan Corporation compound the errors thus made in institution building. As an alternative, it could be argued that the metropolitanwide planning functions (social and economic, as well as physical) should be undertaken on an advisory basis by the proposed coordination council, which could also advise the federal and provincial governments on the crucial questions of budgeting and the allocation of resources for related metropolitan development. The corporation could then confine its activities to the implementation of development projects allotted to it (the work would be done mainly by its subsidiaries, the Development Authority and Water Board), to the operation and maintenance of essential metropolitan services, and to regulatory activities (including town planning and physical development).

It is also not clear whether a massive infusion of financial investment is an appropriate response to the existing service deficiencies. Although it is true that in most Asian metropolitan cities the tax base is by and large exploited by federal and provincial governments, the resources mobilized at the city level are not insignificant. A 1977 study of municipal finances indicated that the assessment values of all properties in Karachi amounted to less than one-third of their market value. As much as 55 percent of taxable properties were not taxed at all for various reasons. As a result, property taxes account for less than 15 percent of the city's total receipts, which is well below the amount collected in many other cities in Asia. Rates and fees have not been charged for fifteen to twenty years, and more than one-quarter of the population pay nothing, directly or indirectly, for water received. The proposed transfer of betterment, capital gains, and motor vehicle and profession taxes would also require detailed consideration of the implications for provincial finances.

In the past two decades, Karachi has taken several steps to reorganize its metropolitan institutions and their functions. As in Calcutta, the steps taken in Karachi toward upgrading slums and providing serviced sites represent pioneering initiatives. The creation of the Metropolitan Water and Sewerage Board has been a major reform and the establishment of the Metropolitan Corporation a significant step toward local public participation in city government. The problem of providing and sustaining basic services in a rapidly expanding metropolis thus continues to be mainly financial in character, rather than institutional.

14

Madras

MADRAS, THE CAPITAL of the state of Tamil Nadu and the largest city in southern India, originated as a group of fishing villages, which in 1639 became a trading post of the British East India Company. Since then, commerce has played a central role in the city's economic and social development. By 1791, Madras had emerged as one of the subcontinent's principal commercial ports, and today it shares the greater part of India's external trade with Calcutta and Bombay.

Growth of the City

During the 1800s, manufacturing commenced in the area, and by 1900 the city could boast a sizable textile mill, a number of engineering industries, and the first railway workshop. Its status as a provincial headquarters was an additional stimulus to growth, so that by 1911 the urban population had increased to some 500,000. The city's emergence as a seat of higher education helped to bring about further growth in the 1930s. Most of the industrial growth in Madras came after independence, however, with the shift in national policies, such as equalization in the shipping charges for coal and steel, which kept prices more or less the same in different parts of the country. Between 1951 and 1961, about 29,000 factory jobs were added in Madras City alone. The establishment of large automobile industries was soon followed by the arrival of numerous ancillaries. A refinery and fertilizer plant were also attracted to the port. Between 1961 and 1971 manufacturing increased by a further 36 percent, and the secondary and tertiary sectors expanded by an even greater amount. By the 1960s, the suburbs had expanded and the rural fringes had become industrialized.

The Madras Metropolitan Area (MMA) now covers about 1,167 square kilometers and takes in the city of Madras, four municipalities, four townships, and twenty semiurban local authorities. The city proper (which has

Madras.   Anna Salai, formerly Mount Road, is the principal corridor to the suburbs in the south, and most business offices are located along it. Highrise buildings are a recent phenomenon and there are only a few.

Map 14-1. Growth of Madras, 1733–1964

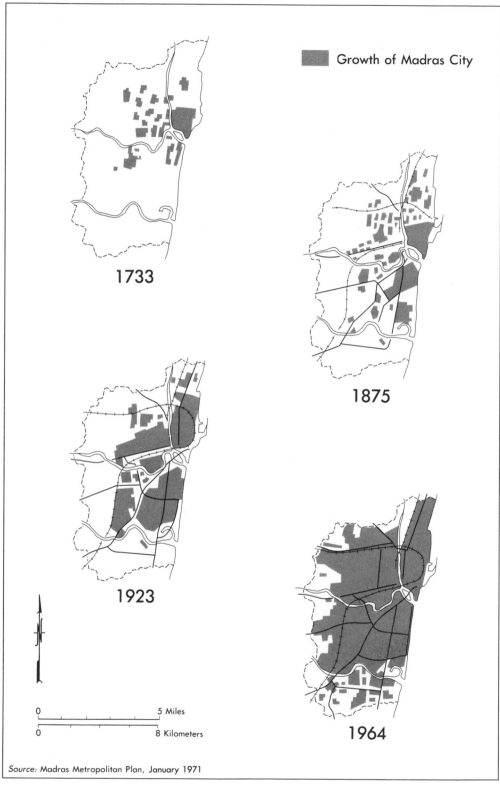

Growth of Madras City

1733

1875

1923

1964

0 ——————— 5 Miles

0 ——————— 8 Kilometers

Source: Madras Metropolitan Plan, January 1971

Map 14-2. Madras, 1764

Photo: Library of Congress, Washington, D.C., from S. Bellin, *Le Petit Atlas Maritime* (1764).

Map 14-3. Madras Urban Area, 1984

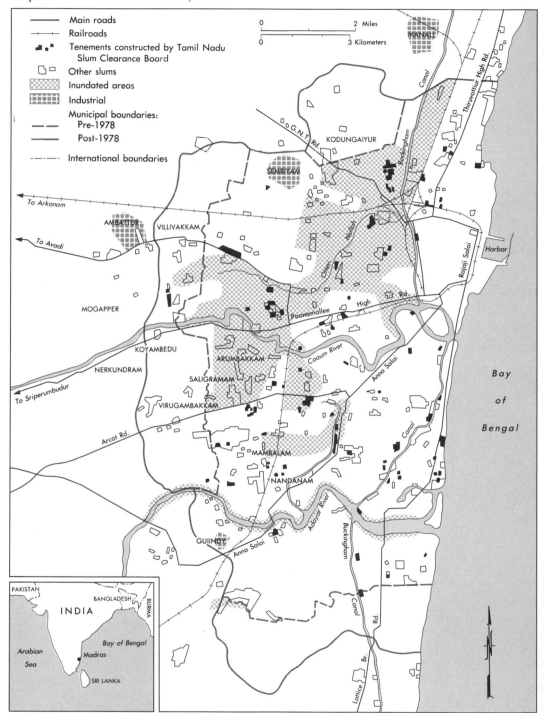

an area of about 150 square kilometers) is the center for all commercial and social activities and is also the home of two-thirds of the metropolitan population of 5.14 million. The MMA is the fourth most populous urban agglomeration in India. During 1961–71, it had the highest annual population growth (about 5 percent) among all the metropolitan centers in the country; about 43 percent of this growth was due to migration.

Today Madras is the trade and commercial center of southern India and contains the fourth largest port in the country. In 1978 more than 56 percent of the income of the MMA was derived from the tertiary sector (estimated at Rs2,954 million, or US$354.4 million); the secondary sector accounted for nearly 39 percent (Rs1,971 million, or US$236.5 million) and (as of 1971) for 130,000 jobs. Unregistered small-scale industrial units accounted for 30,000 jobs (23 percent), and registered large-scale machinery, transport, rubber, and chemical industries together accounted for nearly 90,000 jobs (69 percent), as well as for 80 percent of the value added. By contrast, nonmanufacturing employment provided 503,000 jobs (as of 1971), of which services accounted for 190,000. The fastest-growing sectors with respect to employment were transportation, storage, and retail trade.

Metropolitan Problems

The location of Madras, like that of many other Asian cities, was not an ideal site for urban development. Four rivers flow through metropolitan Madras, three from west to east and one from south to north. Its low-lying flat terrain is also studded with canals and many chains of water tanks. Flooding is widespread during the monsoon season from October to December each year, especially along the rivers, canals, and tanks. Despite the heavy rainfall, however, there is a severe shortage of potable water. The estimated reliable yield of water from all sources is about 290 million liters a day, which is less than half of the supply needed.

The core of the present water distribution system was built in 1911, but the population it was designed for was exceeded thirty years ago. Moreover, 40 percent of the system is more than fifty years old. The lack of clean water for both domestic consumption and industrial use is now the most critical problem facing metropolitan planners. Only 2 million of the 3.7 million residential consumers within the service area of the Madras Metropolitan Water Supply and Sewerage Board (MMWSSB) are connected to the system. They receive some 36 liters per capita daily, whereas the desirable level would be 180 liters. The remainder must use public taps, which serve about 240 persons per tap. Another million consumers outside the service area must rely on wells, but the supply there, too, is less than adequate because of falling groundwater levels. In 1969, 1975, and again in 1983, Madras suffered severe water shortages and drastic rationing. Even schools had to close because of the shortages. Although the overall volume of water supplies throughout the country had doubled between 1931–32 and 1968–69, the problem in Madras was more severe than in any other large city in the nation.

Sewerage facilities are also inadequate. Only 75 percent of Madras City itself has such facilities, and the system serves no more than 1.6 million people, or 31 percent of the metropolitan population. Furthermore, raw sewage flows freely into the Metropolitan Area's natural watercourses at many points. Inadequate shelter is another great problem. More than three-quarters of the population live in slums (30 percent) and substandard housing (47 percent), and the natural increase in population alone raises the demand for housing by 30,000–40,000 dwelling units a year. Until recently, however, no more than 8,000 units a year could be produced. Thus, little could be done about the backlog of slums and substandard housing, and some 22,000–32,000 families had to be absorbed by the existing inadequate stock or by informal housing. Furthermore, the housing program tended to serve mainly middle-income groups and thus did little to check the growth of the slums.

Buses provide the principal means of public transport (they account for 42 percent of total trips), and between 1965–66 and 1975–76 daily bus traffic in the Metropolitan Area rose from 762,000 to 1,693,000 passengers. The average annual increase in ridership is estimated to be greater than 7 percent. Overcrowding of buses, particularly at peak hours, is thus a serious problem, as is the lack of depot and terminal facilities. Suburban trains—which carried 11 percent of the volume of passengers in 1970—are also greatly overcrowded during peak hours, and the road network is incomplete, congested with hazardous bicycle traffic, and poorly maintained. Public authorities have been able to improve the bus fleet and traffic in recent years, however, and have managed to prevent services from deteriorating further.

Other essential services failing to respond adequately to the metropolitan challenge include power supplies, solid waste disposal, and public health and education. A common problem is the lack of financial resources needed to operate and maintain these services, let alone improve them. In 1978, per capita income in the Metropolitan Area averaged about Rs1,103 (US$132.4), but the monthly income of more than 46 percent of all households was less than Rs350 (US$41) and could not begin to pay for standard essential services. Moreover, although employment grew by about 45 percent between 1970 and 1980, most of this growth took place in the small-scale informal sector and was accompanied by a great deal of marginal employment and underemployment. Formal sector employment has experienced very little growth in recent years, and increases in income generation have depended mainly on crafts and unorganized industry. The gap between the demand for and supply of services has thus been widening.

Structure of Government

In Madras, as in other metropolitan cities, several levels of government are involved in metropolitan planning and development, from the national and state levels through the metropolitan, submetropolitan, and village levels. The Madras Metropolitan Area as delineated in the 1967 Interim Plan covered the area under the jurisdiction of the Madras Corporation (MC), four municipalities, four townships, twenty semiurban areas, and several urbanizing villages. A more elaborate Madras Metropolitan Plan for 1971–91 published by the Tamil Nadu government early in 1971 projected a population of 5 million by 1991, of which 3 million would be accommodated in the MC area and the rest in existing and new nodes of growth expected to form a radial pattern along the principal corridors of movement. The plan also envisaged the building of three new towns outside the Metropolitan Area that would be linked to the corridors. In 1973, the Madras Metropolitan Development Authority was established by statute to interpret and implement the plan.

The responsibility for the execution of development projects and operation of urban services rests with more than fifty governmental, parastatal, and municipal organizations (see table 14-1). The Madras Corporation, set up in 1919, is one of the oldest city governments in the country. Its primary functions are to develop and maintain infrastructure facilities, including roads, drainage, street lighting, and solid waste disposal. It also maintains public health, elementary education, and parks and playground facilities. The corporation has normally been governed by a council of 120 elected members, but it has been administered by a state-appointed special officer since 1974. The commissioner who is executive head of the corporation is also appointed by the state government. In 1977, responsibility for water supply and sewerage was transferred from the corporation to the Madras Metropolitan Water Supply and Sewerage Board.

By law, the corporation is required to raise sufficient resources to meet current costs, including the cost of debt servicing and of operating and maintaining services. Property and entertainment taxes constitute the main tax revenues. The corporation also receives grants and subsidies from the state government for education, health, and family planning services. Capital expenditure is financed by loans from the state government and to a limited extent from financial institutions. Until 1976–77, the corporation consistently incurred annual deficits on its current account, mainly as a result of deficits in water supply, drainage, and education services, where revenues covered only 75 percent of the costs. As a result, expenditure on other services such as road maintenance, public health, and conservancy services decreased in real terms.

The other municipal and nonmunicipal authorities in the Metropolitan Area are concerned with local roads, street lighting, conservancy, drainage, and the like, but most new investment is undertaken by state government departments and enterprises. The departments of Public Works, Highways and Rural Works, Education and Health, and Social Welfare are the principal state agencies responsible for the development and administration of the principal urban services. In addition, however, a host of parastatal organizations have special metropolitan functions. The Tamil Nadu Housing Board, established in 1961, is probably the oldest to be involved in urban development. It operates programs throughout the state,

Table 14-1. Madras Metropolitan Area Institutions, 1978

Departments and directorates of the state and central governments concerned with infra-
    structure planning and investment activities in the Metropolitan Area
  Defense Ministry (defense cantonments, factories, and townships)
  Posts and Telegraphs
  Civil Aviation
  Telephones
  Port Trust
  Railways (long distance and suburban)
  Fisheries
  Social Welfare
  School Education
  Tamil Nadu Dairy Development Corporation (milk supply)
  Tamil Nadu Small Industries Corporation (industrial estates)

Statutory entities with specific functions of planning or control for the Metropolitan Area
    or a large part of it
  Madras Metropolitan Development Authority
  Directorate of Public Health
  Inspectorate of Factories
  Police Department
  Regional Transport Authority
  Labor Department
  Fire Services Department
  Civil Aviation Department

Statutory bodies or utilities with statewide or larger jurisdiction, also functioning in the
    Metropolitan Area
  Tamil Nadu Housing Board
  Tamil Nadu Water Supply and Drainage Board
  Electricity Board
  Pallavan Transport Corporation
  Town and Country Planning Board

Statutory bodies with metropolitan or local jurisdiction
  Madras Metropolitan Development Authority
  Madras Metropolitan Water Supply and Sewerage Board
  Slum Clearance Board
  Madras City Municipal Corporation
  4 municipalities
  4 townships
  16 town panchayats

Source: Abhijit Datta and others, ''Organization Framework for Metropolitan Planning and Development, Preliminary Report: City Surveys'' (New Delhi: Indian Institute of Public Administration;
Calcutta: Indian Institute of Management, June 1978), pp. 60–61.

and in the Metropolitan Area it has carried out a number of housing and
land development schemes, including sites and services for low-income
families. The Tamil Nadu Slum Clearance Board, established in 1971,
took over all activities for slum improvement and clearance of resettlement
within the city of Madras from the Housing Board. The Pallavan Transport Corporation (PTC), incorporated in 1972 as a public sector company,

operates all local and long-distance bus services to and from Madras, and its metropolitan wing is responsible for services within the Metropolitan Area. Although the corporation is semiautonomous, the state government exercises substantial control over its budget, including fares and borrowings. The Tamil Nadu Electricity Board, another parastatal organization, is responsible for the generation and distribution of electricity in the state, including the Metropolitan Area. The Small Industry Development Corporation is still another government enterprise that serves the metropolitan area; it provides technical and marketing services to small-scale entrepreneurs, procures and distributes essential raw materials, and makes available machinery, workshops, and financial support.

In the field of planning and monitoring metropolitan development, however, the most significant institution is undoubtedly the Madras Metropolitan Development Authority (MMDA). As outlined in the Tamil Nadu Town and Country Planning Act, 1972, the MMDA's functions are to carry out surveys of the Metropolitan Area; prepare master plans, detailed development plans, and new town development plans for the area; prepare land use maps and other maps needed for development plans; ensure that the works contemplated in development plans are carried out; designate the whole or any part of the Metropolitan Area as a new town and prepare development plans for the area concerned, develop the new town as planned, and perform any other function entrusted to it by the government; and entrust to any local or other authority, by order, the execution of the development plans prepared.

The MMDA is headed by the ministers of the Department of Town and Country Planning (chairman) and the Department of Local Administration (vice-chairman), and its members are representatives of the state departments of Finance, Transport, Industries, Public Works, Local Administration, and Town Planning and of the Madras Corporation, Housing Board, Slum Clearance Board, Water Supply and Drainage Board, and the state legislature. It also has an advisory council made up of representatives of various professions and both the private and public sectors. Its chief executive is a senior state administrator.

Although its principal function is to oversee land and urban development planning, since 1977 the MMDA has also been entrusted with supervising the execution of multisectoral programs or urban development projects sponsored by the World Bank. It is not responsible for the actual routing of funds to the various agencies concerned, nor does it exercise any administrative control over them. However, in supervising the programs of many sectors and agencies, the MMDA has been able to promote metropolitan management and improve the financial administration of the agencies.

Fiscal Situation

In contrast to Calcutta, where infrastructure received little investment before the CMDA program was launched in 1970, the Madras Metropolitan

Area has been receiving a modest outlay for improvements from the Tamil Nadu government for several years. Before 1970–71, annual investment averaged about Rs100 million. Between 1970–71 and 1976–77, the amount ranged from Rs180 million to Rs220 million. With the start of the World Bank–financed program, it rose to Rs300 million in 1977–78 and to about Rs920 million in 1981–82. Even so, the investment in the Metropolitan Area accounted for only about 13 percent of the total infrastructure investment in the state during the five-year period. Transport and communication (that is, road networks and the bus fleet) accounted for one-quarter of this investment, which in turn facilitated the expansion of the urban area. Water supply and housing each accounted for about 15 percent. Close to 40 percent of the investment was incurred by the state government and 44 percent by state agencies such as the Water Board, Housing Board, and Transport Corporation, whereas the Madras Corporation accounted for only 9.5 percent.

Whereas the state departments are funded through the five-year plan, the functional agencies are financed mainly through loans from national and other institutions. The Housing Board, for example, is the largest borrower from the national Housing and Urban Development Corporation. The MMDA itself does not have any significant source of revenue other than a small development cess (a surcharge on municipal taxes) and contributions by local authorities. Since the schemes are funded individually by the state departments concerned, the concept of a metropolitan fund has not yet taken shape.

The Madras Corporation is the most important of the local authorities. In 1979–80 its annual revenue was about Rs204.5 million, of which government grants accounted for only Rs12.3 million. Its main sources of revenue are local taxes, including a property tax, profession tax, and other small taxes. The revenue from nontaxes contributes only about 14 percent of its total income. The corporation has been incurring deficits for several years, mainly because of the deficits in water supply, drainage, education, and other services (see tables 14-2, 14-3). Revenues in these sectors have covered only about 75 percent of the costs in recent years. Since 1978, water and sewerage revenues have been allocated to the MWSSB. Property taxes, which are the corporation's principal source of revenue, have declined owing to underassessment and poor collection. The local authorities as a whole raise about 70 percent of their revenues from their own tax resources and depend on revenues assigned by the state government and grants-in-aid for the remaining 30 percent. The state government also controls their borrowing powers, by way of both debentures and loans from financial institutions. Local authorities receive no revenue transfers from the national government, except in the case of certain national programs, such as the family planning program, or schemes of a specific nature, such as supplementary feeding. Thus, neither the Madras Corporation nor the other local authorities have a significant role in capital or revenue expenditure in the Metropolitan Area.

Table 14-2. Revenue of Madras Corporation, 1976–77 to 1979–80
(100,000 rupees)

Source of revenue	1976–77	1977–78	1978–79	1979–80
Taxes				
Property tax	1,213	1,148	1,400	1,450
General	552	483	611	632
Water	64	62	76	79
Drainage	235	229	280	290
Sewerage	149	146	178	185
Education	213	228	255	264
Entertainment tax	324	345	325	325
Duty on transfer of property	41	13	72	72
Other	94	150	148	148
Subtotal	1,672	1,656	1,945	1,995
To MMWSSB[a]	—	—	– 295	– 351
Total tax revenue	1,672	1,656	1,650	1,644
Nontax revenue				
License fee	44	45	49	49
Excess water charges	62	68	7	n.a.
Rents on land and buildings	9	10	9	9
Revenue from investments and deposits	41	32	34	25
Other	101	108	319	195
Subtotal	257	263	418	278
Government grants				
Education	29	35	38	65
Compensation for loss of tolls	4	4	4	4
Health and family planning programs	15	2	14	54
Other	n.a.	1	1	n.a.
Subtotal	48	42	57	123
Total current revenue	1,977	1,961	2,125	2,045

— Not applicable.

n.a. Not available.

Note: Revised estimates for 1978–79; budget estimates for 1979–80.

a. Water and drainage tax to be transferred to the Madras Metropolitan Water Supply and Sewerage Board.

Source: Madras Corporation.

Response to Metropolitan Problems

Given the background of the Madras Metropolitan Plan exercise of 1971, it is not surprising that at first the MMDA concentrated on land use planning. When entrusted with the task of assembling a multisectoral project for World Bank assistance, however, it began to expand its activities into development programming and administration. Almost immediately, it had to contend with an array of state government departments and func-

Table 14-3. Madras Corporation Revenue and Capital Expenditure,
1976–77 to 1979–80
(100,000 rupees)

Expenditure	1976–77[a]	1977–78[a]	1978–79[a]	1979–80[a]
Revenue expenditure				
Management	157	178	232	232
Education	83	95	116	123
Communications	133	140	148	153
Mechanical engineering	146	177	236	235
Public health and conservancy	501	516	614	643
Lighting	103	118	145	148
Water supply	133	161	63	7
Sewerage	140	165	72	16
Remunerative enterprises	11	12	16	14
Debt service	375	296	317	309
Other expenses[a]	11	23	34	95
Total	1,793	1,881	1,993	1,975
Capital expenditure				
Public health	108	27	80	114
Communications	256	211	596	275
Lighting	45	4	19	42
Water supply and sewerage	375	437	80	23
Remunerative enterprises	183	2	5	18
Town planning	2	n.a.	3	3
Education	36	n.a.	8	10
General	8	1	10	19
Total	1,013	682	801	504
Current account				
Surplus (deficit)[b]	(136)	38	75	(53)
Debt service as percentage of self-generated revenues	19.4	15.4	15.3	16.1

n.a. Not available.
Note: Revised estimates for 1977–78 and 1978–79; budget estimate for 1979–80.
a. Mainly Town Planning and Building Department.
b. Total self-generated revenue minus total revenue expenditure.
Source: Madras Corporation.

tional agencies with a proven record in formulating and implementing sectoral projects. The MMDA's principal task was therefore to relate the sectoral projects to an overall strategy, integrate them in a time-bound program, and monitor their progress. The first Madras Urban Development Project (which was expected to cost Rs540 million) included the following components: sites and services for about 13,500 low-income households in three locations and slum improvement to benefit some 30,000 households; serviced sites, workshops, loans, and training for small-scale business to create 9,000 jobs; priority rehabilitation of the citywide water supply and sewerage systems; citywide traffic and transport improvements; and strengthening of development planning, capital programming, project monitoring and evaluation, and municipal administration and finance, within the MMDA and Madras Corporation.

Following this approach, the MMDA's work program for 1978 and 1979 envisaged:

- Monitoring and evaluation of the implementation of the Madras Urban Development Project
- Review of the existing investment programs and policies in the main sectors to determine their appropriateness and financial implications for the state government and the various local bodies
- Review of local government finances in the Metropolitan Area and advice and assistance in augmenting financial resources
- Preparation of a ten-year indicative development program for the Metropolitan Area, including a capital budget for the next five years, analysis of the financial implications of the proposed program for the state government and the various local bodies, and further proposals for generating the requisite resources, and
- Continued work on land use planning for the Metropolitan Area.

A 1980 review concluded that the project was progressing well and had demonstrated the overall feasibility of its basic objectives and the effectiveness of its design. Implementation of physical works was proceeding roughly on schedule. By 1982, 60 percent of the serviced sites were marketed, improvements had been made to 25,000 slum households, all industrial sites and workshops had been allotted, the bus fleet had been augmented, and traffic engineering projects had been completed. Although the overall physical progress confirmed that sectoral agencies were capable of managing construction, problems persisted in other areas, such as the granting of legal land tenure, collection of charges from slum households for improvement and maintenance, conclusion of lease agreements for serviced sites, improvements in accounting practices and financial management of the Madras Corporation, and capital budgeting for the Metropolitan Area. The most sweeping organizational change was brought about with the establishment of the Metropolitan Water Supply and Sewerage Board in 1978. The responsibilities and staff for the Metropolitan Area, hitherto belonging to the Madras Corporation, the Groundwater Directorate of the state Public Works Department, and the state Water Board were transferred to the MWSSB.

Early in 1981, encouraged by the physical progress and seeking to strengthen the programming and management processes, authorities launched a second Madras Urban Development Project at an estimated cost of Rs740 million with World Bank assistance. Its main goals were to add another 15,000 sites and services plots, improve slum areas populated by 50,000 families, augment bus transport with 555 buses, bus workshops, and depots, provide loans for infrastructure and machinery for small industries, and improve solid waste management. Technical assistance and training for project identification, preparation, and appraisal and investment programming, especially in the MMDA, were additional goals.

Experience to date has demonstrated once again the ability of the sectoral agencies to complete physical works and the ability of the MMDA to resolve problems of interagency coordination in works management. With respect to sectoral investment, this project, like the earlier one, sought to achieve extensive changes in shelter and public transport. The first project succeeded in this regard, whereas the second met with considerable problems in recovering costs. As for the MMDA itself, its capacity as an institution for programming, policy planning, and evaluation has yet to be demonstrated.

Pending Issues

The functions assigned to the MMDA under the Madras Urban Development Project were intended to modify the organization's traditional role as a land use planning agency and give it a central position in metropolitan management. Apart from monitoring the project itself, its main functions were to review existing sectoral programs, reform local government finances, and prepare a capital budget for the Metropolitan Area. The experience with two sectors—housing and public transport—will illustrate both the opportunities and limitations in this regard.

The 1971 census estimated a deficit of about 140,000 houses in the Metropolitan Area. In addition, about 21 percent of the existing housing was classified as *kutcha*, or temporary huts without basic services. It was estimated that each year from 30,000 to 35,000 houses would be needed to meet the anticipated population increases. The Tamil Nadu Housing Board established in 1961 was one of the first organizations in the country to construct housing and provide serviced land on a large scale. Its housing units tended to be expensive, however. The average cost of the cheapest housing unit for the economically weaker sections (officially defined as households with monthly incomes of Rs350 or less) was about Rs12,000, which was about three times the affordable price. By 1975, the Housing Board had completed more than 25,000 housing units and 50,000 serviced housing sites, mainly in the Metropolitan Area and its surroundings, intended principally for middle-income households. The output was obviously far below the need, and inevitably slum population increased. The Tamil Nadu Slum Clearance Board established in 1971 began a major program of replacing slum huts by storied tenements. Although the board was prompt in completing the tenements, allotting them, and shifting slum households to the new units, annual production was only about 4,000 units.

The shelter component of the Urban Development Project was therefore designed to provide serviced sites to low-income families on a large scale as well as basic services to existing slum households. Both the Housing Board and the Slum Clearance Board were expected to redirect their investment accordingly. The proportion of the Housing Board's investment in housing and sites for economically weaker sections was to increase from zero percent in 1976–77 to 20 percent in 1978–79 and 45 percent in 1982–83, by which time the board would be catering to 6,000 such households annually. The Slum Clearance Board was to limit its tenement program to households in areas that could not be improved or that were required for other projects and was to redirect its allocations to slum improvement. These changes were expected to provide housing for about 22,000 families in the economically weaker sections, which would be sufficient to begin reducing the number of households in unserviced slums to only 10 percent of the total population by 1991. One of the main justifications for the proposed program shifts was that without them about one-third of the Metropolitan Area's population would be living in unserviced huts. Accordingly, the shifts were agreed to as part of the loan agreement for the project. Encouraged by its success, the Housing Board drew up a ten-year program that was to provide upwards of 100,000 plots or units primarily for low-income and economically weaker groups from 1982 to 1987. A March 1984 review of performance indicated that by 1985 the supply of serviced sites, in both the public and private sectors, and the pace of improvements to slum households would, for the first time, slightly exceed the demand for 30,000 units annually. Although the MMDA was deeply involved in reshaping the shelter strategy, the Housing Board has proved its competence in meeting the physical goals.

The outcome with respect to the transport component of the project has been quite different. As noted earlier, nearly half the transit trips in the Metropolitan Area are by bus. Under the first Urban Development Project, the bus fleet was to be increased by 285 buses; the second project envisaged a further addition of 550, and 200 more were to be purchased by the bus company from its own funds. The expansion of depot, communication, and workshop facilities was to be another component of the project. The Pallavan Transport Corporation (PTC) had already demonstrated its efficiency in operating and maintaining the existing fleet. It was able to bring down the ratio of its operating costs to revenues from 1.12 in 1975–76 to 0.98 in 1978–79. Its staff ratio of nine per bus was also one of the lowest in the country. In the next year, however, the operating ratio just exceeded 1. Improvements in efficiency could no longer compensate for the large increases in fuel, maintenance, and other operating costs since the last fare increase in 1976. As part of the project negotiations, the Tamil Nadu government agreed to the World Bank's proposal for fare increases and a revision of capital structure. The operating ratio was to be kept at a maximum of 0.95. Between 1980 and 1983, as the PTC endeavored to keep up its efficient record and even reduced the staffing ratio to 7.5, action on the stipulated fare increases and reimbursement of subsidized student fares were less than what was needed. In March 1983, the operating ratio rose to 1.09, the PTC ran into serious financial difficulties, and the World Bank threatened to suspend payments. At the time of writing, a revised action program has been agreed upon and the suspension has been lifted.

The PTC experience clearly illustrates both the opportunities and the limitations of a project as an instrument for policy change. The MMDA's role of sectoral review and program coordination could not help secure the project objectives. The experience also illustrates the basically political nature of policy and program shifts and the ineffectiveness of a metropolitan planning or development group such as the MMDA in this type of situation.

From the standpoint of metropolitan management, another important issue still pending may well be the consolidation of the Madras Metropolitan Development Authority's de facto role and the reorganization of local government. With the reorientation of its objectives from emphasis on physical planning and land use control toward emphasis on the preparation, programming, and coordination of urban development projects, the MMDA has already begun to tackle one of the basic issues still facing urban management in other metropolitan complexes. Unlike its counterparts in Calcutta and Bombay, for instance, the MMDA has resisted the temptations and pressures to assume responsibility for the actual execution of projects. It continues to be involved in the development of a new town and in the application of land use controls, however, because of statutory requirements of the Town and Country Planning Act. In these respects, therefore, it is still a hybrid institution. Indeed, the reorientation of its objectives appears to have been fortuitous in that it coincided with the preparation of the first Urban Development Project.

Although the MMDA is controlled by the state Department of Housing and Urban Development, which is responsible for the application of the Town and Country Planning Act, it undertakes nonstatutory capital budgeting and monitoring tasks for the Metropolitan Area on behalf of the Finance Department. From the standpoint of urban management, the MMDA's nonstatutory functions are possibly the more crucial, and for long-run effectiveness they need to be consolidated and given the stamp of authority. Up to now, the MMDA has exercised these functions only by means of discussion and persuasion. It has greatly depended on the consistent support of the state government, and in particular on the willingness of the Finance Department to act on the MMDA's advice in allocating funds to executing agencies. In turn, this support has been influenced by the requirements of the World Bank and its endorsement of the MMDA's role in the urban development programs.

In the long run, another issue that will have to be tackled is the role of local government institutions in metropolitan development. Overwhelmingly, metropolitan priorities are currently being set by the Tamil Nadu government on the advice of a technoadministrative institution (the MMDA) appointed by itself and in consultation either with its own ministries or with other technoadministrative institutions also appointed by itself. The MMDA consists of seventeen members, of whom only one—the commissioner of the Madras Corporation—represents local government, and he too is a state-appointed administrative official. Its advisory council consists of twenty-seven members, only five of whom can be elected representatives of local government. In both cases, the vast majority of the members are state-appointed officials, and they are seldom involved in the decisionmaking process of institutions that are traditionally supposed to act as the eyes and ears of local communities. If the reasons for bypassing these communities are a lack of faith in their political abilities and a progressive denuding of their responsibilities and finances by the substitution of state-appointed special agencies, urban management in Madras still has to resolve a fundamental issue of representative government.

15

Manila

MANILA IS A FOREMOST example of a primate city that dominates the nation economically, socially, and politically. From 12 to 15 percent of the population of the Philippines now lives within the city's metropolitan area, which accounts for almost 40 percent of the country's gross national product. Metropolitan Manila is also the location of 90 of the country's 100 largest business corporations and 60 percent of the manufacturing firms, and it employs 45 percent of the nation's nonagricultural labor force. Furthermore, it operates the country's only international airport and handles 70 percent of all imports.

Growth of the City

Manila began as a Malay settlement at the mouth of the Pasig River on the island of Luzon. For 250 years before the Spanish arrived, it traded with neighboring China, Viet Nam, Indonesia, Malaysia, Borneo, and Kampuchea, and with Acapulco. Because Manila was a prosperous cosmopolitan city with a rich agricultural hinterland, the Spanish made it the capital of the Philippine archipelago in 1571, renamed it Intramuros, and made it the political, cultural, and economic center of Spanish rule for 377 years.

Manila's basic community structure of barangays, each of which originally formed a clan neighborhood ruled by a local rajah, dates back to these early centuries. The Spanish were responsible for the gridiron pattern of its streets, which have as their nucleus Intramuros proper, a walled city of 120 hectares; radiating from this nucleus are axial arteries focused on churches and adjoining plazas.

In 1898, the Philippines became a colony of the United States, and Manila, the Pearl of the Orient, was reconstructed along the lines of an American city—that is, with physical development focused more on schools than on churches. During the Second World War, however, the city suffered severe and widespread damage. After the Philippines achieved independence in 1945, Manila was named the capital of the new nation and rapidly recovered from its war damage, although in-migration from the poverty-stricken provinces grew apace. Quezon City, originally conceived at the turn of the century as the means of absorbing urban spillover from Manila, was declared the official capital in 1950, but Manila continued to act as the national center of government, financial affairs, and commerce and attracted migrants from all over the country.

By the end of the Second World War, Manila had a million or more people, and the metropolitan area began to expand rapidly in the 1950s. Quezon, Pasay, and Caloocan cities developed together with fourteen adjacent towns, and by 1957 the population had grown to 1.84 million. Today, only two decades later, the metropolitan population is close to 8.2 million, and Metropolitan Manila officially takes in Manila, Quezon, Caloocan, and Pasay and the thirteen municipalities of Makati, Navatos, Malabon, San Juan, Mandaluyong, Valenzuela, Marikina, Pasig, Muntinlupa, Parañaque, Las Piñas, Taguig, and Pateros. Their contiguous areas cover 636 square kilometers.

The four cities and first five municipalities of the preceding list make up a densely settled inner core that contains more than 60 percent of the population; this core doubled in size between 1948 and 1970. The Ayala development in the Makati area and the ring road known as EDSA have been instrumental in fostering this growth. A less densely populated ring of eight municipalities is now rapidly expanding along linear transportation routes at an average rate of 7 percent a year. Beyond this intermediate area stretches an extensive peripheral fringe or outer area of twenty-six municipalities, the character of which, although still predominantly rural, is progressively changing because of industrialization, housing resettlement schemes, and the development of transport and communication links.

Since independence, the metropolitan economy has diversified rapidly. About 60 percent of the country's large manufacturing firms and almost 50 percent of its small firms are now located in the metropolitan area. In 1974, industry accounted for 38 percent of the area's value added and 25 percent of its employment, commerce for 30 percent of value added and 17 percent of employment, and services for 17 percent of value added and 38 percent of employment. The other important sectors of the metropolitan economy were transport and construction. Since then, the rapid growth in services—particularly informal domestic service and personal services in the fields of communication, recreation, water distribution, and sanitation—has continued to absorb a great deal of immigrant labor. The many small, informal cottage industries have also shown a high employment capacity.

Metropolitan Problems

Like so many other cities of South and East Asia, Manila has a hot and humid climate. It is located on a flat, alluvial, and deltaic terrain that

Manila.   Pasig River and the port from which the city grew. The old city (Intra-muros), now government offices, is to the left; new office development to the right; Manila Bay and the harbor in the background.

Map 15-1. Manila City, 1898

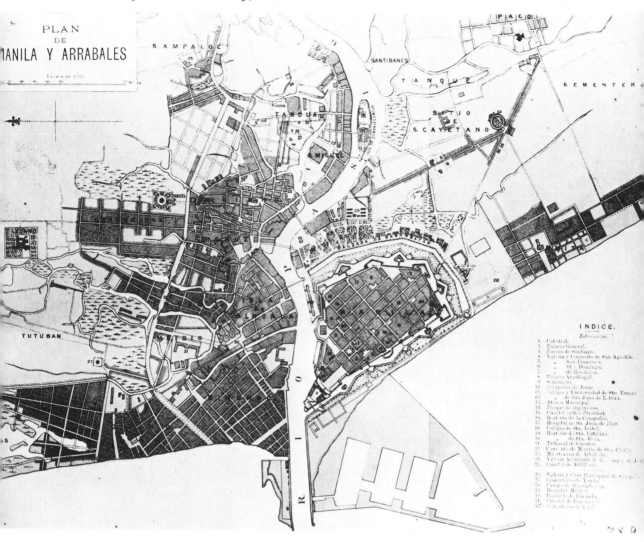

Photo: Library of Congress, Washington, D.C.

Map 15-2. Manila Urban Area, 1984

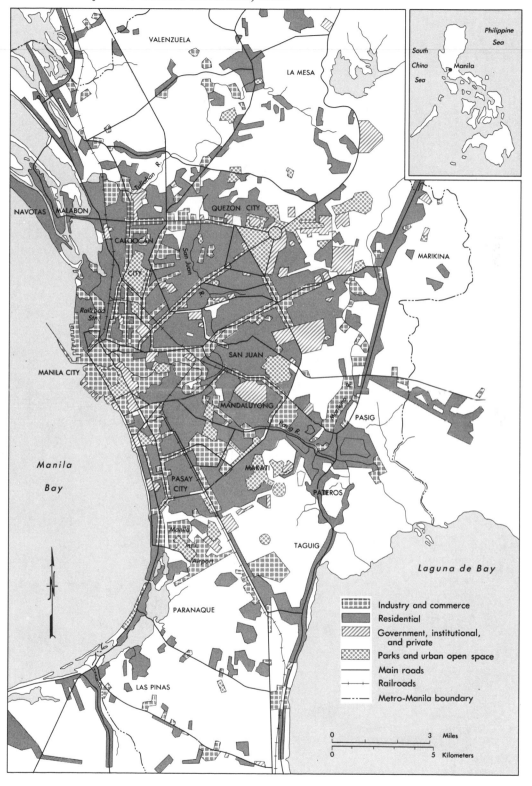

Legend:
- Industry and commerce
- Residential
- Government, institutional, and private
- Parks and urban open space
- Main roads
- Railroads
- Metro-Manila boundary

Map 15-3. Metropolitan Manila Area: Cities and Municipalities

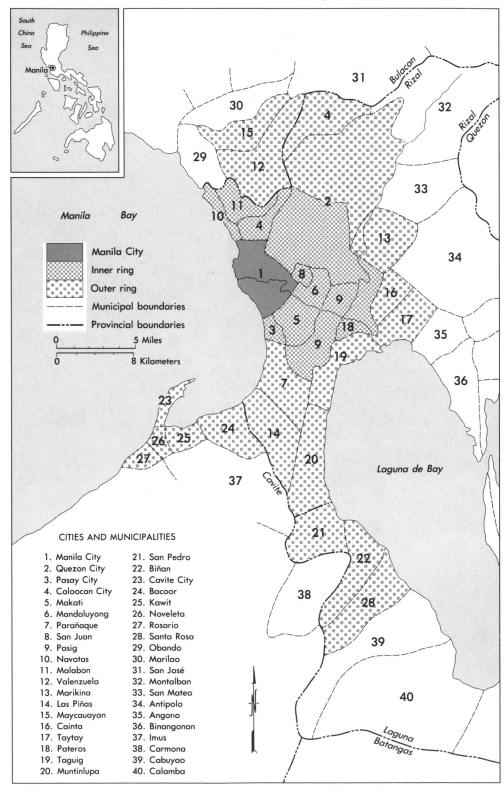

CITIES AND MUNICIPALITIES

1. Manila City	21. San Pedro
2. Quezon City	22. Biñan
3. Pasay City	23. Cavite City
4. Caloocan City	24. Bacoor
5. Makati	25. Kawit
6. Mandaluyong	26. Noveleta
7. Parañaque	27. Rosario
8. San Juan	28. Santa Rosa
9. Pasig	29. Obando
10. Navotas	30. Marilao
11. Malabon	31. San José
12. Valenzuela	32. Montalban
13. Marikina	33. San Mateo
14. Las Piñas	34. Antipolo
15. Maycauayan	35. Angono
16. Cainta	36. Binangonan
17. Taytay	37. Imus
18. Pateros	38. Carmona
19. Taguig	39. Cabuyao
20. Muntinlupa	40. Calamba

floods regularly in the monsoon season. Furthermore, the soil is unstable except on the higher ground to the east, where the Sierra Madre mountains lie. The metropolitan area is divided by the Pasig River and is crisscrossed by creeks and esteros. Expansion is restricted by Manila Bay in the west and Laguna de Bay in the southeast, and the fertile agricultural planes of central Luzon form its northern border. In part because of these restrictions, extensive foreshore reclamation has begun in Manila Bay (Dagat Dagatan) and is expected to continue in order to accommodate further commercial and cultural development along with tourism. Population density tends to be low outside the inner core, where considerable tracts of land remain unutilized. Peripheral fringe development beyond the intermediate area tends to be sporadic and uneconomic—that is, it preempts good agricultural land, and the costs of providing urban services and facilities in a primarily rural setting are quite high.

Because little control has been exercised over this development, land uses have been mixed indiscriminately, prime agricultural land has been converted to urban uses prematurely, and the subdivision of peripheral fringe areas has been excessive and uncoordinated. Further problems are the ribbon commercial and residential development along major transport axes, the lack of public open spaces and recreational areas in the inner core, and the polarization of the low- and high-income areas between the inner and southern and eastern parts of the surrounding intermediate area, respectively.

Migration to Manila is close to the rate of natural increase and thus remains one of the main determinants of metropolitan growth and economic and social conditions. Furthermore, the high influx of rural poor has widened the gap between the need for and the availability of essential services. At least 140,000 families live in makeshift housing, and slum conditions prevail in 415 squatter and blighted areas, mainly in the inner core, where both the indigenous and migrant poor tend to be concentrated.

In spite of its industrial and commercial dominance, strong economic base, and higher than average levels of income, the metropolitan area contains substantial poverty. Although unemployment is officially reported to be only 4 percent of the work force, there is widespread underemployment and a great deal of work sharing. In 1975, not more than 1.64 million out of a total labor force of 3.66 million were estimated to be fully employed, and the highest unemployment rates today are to be found in the three inner cities of Quezon, Caloocan, and Manila itself.

In addition, although the average income in the metropolitan area was double that of the nation as a whole in 1975, the difference has been narrowing, metropolitan disparities in incomes are very wide, and it is officially estimated that about 25 percent of all families in the metropolitan area live below the local poverty line. Real wages for unskilled workers have been declining substantially because of inflation, and the inadequate income earned by a large segment of the urban population continues to be a basic cause of the difficulties experienced in the provision of housing, transport, water, health, sanitation, and drainage services at even minimally acceptable standards.

As a result, some 1.8 million people lack adequate water supplies and educational, community, health, and sanitary services. Flooding remains a chronic problem, too. In the inner core, where residential densities are high and reach more than 1,700 persons per hectare, there is considerable overcrowding; in some areas, occupancy rates are as high as nine persons per room. Because fiscal resources are uneven from city to city and even among municipalities, services are unevenly distributed and developed, and the maintenance of infrastructure also varies widely.

This disparity throughout the metropolitan area has been made worse by the proliferation of governmental authorities. As a result, functions are duplicated or overlap, roles have become confused and loyalties divided, and the pressures on financial and human resources have increased. As already indicated, there has also been little effort to control the use and price of land. As early as 1958, the National Planning Commission reported that city zoning regulations adopted in 1940 "had been found obsolete and totally ineffective."[1] At that time, more than 50 percent of Manila proper already suffered from an indiscriminate mixing of land uses, partly because of laxity in the enforcement of local regulations for temporary building permits; and land prices were three to ten times higher than prewar levels, partly because of speculation by large-scale owners. In addition, property rights had been flagrantly violated by the in-migrants from the provinces, who squatted on vacant land and built shacks without the owner's consent, with the result that substandard housing had spread far and wide.

Structure of Government

Until 1975, the structure of Metropolitan Manila's government barely reflected the regional nature of the vast urban complex that had arisen since the 1940s. For administrative purposes, the country was divided into 72 provinces, 61 chartered cities, 1,440 municipalities, and 34,000 barangays. Metropolitan Manila fell within the jurisdictions of Rizal and Bulacan provinces, both of which were responsible for the collection of taxes, construction of highways, bridges, and public buildings, and the supervision of municipalities. Each province had a governor, vice-governor, provincial council, treasurer, assessor, engineer, and health officer, all of whom—except for the provincial council—were representatives of the central government.

The metropolitan area also fell under the jurisdiction of four chartered cities (Manila, Quezon, Pasay, and Caloocan), each of which was administered independently of the province and linked directly to the central government. Each had a mayor, a vice-mayor, a city council, and various departments, but the city auditor and superintendent of schools were rep-

1. A. T. Alquinto and M. Y. Garcia, "Growth of Greater Manila," paper presented at the United Nations seminar on Regional Planning, Tokyo, 1958.

resentatives of the central government. In addition, there were the thirteen municipalities of Makati, Mandaluyong, San Juan, Las Piñas, Malabon, Navetas, Pasig, Pateros, Parañaque, Marikina, Muntinlupa, Taguig, and Valenzuela, all of which, except Valenzuela, fell within Rizal province. Like the cities, they were responsible for the collection of taxes, street lighting, police forces, traffic control, local courts of justice, local markets, public utilities, fire control, health services, recreation and social services (including housing and relocation), and refuse collection.

The cities and municipalities were divided into neighborhood barangays comprising about 1,500 households each, which elected a barangay captain and six councilmen. Initially established for citizen consultation and participation in connection with both national and local issues, they had become primarily political units with the power to initiate and facilitate community action in local sanitation, health, education, beautification, and information services. Barangays had no revenue-raising powers of their own, however, and depended upon mandatory 10 percent allocations from city and municipal revenues.

Certain attempts had been made to introduce integrating regional elements into this otherwise hierarchical and compartmentalized structure of government. METROCOM, a metropolitan police force covering the seventeen local jurisdictions, had been established and financed by the central government. Coordination had also been introduced in fire services, the Metropolitan Water and Sewerage System (MWSS) had been established covering twenty local jurisdictions, and the Metropolitan Mayors Coordinating Council had been set up to represent fourteen local governments. The latter had agreed to coordinate flood control, drainage, and solid waste disposal, but had no operating budget.

In addition, the web of government included many central government departments and agencies. For example, nine different national agencies and two departments shared responsibility for the construction and financing of housing and for the provision of sites and services. These included the People's Homesite and Housing Corporation established in 1948, Presidential Assistance on Housing and Resettlement Agency of 1964, Home Finance Commission of 1956, Central Institute for the Training and Relocation of Urban Squatters, Presidential Committee on Housing and Urban Resettlement, National Housing Corporation of 1968, Government Service Insurance System, Social Security System, Development Bank of the Philippines, Department of Public Works, Transportation and Communications, and Department of Social Welfare.

Other central government departments and agencies had major responsibilities for flood control and drainage, construction and maintenance of roads, port facilities, air and rail transport, health, education, welfare, pollution control, and physical planning. Furthermore, the private sector operated certain services, such as hospitals and road passenger transport.

In 1975, Presidential Decree no. 824 introduced an important catalyst of change into this vast, fragmented array of central, provincial, and local government. It explicitly recognized that the rise of an urban region called for "simultaneous and unified development," and for the coordinated planning, administration, and operation of many public services. For these purposes, the decree created a public corporation, to be known as Metropolitan Manila and to be administered by a commission with jurisdiction over the four chartered cities and thirteen municipalities, "all of which together shall henceforth be known as Metropolitan Manila" (and be removed from the jurisdictions of Rizal and Bulacan provinces). The commission is composed of a governor, a vice-governor, and three commissioners for planning, financial control, and operations, respectively, all of whom are appointed by the president (the commissioner for operations has not yet been appointed, however). Its powers and functions are:

- To act as a central, metropolitan government for the establishment and administration of common programs and the provision of common services
- To levy and collect taxes, borrow money, and issue bonds and certificates
- To charge and collect fees for the use of public service facilities
- To appropriate money and review (with the power to disapprove) city and municipal appropriations
- To pass ordinances and resolutions, and perform general administrative, executive, and policymaking functions
- To centralize control over city and municipal fire services, garbage disposal, and traffic control activities
- To coordinate and monitor governmental and private sector activities pertaining to essential services such as transportation, flood control and drainage, water supply, sewerage, social health and environmental services, housing, and park development
- To ensure and monitor metropolitan planning and development (social, economic, and physical)
- To study and make recommendations on the feasibility of increasing barangay participation in local government affairs.

The establishment of the Metropolitan Manila Commission (MMC) appears to have initiated a fundamental process of change in the structure of government. Thus far, the responsibilities of the local and other authorities for the delivery of services have not been substantially modified. The commission has been concerned primarily with coordinating and regulating the existing provision of services (particularly those of local government) and with facilitating the execution of major priority programs cutting across traditional administrative boundaries. However, the commission has also been frequently involved in special projects such as improving street furniture, organizing additional labor for street cleaning, and mounting demonstration schemes. Though on a small scale, these activities have taken up a great deal of the MMC's time.

Fiscal Situation

The chartered cities and municipalities derive their revenue mainly from property taxation (31 percent), business taxes (23 percent), and profits and receipts from the operation of public utilities and commercial enterprises, such as municipal markets and slaughterhouses (17 percent). Other taxes (10 percent) include those on residences and entertainment and parking fees. National shared revenues (9 percent) and allotments of the specific tax on petroleum products (9 percent) account for the balance. The income of local authorities is expected to amount (in pesos) to ₱1,330.7 million (US$179.8 million) overall in 1981 (see table 15-1).

Twenty percent of this revenue is earmarked for the Metropolitan Manila Commission, which derives nearly 52 percent of its income from this single source and is otherwise dependent mainly on property taxation (30 percent) and a number of miscellaneous taxes, including corporate, residential, franchise, and occupation taxes (9 percent). Thus 88 percent of the total combined income of the local and metropolitan authorities is in fact derived from chartered city and municipal resources, and the fiscal performance of municipalities is of crucial importance to the metropolitan areas's public sector development. Furthermore, because of the wide range of incomes from one local authority to another, the burden falls mainly on six authorities, especially Manila itself, Quezon City, and Makati, which account for nearly 70 percent of total local income (see tables 15-2, 15-3). Central assistance usually accounts for 25 to 55 percent of the current income of local governments in the Philippines. This is not the case for metropolitan Manila, however.

Although anticipated current expenditure appears to fall below anticipated revenue, this is not so when capital outlays are added (table 15-4). More to the point, only about 17 percent of the total expenditure is represented by capital outlays. The proportion for 1981 was in fact about 22 percent, whereas the total revenue of the local governments and the MMC combined remained at ₱1.5 billion, as estimated. In practice, capital outlays have been financed by central government investment and account for a significant part of the national infrastructure outlays (see table 15-5). Projections of capital outlays and likely resources for the 1983–87 period indicate that the contributions of the local governments and the MMC could be less than 10 percent of what is expected from national agencies (see table 15-6).

Thus, although Metropolitan Manila's current revenues are not greatly dependent on central assistance, they fall far short of providing the capital needed for development. Moreover, they will continue to do so in the foreseeable future, even if additional local revenue resources can be found through user charges (for example, in garbage collection) and fees (for example, in markets and excavations), as recently suggested by the finance

Table 15-1. *Annual Budget of Metropolitan Manila: Estimated Financial Resources, 1981*

Financial resources	Pesos	Percentage distribution
Cities and municipalities		
Tax revenue		
Internal revenue allotment	114,677,617	8.62
Specific tax allotment	124,615,338	9.36
Real property tax	418,354,830	31.44
Business tax	309,512,500	23.25
Other	129,981,570	9.78
Subtotal	1,097,141,855	
Earnings and other credits	233,530,344	17.55
Total income	1,330,672,199	100.00
Metropolitan Manila Commission (MMC)		
Tax revenue		
Internal revenue allotment	13,914,146	3.65
Specific tax allotment	7,238,437	1.90
Real property tax	115,669,300	30.32
Other (corporate, residential, franchise, occupation, etc.)	33,078,817	8.67
Subtotal	169,900,700	
Earnings and other credits		
National aid	7,500,000	1.97
Building permit fees	6,733,810	1.76
Contribution to MMC	197,372,790	51.73
Subtotal	211,606,600	
Total income	381,507,300	100.00
Summary		
Income of local governments (net of contribution to MMC)	1,133,299,409	74.81
Metropolitan Manila Commission	381,507,300	25.19
Total	1,514,806,709	100.00

Source: Manila Budget Operations Service.

commissioner: ''Financing and delivery of services will never be adequate relative to the constantly increasing demands.... In view of the pressing need to expand financial resources to support development programs for the metropolitan area, it is of major importance that a reexamination of the existing tax structure of the individual local units be made.''[2]

2. Mauro G. Calaguio, ''To Meet Development Needs, MMC Must Raise More Funds,'' paper presented at World Bank Economic Development Institute/Asian Development Bank seminar, Manila, January 1981.

Table 15-2. *Actual and Estimated Income, Metropolitan Manila, 1971–80*
(millions of pesos)

City or municipality	1971	1972	1973	1974	1975	1976	1977	1978	1979	1980
Manila	137.0	135.9	166.0	192.0	237.3	306.5	350.1	355.7	390.3	415.0
Quezon City	36.7	39.5	46.1	60.0	82.0	90.0	112.2	146.7	167.3	190.0
Makati	30.1	40.2	44.6	70.0	56.6	76.7	70.6	85.0	109.2	129.0
Caloocan City	11.0	12.0	15.0	22.0	25.0	27.8	33.7	16.3	47.7	58.0
Las Piñas	1.8	2.1	2.5	2.1	2.2	4.8	4.8	7.3	10.6	15.0
Malabon	3.0	3.0	4.1	6.2	6.3	10.4	10.4	14.6	19.6	24.0
Mandaluyong	10.7	15.3	10.0	12.0	11.5	14.3	17.7	25.5	30.3	38.0
Marikina	3.1	3.8	3.9	4.4	4.1	7.3	9.2	9.8	12.7	15.0
Muntinlupa	2.9	3.6	2.5	3.2	3.5	3.9	4.4	7.3	11.9	16.0
Navotas	1.0	1.2	1.6	2.5	2.5	4.5	4.1	6.3	6.0	7.0
Parañaque	6.3	10.4	7.0	7.2	8.3	10.7	13.6	17.5	25.2	30.0
Pasay City	9.2	9.5	11.1	16.3	18.4	25.0	26.5	33.2	37.6	42.0
Pasig	11.4	18.0	13.3	13.6	14.6	18.6	24.4	29.7	39.3	48.0
Pateros	0.3	0.4	0.2	0.4	0.4	0.5	0.9	1.2	1.3	2.0
San Juan	4.1	3.5	4.4	4.5	5.3	6.6	8.8	12.5	12.6	14.0
Taguig	0.4	2.4	1.2	1.7	1.8	2.0	2.9	4.4	4.6	5.0
Valenzuela	2.6	3.1	3.4	4.6	6.1	8.5	11.3	14.2	14.4	17.0

Source: World Bank data.

Table 15-3. *Estimated Revenue, Metropolitan Manila, 1978, 1979, and 1980*
(millions of pesos)

City or municipality	1978	1979	1980
Manila	346.344	381.178	430.094
Quezon City	140.347	160.951	207.607
Makati	83.621	108.732	126.690
Caloocan City	43.371	45.039	52.679
Pasay City	30.000	36.146	43.430
Pasig	29.535	33.265	45.540
Mandaluyong	25.295	30.068	39.587
Parañaque	17.365	25.084	35.990
Valenzuela	13.766	14.352	17.775
Malabon	13.580	19.405	20.860
San Juan	12.317	12.434	15.357
Marikina	9.518	12.425	16.685
Muntinlupa	7.198	11.822	16.805
Las Piñas	6.982	10.465	14.120
Navotas	6.253	5.775	7.367
Taguig	3.967	4.471	6.492
Pateros	1.165	1.200	1.457
Subtotal	790.624	912,812	1,098,535
Metropolitan Manila Commission	205.660	259.064	335.000
Total	996.284	1,171,876	1,433,535

Source: Manila Budget Operations Service.

Table 15-4. Annual Budget of Metropolitan Manila: Estimated Expenditure, 1981
(pesos)

City or municipality	Current operating expenditure	Capital outlay	Total	Percentage distribution
Manila	447,087,839	47,444,250	494,532,089	30.05
Quezon City	224,052,969	52,803,562	276,856,531	16.82
Makati	121,609,302	12,923,000	134,532,302	8.17
Caloocan City	59,233,926	15,187,858	74,421,784	4.52
Las Piñas	13,868,007	1,039,000	14,907,007	0.91
Malabon	22,276,288	4,003,590	26,279,878	1.60
Mandaluyong	30,329,129	2,778,300	33,107,429	2.01
Marikina	17,205,522	2,325,916	19,531,438	1.19
Muntinlupa	14,832,544	3,178,460	18,011,004	1.09
Navotas	7,780,394	518,650	8,299,044	0.50
Parañaque	32,667,464	6,473,443	39,140,907	2.38
Pasay City	53,243,961	3,694,000	56,937,961	3.46
Pasig	33,224,472	13,128,500	46,352,972	2.82
Pateros	1,806,292	18,000	1,824,292	0.11
San Juan	16,535,387	2,524,000	19,059,387	1.16
Taguig	7,606,720	2,001,995	9,608,715	0.58
Valenzuela	20,144,570	2,287,000	22,431,570	1.36
Subtotal	1,123,504,786	172,329,524	1,295,834,310	78,73
Metropolitan Manila Commission	245,000,000[a]	105,000,000[a]	350,000,000	21,27
Total	1,368,504,786	277,329,524	1,645,834,310[b]	100.00
Percent	83	17	100	

a. Figures for the Metropolitan Manila Commission are approximate amounts only.

b. This represents total expenditure including a 20 percent contribution to the Metropolitan Manila Commission.

Source: Manila Budget Operations Service.

Table 15-5. Public Sector Capital Expenditure in the Philippines and Manila, 1977–83
(millions of pesos, current prices)

Item	1977	1978	1979	1980	1981	1982	1983
1. Philippines GNP	154,280	178,067	220,957	264,973	305,499	347,700	395,000
2. Infrastructure program	8,027	7,335	10,791	11,768	13,946	23,346	23,739
3. Row 2 as percentage of GNP	5.2	4.1	4.9	4.4	4.6	6.7	6.0
4. Manila[a] infrastructure	1,383	638	732	980	1,603	3,608	3,201
5. Row 4 as percentage of row 2	17.2	8.7	6.8	8.3	11.5	15.5	13.5
6. Row 5 excluding electricity	31.8	16.2	14.4	18.0	23.5	25.5	22.8

a. National Capital Region.

Source: National Economic Development Agency. Actual figures for 1977–81; capital investment folio estimates for 1982–83.

Table 15-6. Projected Financial Resources in the Manila National Capital Region,
1983–87
(millions of pesos, 1982 constant prices)

Source	1983	1984	1985	1986	1987	Total
Low projection						
National agencies[a]	1,640	1,650	1,730	1,780	1,860	8,660
Local government and MMC[b]	150	160	160	160	160	790
Total	1,790	1,810	1,890	1,940	2,020	9,450
High projection						
National agencies[a]	2,730	2,890	3,080	3,210	3,420	15,330
Local government and MMC[b]	200	210	220	230	250	1,110
Total	2,930	3,100	3,300	3,440	3,670	16,440

a. The low projection for national agencies reflects only a modest increase over 1980 expenditures; the high projection implies steady growth on the basis of 1981 actuals and 1982 estimates.

b. The low projections for local governments and the Manila Metropolitan Commission are based on the average from 1979 to 1981; the high projection assumes 10 percent of the estimated income.

Source: Metropolitan Manila Commission and Halcrow Fox and Associates, "Metropolitan Manila Capital Investment Folio Study" (Manila: Office of the Commissioner for Planning, November 1982).

Response to Metropolitan Problems

One of the first institutional changes that came about with the establishment of the Metropolitan Manila Commission was the division of the metropolitan area in 1976 into four local treasury and assessment districts centered on Manila, Quezon City, Caloocan City, and Pasay City. The treasurers and assessors of these cities assumed the duties of the provincial officers of Rizal and Bulacan provinces with respect to the general supervision of the municipal treasurers and assessors working in their districts. In addition, the finance commissioner of Metropolitan Manila was empowered to appoint the latter officers, and the city treasurers and assessors were henceforth to be appointed by the president. The Metropolitan Manila Commission thus assumed provincial fiscal powers and responsibilities. When the new Ministry of Human Settlements was created in 1978, the metropolitan area was designated the National Capital Region, the commission was attached to this ministry, and the latter's minister was made governor of the commission. The first lady (wife of the country's president) has been the minister of human settlements and governor of Metropolitan Manila since 1978. Reporting to the governor is a full-time vice-governor supported by a commissioner for planning and a commissioner for finance. The vice-governor has also been serving as commissioner for operations.

The commissioner for planning is responsible for formulating long-range plans for the development of Metropolitan Manila, coordinating the planning and implementation of infrastructure projects of the various local authorities and government agencies, formulating land use plans and implementing planning controls. The commissioner of finance is responsible for income and expenditure planning and control; supervises the local authorities' finances; and administers the commission's staff position, classification, and compensation systems. Two important divisions under the commissioner for finance are the Real Property Assessment Service responsible for property assessment, valuation, and tax administration, and the Budget Operations Service, which looks after the MMC's budget, reviews the budgets of local authorities, and controls the allotments made to them.

One of the more innovative responses to Manila's problems began in the Tondo Foreshore. Tondo, the largest slum in Manila, was created by successive waves of squatters on land that had been reclaimed for developing a port. The slum spread to adjoining lands and consisted almost entirely of shacks built along drainage canals. After several unsuccessful attempts to remove the squatters, an upgrading program was adopted in 1974. Like the programs in Calcutta and Jakarta, this was one of the early efforts in Asia to improve slums. The Tondo Foreshore Development Authority was created that year to implement the improvement project, which was partly financed by the World Bank. In 1975, this authority merged with the newly created National Housing Authority (NHA), which consolidated six existing agencies and thus concentrated governmental housing efforts and resources in a single body. The Tondo project proved to be a success. Community participation was organized effectively for reblocking, a process by which the barangay committees choose between alternative plans for improvement in a slum neighborhood and decide which structures will be removed to make way for utility lines and other services.

The Tondo project led to the initiation of the Zonal Improvement Program (ZIP) in 1977, which is designed to upgrade the environmental social and economic conditions of slum residents with minimum relocation. Fifteen thousand plots are to be upgraded annually over a period of fifteen years. Complementing ZIP is the Metropolitan Manila Infrastructure Utilities and Engineering Program (MINUTE) developed by the Ministry of Public Works in 1978, and a third upgrading program (PROGRESS) for removing sewage from the streets is now being operated by the Metropolitan Water and Sewerage System. Together MINUTE and PROGRESS will provide critical improvements in drainage, sanitation, water supply, and access for 5 million people under an eight-year plan. All three priority programs have involved large-scale capital investments needing overall planning and programming. In addition, major projects for augmenting water supply, expanding and improving distribution systems, and upgrading the sewerage system in the central areas have been continued by the Metropolitan Water Supply and Sewerage Board, with assistance from the World Bank and the Asian Development Bank.

As a first step toward the metropolitanwide coordination of investment, the Ministry of Public Works compiled a list of the infrastructure projects proposed by various government agencies. It was envisioned that several investment options for Metropolitan Manila should be developed and that each option should show a mixture of projects with the corresponding total investment required.[3] The initial investment folio was to contain mainly national agency projects that would be reviewed by an interagency consultative group, and the order of priorities was to be based on accepted criteria. The folio was then to be submitted to the Budget Ministry through the National Economic and Development Authority (NEDA) within the time schedules specified for the national budget.

The principal criteria for determining the priority of projects (and the weights assigned to them) were: social (50 percent), such as expected health, safety, and shelter benefits, equitable income distribution, and employment potential; economic (20 percent), such as increased productivity, contribution to net domestic product, foreign exchange earnings, and savings; and financial (30 percent), such as cost recovery, inflationary effects, and impact on domestic borrowings.

For 1980, for instance, the list of proposed projects originally amounted to ₱5,000 million (US$675.5 million), which meant an increase of 272 percent over the previous year and a jump from 9 to 30 percent of planned national investment. At the other extreme was an option pegged to ₱1,000 million. For both practical and political purposes, such a high increase or freeze would clearly not be approved by the NEDA and would be strongly opposed by other regional interests. The proposed projects were therefore examined by an executive committee formed from the agencies concerned, classified according to relative urgency and status, and then weighted on the basis of social, economic, and financial criteria. The investment of ₱3,336 million (US$450.7 million) finally authorized by NEDA and the Budget Office represented 20 percent of the total national investment. The projects excluded were held over to subsequent financial years, and a five-year capital investment program with three differing options for each year was drawn up by the committee.

The working group assisting the interagency executive committee prepared similar investment options for 1981 and 1982. The consultations resulted in substantial rephasing and reprogramming of projects: the MWSS and NHA 1980 budgets were reduced to more realistic and attainable estimates; some road projects were deferred; some World Bank–financed urban projects were brought forward; and the ports, airports, and other transport projects were rephased. A workshop for Metropolitan Manila and local government officials held in October 1978 to introduce the capital investment folio (CIF) and MINUTE brought forth an encouraging response. By the end of 1979, the 1980–83 CIF was completed and handed over to the

3. For further information on the evolution of the capital investment folio, see Theodoro Encarnacion, ''Metro Manila CIF: History and Process of Formulation,'' paper presented at World Bank Economic Development Institute/Asian Development Bank seminar, Manila, January 1981.

Metropolitan Manila Commission for follow-up and continuation of the exercise for future years.

The proportion of foreign–assisted schemes in the CIF has been significant. In the 1980 exercise, the share came to 74 percent. In the various options for 1981 and 1982, the share ranged from 81 to 84 percent. Because the country attaches considerable importance to foreign investments, a high-level management coordination board was set up in 1980 with the MMC's vice-governor as chairman and representatives of the ministries of Budget, Finance, Public Works, and Human Settlements, the NHA, and the NEDA to coordinate World Bank- and other foreign-assisted projects and to review annual or three-year budgets in the context of the CIF. It was also felt that substantial technical assistance would be needed for the CIF analyses, and consultants were provided as part of the World Bank project.

Although the MMC management appreciates the need for allocating adequate staff to the interagency and corporate-level coordination of the CIF exercises, its resources have been increasingly drawn into execution. Much of the staff, financial resources, and—most important—top management attention are taken up by the MMC's operations centers. The Barangay Operations Center provides a link between the MMC and each barangay and helps the barangays to administer the numerous local improvement schemes. The Engineering Operations Center oversees and monitors all engineering activities, including the construction of roads and drains within the National Capital Region, and it regulates all excavation by issuing permits. The Environment Sanitation Center is the largest operations center and is responsible for refuse collection, disposal, and street sweeping in Metropolitan Manila. The Health Operations Center has the status of a regional office of the Ministry of Health, and it monitors the activities of various health care agencies and attempts a strategic planning role. The Traffic Operations Center formulates traffic management policies and regulations and develops an integrated transport and traffic management service in Metropolitan Manila. The Action Center for Infrastructure Development is now combined with the Plan Enforcement and Regulation Center. Apart from the MMC's directly executed infrastructure schemes, the center is also responsible for issuing building permits, administering the national building code, and issuing certificates of occupation.

Of the total staff of about 14,500, less than 1,000 are in the offices of the MMC's vice-governor, planning commissioner, and finance commissioner. The remaining are employed in the various operations centers. The largest is the Environmental Services Center (responsible for garbage collection and disposal); it has a staff of about 12,700, and its annual expenditure of ₱144 million represents 44 percent of the total MMC expenditure. The nature of the activities undertaken by the operations centers is such that the public perceives the MMC more as a super municipal body responsible for several day-to-day services than as a metropolitan-level planning and development authority. Undeniably, the operations centers also take up a sizable portion of the vice-governor's time in his capacity as commissioner for operations.

Pending Issues

The consultants who were engaged to develop the CIF process submitted their final report in November 1982. The report indicated that whereas the program called for ₱29.8 billion (1982 prices), available resources were estimated to range from ₱9.5 billion to ₱16.4 billion. Committed projects accounted for 98 and 59 percent, respectively, of these two estimates of resources. The report concluded that the opportunity to introduce new projects was limited and that unless the National Capital Region—contrary to what was recommended in the national five-year plan—were to preempt resources from other regions or tap other funding resources, significant parts of the agency programs would have to be cut. After analysis of the impact-scoring system and alternative techniques, the report recommended a three-stage evaluation process for selecting projects. Stage 1 tests projects against five criteria (compatibility with the Regional Development Framework Plan [RDFP], impact on equity, and technical, economic, and financial feasibility) to arrive at a list of "sensible" projects. Stage 2 ranks the projects in order of priority, and stage 3 is an intersectoral review in the context of the RDFP and available resources. The first two stages of the 1983–87 exercise have been carried out and further results are being awaited.

The greatly improved dialogue between public agencies, the spirit of realism in financial and economic planning, and the attainment of an institutional process to carry planning forward are considered to be the main advantages of the CIF. Competition and self-protection are still widespread among some major spending agencies, however.[4] Insufficient commitment to the CIF process is evident from the fact that the members of the interagency technical working group have not been senior officials. Inadequate staffing and organizational support have created further difficulties. Although it has been demonstrated that the CIF can be an important and progressive tool in relating urban planning to expenditure programs, its future depends on whether some important institutional steps are implemented. For example, the MMC should be assigned whatever responsibilities a NEDA regional office would have that pertain to the Capital Region's Development Framework Plan and investment programs; the terms of reference and membership of the interagency technical working group should be defined; adequate staff should be provided for the technical secretariat; and the staff engaged in the CIF exercise should be properly trained. These steps, in turn, depend on the continued acceptance of the MMC's strategic planning and coordinating role in Metropolitan Manila. Although such a role may not be questioned explicitly, it may well be undermined by the MMC's

4. See David Walton, "Manila Case Study," in Desmond McNeill, ed., *Proceedings of the Workshop on the Changing Practices of Urban Planning* (London: University College, Development Planning Unit, July 1983).

increasing preoccupation with operations at the sectoral and local municipal levels.

As already noted, a large share of the MMC's staff and budget are used up in its operations centers. As it is, the MMC relies heavily on local authorities to provide the greater proportion of its revenue. If it becomes more involved in municipal service delivery and project implementation, the funds that are needed will have to come from some other component of local or national government. Given the limits of overall resource availability, such reallocations are bound to be resisted. There is no question that an increased role for the MMC in project implementation will also undermine its neutral role in investment coordination. Present relationships between the various agencies, local authorities, and the MMC are complex and ill-defined. These will become clear only when the MMC's role and responsibilities are explicitly defined and accepted.

At present, the MMC acts as an insert between the two layers of central and local government. Manila has received a significant share of the country's investment in infrastructure and will need to do so again in the future to sustain its dominant role in the national economy. Central government agencies will therefore continue to operate and maintain infrastructure programs on a large scale and are unlikely to surrender their funds or responsibilities to the MMC. The jurisdictions of the local governments are highly disparate in area, population, and resources: Pateros, for example, has an area of 201 hectares and a population of 4,000, compared with Quezon's 15,359 hectares and Manila City's population of 1.63 million. Nonetheless, the municipal councils and chartered cities claim that municipal services can be better performed at the local level and that the MMC should only coordinate and not take over these functions.

In its brief period of existence, the MMC has sought both planning and executive roles. As a strategic planning authority, it has formulated the Regional Development Framework Plan and assumed responsibility for the capital investment folio. In an effort to reduce disparities and improve the delivery of services, it has taken on metropolitanwide municipal functions such as solid waste collection and disposal and traffic operation. It has also assumed for itself basic municipal functions such as building control. Through its Barangay Operations Center, it has tried to establish some direct links with the 1,700 grass-roots political entities. Together these various initiatives are regarded as a threat to preexisting local governments and other agencies. Yet, even the MMC's critics would admit that within a short time it has formulated and projected a metropolitan view of Manila's problems, improved interagency relationships, and brought about significant fiscal and administrative changes toward reducing intermunicipal disparities. These are managerial tasks that the MMC has successfully accomplished, in contrast to some other metropolitan cities in South and East Asia.

APPENDIX A

Managing Metropolitan Growth in Latin America

THIS BRIEF ACCOUNT of a seminar on managing metropolitan growth*
draws from the concrete experiences of eleven metropolitan areas in eight
Latin American countries: Asunción, Bogotá, Caracas, Curitiba, Lima,
Mexico City, Montevideo, Quito, Recife, Rio de Janeiro, and São Paulo.
The report attempts to provide a practical agenda for those in government
and in the private sector who share the responsibility of managing the
future development of the metropolitan areas of Latin America.

The Challenge

The sheer scale of the metropolitan areas of Latin America, the rapid
growth of their populations, the low incomes, and extremely limited infrastructure present an enormous challenge to those trying to achieve effective metropolitan management. As the older cities have grown beyond
their historical administrative boundaries, encroaching upon neighboring

*This appendix is the somewhat revised report of a seminar sponsored by the
United Nations Centre for Human Settlements (UNCHS-HABITAT) and the
Economic Development Institute (EDI) of the World Bank, in Rio de Janeiro,
June 1983. The report was prepared by Roy Gilbert, consultant and rapporteur
for the seminar, in collaboration with John D. Herbert, senior training officer in
the EDI and codirector of the seminar, and in consultation with Charles P. Boyce,
formerly officer in charge of training for HABITAT and codirector of the seminar,
and Diogo Lordello de Mello, director of the Brazilian Institute for Municipal
Administration, which was host for the seminar. Margaret Y. Myers, EDI, col-
laborated on the final preparation of the report.

municipalities and in some cases even on other states, the need has arisen for local and national governments, sectoral agencies, and private sector bodies to consolidate their efforts in a broad approach to the management of metropolitan areas. In addition to allowing more effective coordination, such an approach could take advantage of the economies of scale that the metropolis itself offers, and could also stimulate a more comprehensive management of strategic projects and common problems, such as environmental pollution, that affect the entire metropolis.

The difficulties of achieving sound metropolitan management should not be underestimated, given the involvement of many agencies representing specific, often conflicting, local and sectoral interests. These are not easy to reconcile, because of the weakness of the existing institutional base of the metropolitan areas. With the limited financial autonomy of local metropolitan government and the overcentralization of political power at the national level, it is not surprising that the existing financial, technical, and administrative capacity of metropolitan institutions is simply not up to the task of comprehensive management.

A number of alternative approaches were considered in the seminar for improving metropolitan management. They included, on the financial side, strengthening existing public finances of the metropolitan areas, as well as introducing specifically metropolitan taxes to give these areas greater autonomy and lessen their dependence on national government. On the planning side, a wide range of spatial approaches were reviewed, such as development programs for rural areas and medium-size cities to relieve some of the population pressures on the metropolitan areas and new planned urban centers and subcores to improve internal spatial structure. These discussions are reviewed below.

Strategic Areas for Action

The action-oriented approach of the seminar was structured around six basic themes. Each corresponded to an area in which action is urgently needed to consolidate metropolitan management, and in which opportunities exist to apply practical measures right away, even if only as the beginning of a long-term process. In this spirit, opportunities for action were sought in the following areas:

- Institutional arrangements of the metropolitan areas
- Local finances and their management
- Participation of the formal private sector and the community in planning decisions and the provision of urban services in the metropolitan area
- Metropolitan land management
- Provision of strategic metropoliswide services
- Environmental management.

Opportunities for Immediate Action

Strengthening the Institutional Base

A number of measures were proposed to help consolidate the institutions necessary for effective metropolitan management. Most of the emphasis is on improving the functioning of the existing institutions. At the same time, some adjustments are proposed in the way different institutions interact and coordinate their actions, so that they can better serve the wider interests of metropolitan development.

ASSOCIATIONS OF MUNICIPALITIES. Although municipalities in Latin America usually have their autonomy and independence constitutionally guaranteed, their effective contribution to metropolitan management can be strictly limited by their own financial and technical limitations. Furthermore, in no case in Latin America does a single municipality's jurisdiction cover an entire metropolitan area. Because of this weakness, combined with administrative fragmentation, it was recommended that municipalities form an association so that they can more easily pool limited resources, better coordinate their different activities, and seek to resolve conflicts that might arise between them. This was seen as an interim measure, pending the long-term establishment of new metropolitan institutions.

Eleven municipalities that make up the metropolitan area of Asunción, Paraguay, established the Association of Metropolitan Area Municipalities (AMUAM) in October 1978 in order to strengthen each of its members by fostering mutual support. Even though all municipalities are formally equal, each having one vote in AMUAM's deliberative council, the city of Asunción itself, which accounts for 84 percent of the total metropolitan population, has a key role in supporting the weaker, peripheral municipalities. The latter receive most of the attention from AMUAM's own planning office.

One of the great difficulties in setting up such an association can be the task of convincing politicians, especially those with a strictly local mandate, that this kind of association is at all necessary. Such reluctance can be overcome, however, once the political dividends from more effective administration and greater responsiveness to community aspirations start to appear. In Asunción, attempts are now being made to consolidate the association's legal status, which must take account of the municipal autonomy that is common to the constitutions of most Latin American countries. The successful grouping of the six municipalities that make up the Metropolitan Council of Toronto, Canada, was possible because there were no legal impediments. In Latin America, however, it is necessary to explore the legal implications of such associations.

TECHNICAL ASSISTANCE TO MUNICIPALITIES. If the municipalities that make up the metropolitan areas are to contribute more effectively to their management, it is essential to reinforce their technical capacity through training and technical assistance. Especially important are measures to consolidate the internal management and financial procedures of these municipalities, so that they can use their limited resources more efficiently. Given the diversity of problems faced, it would be necessary to establish precisely, case by case, the current strengths and weaknesses of a municipal administration, and to design the training and technical assistance programs accordingly.

A number of Latin American countries have institutions with varying degrees of experience in preparing and implementing such programs. These include: IBAM (Brazilian Institute of Municipal Administration); FUNDACOMUM (Foundation for Community and Municipal Development—Venezuela); ESAP (Higher School of Public Administration—Colombia); IEM (Institute of Municipal Studies—Uruguay); IULA (International Union of Local Authorities—Ecuador); and ICAP (Central American Institute of Public Administration—Costa Rica). Their experience should be drawn upon to develop efficient and appropriate training and technical assistance programs.

SIMPLIFICATION OF ADMINISTRATIVE PROCEDURES. Measures that reduce bureaucratic delays can remove obstacles to metropolitan development and should be geared toward all public sector agencies that are active in metropolitan management, including of course the municipalities. In particular, the multiplicity of permits required for any development project can stifle private sector investments, especially those by small firms that lack the resources or skills to navigate these lengthy procedures. The simplification of building and planning regulations is a necessary first step.

In an experiment in Caracas, for example, representatives of all the main licensing agencies (such as the municipal building and fire departments, electricity, and telephone companies) were located under one roof. The physical proximity of the licensing authorities can at least simplify the procedures, save a considerable amount of time, and thereby reduce the costs of development.

Another way of controlling excessive bureaucracy is to place a strict limit on the total amount of public sector funding available to finance administrative costs. In the case of the Metropolitan Investment Fund of Lima, for example, such costs were not to exceed 1 percent of the total of any project.

SIMPLIFICATION OF PLANNING. The plan for the metropolitan area and the planning system it upholds must be readily understood by those most affected—communities, developers, and politicians as well as professional planners. A metropolitan plan and its component area plans need to be closely related to the real social and economic conditions of the metropolis itself; furthermore, they must be aimed at realistic targets that can be achieved in the short to medium term. They should avoid the trap of many old-style master plans, whose detailed but unrealizable long-term objectives have consigned them to the realm of fiction. The planning system itself must be kept simple with at most two separate tiers: the first providing the general guidelines for metropolitan development; the second offering specific guidance on the location of investments consistent with the first one.

The plan of Curitiba, Brazil, although not covering the entire metropolitan area, highlights some principles that could well be applied to other metropolitan areas. This plan focused on the key physical components of the city's growth, the basic infrastructure for transport, water, sewerage, and energy. These determined the broad guidelines of the plan, which in turn allowed the identification of opportunities for development, particularly with the participation of the private sector. Emphasis was given to a straightforward presentation of the plan at all levels, with extensive publicity material that could be readily understood by the community at large.

CONSOLIDATED INFORMATION SYSTEMS. Because of the complexity of the development process of metropolitan areas, those responsible for its management must have readily retrievable information on a wide variety of topics, and they must be able to make this information available to interested parties when necessary. In addition to an overview of the social, economic, and physical conditions of the metropolitan area, metropolitan management needs data on financial administration and the information necessary to evaluate the efficiency and likely economic impact of proposed investments.

The organization, storage, and retrieval of this information should make use of the increasingly accessible technology of microcomputers, which have been used in Fortaleza, Brazil, and other metropolitan areas in Latin America. This information should also be made available both to orient potential developers and to create a greater awareness of the challenges of metropolitan development among the community as a whole. Although the traditional media—the press, radio, and television—can be used to disseminate information, an interesting experiment in Curitiba uses taxi drivers. They are trained (as a condition for obtaining their licenses) in the city's history and development to help them explain its planning to a wide public.

DEMONSTRATION PROJECTS. Learning by doing can be an effective way of consolidating the institutional base for metropolitan management. For each country or region, a metropolitanwide demonstration project could give the institutions responsible for its implementation important experience in coordination that could be applied elsewhere. For such cross-fertilization to be effective, it would be important to monitor the demonstration project carefully to determine which lessons could be learned.

In this respect, the World Bank–supported integrated metropolitan development projects in Northeast Brazil were felt to provide relevant examples. In Recife, where a project is already being implemented, World Bank support has been crucial in providing opportunities for FIDEM (Foundation for the Metropolitan Area of Recife) to begin to coordinate the sectoral and local agencies involved in managing the metropolitan area. Further metropolitan development projects are being prepared for Salvador and Fortaleza. In addition to institution building and the improvement of local finances, the goal of these projects is to strengthen the economic base of the metropolis, particularly through the creation of income and employment and the provision of basic infrastructure.

IMPROVED CONSULTATION BETWEEN CENTRAL AND LOCAL GOVERNMENT. As a counterweight to excessive centralization, which can result in ad hoc sectoral interventions unrelated to the needs of the metropolitan areas, regular formal consultation between central and local government was considered an essential ingredient of metropolitan management. Such consultations could provide the basis for collegiate decisionmaking at the level of the metropolitan area itself. Furthermore, to encourage the integration of its technical and political aspects, metropolitan management should include political consultation. This is especially important at the local level, in the planning and budgeting processes of the metropolitan area, to reconcile the long-term implications of technical decisions with immediate answers that politicians are expected to give their constituents.

Improving Financial Management

During the seminar, possible actions were identified to improve the financial performance of public sector agencies and enable them to contribute more effectively to metropolitan management. Some measures would make more efficient use of the limited financial resources presently available; others would increase public revenues and reduce costs in public sector spending in the metropolitan areas.

IMPROVED CAPITAL BUDGETING. To make public sector capital investments more efficient, it was recommended that the responsible agencies establish an integrated system of investment management. This should be based on the metropolitan plan, the budget (including projects already committed, as well as those for replacement), monitoring, accounting, and independent auditing. The investment budget, which should be for a period of three to five years, should be consistent with the operational budget to guarantee, among other things, the necessary funding for the maintenance of the physical assets in place. In both cases, a clear indication of the sources of finance is essential.

A program budgeting approach which relates budgeted expenditure to specific programs or even projects, as was applied in Cali, Colombia, through technical assistance of the U.N. Economic Commission for Latin America (ECLA), helps to rationalize public expenditure through the systematic allocation of resources between different sectors. Since the budget is explicitly related to a program, the financial follow-up and control can be carried out jointly with the program's technical monitoring.

A SPATIAL DIMENSION TO BUDGETING. Because most public sector budgets are prepared without specific reference to where proposed investments are to be made, it may not be clear until work actually begins that a project of a national sectoral agency is to be in a particular metropolitan area. For this reason, it was considered important to introduce a spatial dimension to both sectoral and metropolitan budgets so that the necessary coordination of the locations can become effectively a part of metropolitan planning and management. In the case of Mexico City, this task is undertaken by the (national) Programming and Budgeting Department, which coordinates the city (Federal District) budget with those of sectoral agencies and other authorities in the metropolitan area.

SYSTEMATIC METROPOLITAN FINANCE. The mechanisms of metropolitan finance, which are mostly embryonic at this stage, could be better organized for a more efficient and equitable use of the limited resources available, pending more substantial reforms in local finance.

One suggestion was to establish and operate development funds specifically for financing investments in the metropolitan areas. In Lima, the central government transfers a proportion of road taxes to the autonomous Metropolitan Investment Fund (INVERMET) to finance urban infrastructure. In some of Brazil's medium-size cities, municipal development funds (FMDU) have been set up with resources recovered (through user charges and tax levies) from specific projects. With solid cost recovery mechanisms in place, it is possible to establish permanent revolving funds for making local investments. Such funds are also being set up in some of the metropolitan areas of Brazil. It is important not only to ensure an adequate flow of resources to these funds, but also to make explicit the criteria for selecting the projects to be financed, so that the financing is not diverted from the goal of consolidating metropolitan development.

A second suggestion was to try to reduce inequalities in revenue among the different municipalities that make up the metropolitan area. In the case of the metropolitan region of São Paulo, municipalities with a weak economic base receive transfers through an investment fund (FFI) from those better endowed.

A third way of better organizing local finance in metropolitan areas is to place the criteria for transfers from national and state to local governments on a sound legal basis, thereby removing some of the arbitrariness which can introduce instability into the flow of funds. In Venezuela the law of coordinated payments (Ley del Situado Coordinado) helps ensure that these transfers are made almost automatically.

GENERATING MORE LOCAL REVENUE. The financial autonomy of local governments can be helped by more fully exploiting the potential for revenue collection from the economies under their jurisdiction. A number of proposals for doing this were raised in the seminar.

In Medellín, Colombia, for example, local revenues are considerably increased through betterment taxes levied on property whose value has been raised by infrastructure provided by the local authority. The betterment tax can be paid over a number of years, the amount depending on the size of the property and its proximity to the new infrastructure. The tax is intended to recover the cost of the infrastructure itself plus administrative costs, and it has proved to be effective in other cities of Colombia and in Ecuador.

Also in Medellín, the collection of local land and property taxes was considerably improved by extending the coverage of the land register and updating the information that it contained. There is felt to be a considerable potential for such improvements in many metropolitan areas in Latin America where many of the better-off make a limited contribution to local taxes.

To further enhance revenues, user charges on services provided by public agencies in metropolitan areas ought at least to cover the costs of those services. This would also help ensure a more efficient allocation of the limited resources available to the public sector. Such charges must, however, be in keeping with the users' ability to pay; if lower-income users cannot afford the charges, then consideration could be given to cross-subsidization by levying heavier charges on higher-income users. General subsidies, which also benefit high-income groups, should not be encouraged since they can reduce the overall scope of programs and are a permanent drain on resources.

COST REDUCTION. To ensure that they are getting good value for their money, local authorities in metropolitan areas should always be on the lookout for less costly ways to provide services—such as using appropriate technologies or setting standards that are compatible with the social and economic conditions of the area.

In Asunción, for example, the streets in poor neighborhoods were paved with irregular stones which, although not of high quality, did provide a better service than before. A dramatic example of a potential cost saving was identified in a study of sewage treatment in San Salvador. By taking advantage of the hilly topography of the city, it would be possible to direct the flow of the sewage to achieve natural aeration which would result in a level of purification equal to that of a conventional treatment plant. It was estimated in 1978 that this appropriate technology could save capital costs of US$100,000,000 and annual operating costs of US$2,000,000 (in 1978 dollars).

Fuller Private Sector and Community Participation

The formal private sector accounts for the large majority of urban investments in the metropolitan areas of Latin America, while a good proportion of urban services and low-income housing is provided on a self-help basis through local communities. The seminar identified a series of measures to overcome obstacles to these contributions, and suggested actions to stimulate the full participation of the formal private sector and the community in the decisionmaking process of metropolitan management.

FACILITATING PRIVATE SECTOR INVOLVEMENT. Although private development does need some planning guidance with regard to its location in the metropolitan area and the standards adopted, a plethora of official regulations and licenses can delay—if not effectively restrict—private investment. Furthermore, in Latin America the lack of clear commitment by public authorities to their own plans has left private developers with little guidance as to the most appropriate locations for their own investments. Some of the relevant measures were discussed in a preceding section (Simplification of Administrative Procedures), while some complementary actions are proposed here.

It was felt necessary to lower the high and costly standards, which, together with the complexity of the licensing procedures themselves, lead to delays and actively encourage unlicensed urban development of very mixed standards. Less exacting technical norms, with standards more closely related to the economic and social conditions of low-income areas, would allow the formal private sector to increase the supply of urban infrastructure and housing at lower unit costs, which would be more affordable by the poor. In Bogotá, for example, the acceptance of ''normas minimas'' by the local authority allows lower than normal standards of building and services for the private subdivision and development of areas for low-income housing.

In particular, simplified procedures for the provision of titles of land ownership could considerably help private sector participation. Although the granting of land titles is a lengthy process in most countries, efforts have been made to speed it up in Lima, especially to regularize the situation of low-income residents in the metropolitan area.

Sometimes the obstacles to urban investment are found within the private sector itself. A private owner who is unwilling or unable to make effective use of well-located land could be encouraged to do so through the appropriate adjustment of property and land taxes. In Brazil the National Housing Bank's CURA project, which provides serviced land for private housing development, requires that land taxes be progressively raised the longer the serviced land remains undeveloped and unoccupied. Conversely, the owner who builds his house quickly faces a lower tax burden. A similar approach was applied more broadly in Curitiba to penalize idle land speculation and reward its productive use.

PRIVATE SECTOR PROVISION OF URBAN SERVICES. Given the profitable nature of some urban services, there is considerable scope for attracting private capital to finance them and private firms to operate them. Although such operations have proved to be efficient and cost-effective, it is still necessary for the public authorities to ensure that the service is provided equitably throughout the metropolitan area and to supervise cost recovery so that it can continue to be financed.

Garbage collection and disposal have been successfully provided at lower unit costs by enterprises in Caracas, Maracaibo (Venezuela), and São Paulo that are in part state-owned and in part privately owned. Although the ratio of public to private equity varies, these mixed companies have in common the ability to issue shares to raise private capital for financing metropolitan development and services.

CREDIT MECHANISMS. Through credit management, the public sector can stimulate private sector activity either directly by providing loans or indirectly by providing guarantees for private credit to borrowers, especially those of low income, who would otherwise present too high a banking risk.

In Lima the Peruvian Builders Bank (Banco Peruano de los Construtores) provides credit to small firms and self-help builders in the form of materials. This program is effectively administered to benefit mostly the low-income population, and problems with delinquent repayments are minimal. Also in Lima, some 60 percent of the low-income population receive electricity, thanks to private bank loans underwritten by the government that enable low-income consumers to pay for the installation of the service.

PARTICIPATION IN POLICYMAKING. To ensure that metropolitan development policies take full account of the potential contribution of the private sector and enjoy its support during the execution of projects, representatives of the private sector need to be involved in policymaking commissions and special committees. The National Council for Urban Development (CNDU) in Brazil, for example, not only brings together representatives of different ministries and sectoral agencies with direct interests in urban development policy, but also has the active participation of representatives of the private sector.

STRONG COMMUNITY ORGANIZATION. Community organization is an essential complement to metropolitan management because it helps to inform public authorities about the needs of the population. Community associations must of course develop spontaneously and operate freely if they are faithfully to present the case of the people they represent, but public authorities can take steps to help consolidate them without threatening their independence.

First, public authorities could formally recognize community organizations by awarding them an appropriate legal status, as is done in Venezuela, for example, through the municipal government law (ley de regimen municipal). In addition, this law requires that each municipality establish a community affairs commission to deal directly and regularly with the associations in its area. With the assistance of IBAM, the municipal council of Rio de Janeiro has established a similar commission, one function of which is to guarantee the public debate of important matters such as the municipal budget and the local land use plan. In Mexico City, consultation with local communities by municipalities is a formal requirement of the planning process.

Once community associations are in place, local authorities should establish formal and informal contacts with them, including regular meetings in the neighborhoods themselves. The Rio de Janeiro Federation of Community Associations (FAMERJ) maintains regular contact with local governments and has brought about important changes in metropolitan investment plans, while the Civic Transport Committee in Cali (Colombia) enables local associations to participate in decisionmaking about traffic measures before they are implemented.

To have a sound base on which to operate, community organizations need access to a free flow of management information, especially regarding the public authorities' plans for the metropolitan area. This can be accomplished in various ways, such as the periodic campaigns mounted in Curitiba, the use of marquees for public meetings in low-income areas of Recife, or the regular meetings of parish councils in Venezuela.

Since community associations usually have inadequate professional skills, they need technical assistance. Technical assistance for building has been provided in San Salvador by the Salvadorean Foundation for Minimum Housing (Fundacion Salvadorena de Vivienda Minima) and in Venezuela by the National Housing Institute (INAVI).

EFFECTIVE COMMUNITY ACTION. If community participation is to be meaningful, the associations must have legitimate spheres of action in which they can operate. Local authorities can help foster community action through the following measures.

With their legal status clarified, the community associations can become either direct borrowers or intermediaries for on-lending. In Venezuela, INAVI provides small-scale credit through local community groups to finance self-help construction. Similar action has also been taken by the Peruvian Materials Bank (Banco de Materiales del Peru) in Lima.

Another way of stimulating community participation is through joint local authority and community action in the provision of urban services. This is how much recreational infrastructure has been supplied in Cali, where the municipality provides the land and basic infrastructure, while community associations provide the equipment and undertake to maintain the parks. The costs of such maintenance are levied on the community itself at a rate that is democratically decided.

Community action can become more effective if it is related to the development priorities of metropolitan management. In this respect, civic education campaigns—such as the ''Educación a Distancia'' in Venezuela and the popular programs of culture in Recife—have an important role in guiding the interests of the community.

Improved Land Management

Land use planning provides an essential spatial dimension to metropolitan management. Although precise zoning ordinances based on detailed master plans may have been appropriate for the slow-growing European cities for which they were designed, they do not always have the flexibility needed in Latin America, where the rapid growth of metropolitan areas makes frequent demands for changing land use. For this reason, the seminar considered several measures to help make land management more effective in these specific conditions. The actions proposed here are in addition to those presented in earlier sections (Simplification of Administrative Procedures, and Simplification of Planning).

PUBLIC SECTOR INVESTMENT IN STRATEGIC INFRASTRUCTURE. Direct public investment in strategic infrastructure, by laying down the broad lines of a land use strategy, can help to consolidate what might otherwise be a series of ineffective land use zonings. With such investment in effect, the local authority declares its firm commitment to act in accordance with the proposed land use of its plan. In Curitiba, for example, major public investment in roads was able to give credence to the land use strategy at least along the main highways. Furthermore, the infrastructure itself, by providing the necessary services for industry, commerce, and housing can, if accompanied by consistent land use zoning, actually create favorable conditions for private sector investment in metropolitan development.

PUBLIC SECTOR ACQUISITION OF STRATEGIC LAND. Large-scale land acquisition by the public sector can impose heavy financial costs on local authorities and a high opportunity cost on the metropolitan economy if the land acquired is not put to timely and productive use. Land acquisition must therefore be used selectively as an instrument of land management, and the establishment of large public sector land banks, which can leave costly land idle for long periods, was not recommended. Instead, local authorities should concentrate their limited resources on acquiring strategic sites that can be developed in the short to medium term to consolidate the metropolitan plan.

Under the Agrarian Reform Law of Peru, uncultivated agricultural land in the expansion zones on the periphery of Lima reverts to the state. These strategic areas can subsequently be transferred to the local municipalities, which can develop them either jointly with cooperatives and non-profit-making institutions or by themselves. In the case of Curitiba, the centrally located land acquired with funds from the National Housing Bank (BNH) allowed for the subsequent development of bus terminals.

ISSUANCE OF TEMPORARY DEVELOPMENT RIGHTS. Where land has not been and is unlikely to be developed in the short term in accordance with the prevailing land use and building regulations, temporary development rights might be granted. Such rights allow either permanent buildings at lower than normal standards, on the understanding that improvements will be made within an agreed period, or temporary installations for particular events which will later be removed.

Under "progressive urbanization" in Bogotá, low-income housing is developed at lower than normal standards through the application of *normas minimas*, which allows for subsequent upgrading *(politica correctiva)* and the establishment of new settlements with adequate albeit low standards *(politica preventativa)*. Similar progressive urbanization has been tried in São Paulo and Curitiba, where low-income development was authorized even though the necessary urban services were not in place right at the beginning.

TRANSFER OF DEVELOPMENT RIGHTS. The transfer of development rights from one location to another involves direct negotiation between the public sector authority responsible for land use and the private developer or owner. In New York, for example, the local authority can offer an owner land and/or development rights in an area it wishes to expand in exchange for the resignation of those rights in an area where it wishes to control development.

RATIONAL PRICING. Public sector real estate is a valuable asset. It can generate important revenue for local authorities and thereby provide a surplus to finance less profitable social investments. A careful review of policies and laws regarding subsidies is necessary, however, to see to what extent those who can afford to pay are being subsidized inappropriately. It should also be borne in mind that the overall reduction of subsidies can increase the supply of urban services and housing in metropolitan areas.

Provision of Strategic Metropolitan Services

Some urban services, because of their scale and impact, have strategic importance; without them the metropolis could not function. Their efficient and equitable operation therefore becomes a matter of crucial concern for metropolitan management. The seminar discussions identified several ways in which the management of some of these services might be improved.

IMPROVEMENTS IN WATER SUPPLY SYSTEMS. A metropolitan water supply system should be monitored regularly to ensure, among other things, that losses through leakage are minimal. Regular maintenance, the periodic renewal of weak points of the system, and the establishment of well-equipped teams to deal with emergencies can help the system function more efficiently. The savings that such improvements can bring are illustrated by the case of Mexico City, where a 10 percent reduction in water losses from the distribution system would increase the supply by 10 cubic meters of water per second without any extra production. It has been estimated that such a measure would lead to capital and operational cost savings of US$350 million in ten to twenty years.

RATIONALIZING CONSUMPTION OF WATER AND ENERGY. In many metropolitan areas of Latin America, the price charged for water consumption is below that needed to cover costs. Pricing policies need to take payment capacity into account, but a low charge itself can induce the wasteful use of water by consumers. Energy is more often, but not always, charged to cover costs and therefore results in a more rational pattern of consumption. Periodic campaigns and educational programs can encourage the conservation of water and energy and reduce per capita consumption.

RECYCLING LIQUID WASTE. The metropolitan areas of Latin America, in spite of the limited extent of their sewerage and drainage systems, still produce a considerable amount of liquid waste. One way to use the liquid waste productively and gain some return from the costs incurred is to use it for irrigating agricultural land on the periphery of metropolitan areas. In Lima some 300 hectares of land have been thus irrigated for the past twenty years. A current project is to use the outflow from one of the city's biggest drains to increase the irrigated area to 1,500 hectares in the southern part of the metropolitan area.

RECYCLING SOLID WASTE. Again, although the garbage collection and disposal systems of metropolitan Latin America are limited compared with those of industrialized countries, they produce a considerable quantity of solid waste, which is expected to increase.

An example of recycling solid wastes is the Iraja plant in Rio de Janeiro, which processes 250 tons of garbage a day to produce compost for agricultural use. Another case is the production of biogas at special garbage disposal points in São Paulo (similar production units are projected for other metropolitan areas in Brazil). The gas is used primarily as fuel for the collection vehicles and can lead to significant operational cost savings.

Opportunities to Initiate Long-Term Changes

New Metropolitan Institutions

The prospect of a full-fledged metropolitan government was viewed with some caution by the seminar because of the risk that introducing a fourth, specifically metropolitan tier (in addition to the national, state, and municipal levels) would overcomplicate the federal systems of most Latin American countries. Furthermore, it was felt that political accountability was best handled through some intermediate collegial arrangement of metropolitan management, which to a large extent incorporated existing authorities. Efforts at establishing metropolitan structures of government have been made in Colombia, Peru, Mexico, and Brazil. A preliminary step toward identifying the appropriate structure for a particular metropolis would be to review the experiences already acquired, both in Latin America and elsewhere.

An example of such an intermediate step is the establishment by the state government of São Paulo of a special secretariat of metropolitan affairs (Secretaria de Negocios Metropolitanos). As part of the state government, it is well placed to help coordinate sectoral and local decisions about state and municipal investments in the metropolitan area. In other metropolitan areas in Brazil, foundations and other entities have been established (FUNDREM in Rio de Janeiro, CONDER in Salvador, FIDEM in Recife, and AUMEF in Fortaleza) to act as technical agencies for the deliberative metropolitan councils that were set up when Brazil's metropolitan regions were legally instituted. In spite of being created under the auspices of their respective state governments, these metropolitan agencies have a special responsibility toward the local municipalities represented on the deliberative councils. An alternative approach, which relies directly on the central government, has been adopted in Mexico City, where the national Programming and Budget Secretariat (Secretaría de Programación y Presupuesto) is responsible for coordinating investment and planning decisions among the various state and municipal governments that are active in the metropolitan area.

Outside the region itself, some cases of metropolitan management that are worthy of study include those of London (Greater London Council), Toronto (Toronto Metropolitan Council), and Madras (Madras Metropolitan Development Authority). In examining the successes and failures of these particular experiences, one should of course focus on those aspects which are strictly relevant to the management challenges posed by the rapidly growing and changing metropolitan areas of Latin America.

New Methods of Finance

Financial resources will continue to be scarce in relation to the needed investments and recurrent expenditures in metropolitan Latin America. For this reason, the seminar sought to explore ways to widen local (especially municipal) governments' access to finance. One method worthy of study is the public issue of local municipal bonds, especially to finance particular projects. Although the present time of financial restraint is not the ideal moment to implement such a proposal, the often lengthy preparatory studies of the legal, institutional, and technical conditions could well begin now. A review could also be made of the experience with municipal bond issues in other countries—particularly the extensive experience of local governments in the United States—to determine to what extent this method could be applied in Latin America.

New Methods of Land Management

Inasmuch as land management in the rapidly growing cities of Latin America is likely to present an ever greater challenge for metropolitan management, new techniques and methods need to be considered. Land readjustment is a new method of increasing the supply of urbanized land in the metropolitan area by bringing more privately owned land into effective use. Using this method, a local authority develops private land without expropriating it and, in common agreement with the owner, retains a portion of the total after it has been developed. This portion is in effect the owner's contribution to the costs, borne by the public sector, of developing the land. In some cases, even after conceding as much as 45 percent of their land, the owners have found that the remaining 55 percent is more valuable real estate than the original 100 percent in its undeveloped and unserviced condition. For this reason, land readjustment has proved attractive to private owners in the metropolitan area of Seoul (Republic of Korea), and it offers considerable scope for negotiating between the public and private sectors.

Participants

Brazil

Almino Monteiro Afonso, state secretary of metropolitan affairs, São Paulo

Candido Malta Campos Filho, former secretary of metropolitan planning, São Paulo

Diogo Lordello de Mello, director, Brazilian Institute of Municipal Administration, Rio de Janeiro

Domingos Theodoro de Azevedo Netto, director, Metropolitan Land Use Planning, EMPLASA (State Metropolitan Planning Company), São Paulo

Gustavo Krause, vice-governor of state of Pernambuco and former mayor of Recife

Jaime Lerner, former mayor of Curitiba

Jo Resende, president of FAMERJ (Community Associations' Federation of Rio de Janeiro)

Joao Fortes, president of Joao Fortes Engineering and Construction Company, Rio de Janeiro

Militao de Morais Ricardo, executive secretary of the National Urban Development Council, Brasilia

Rodolfo Costa e Silva, superintendent of EMPLASA (State Metropolitan Planning Company), São Paulo

Yojiro Takaoka, president of Albuquerque Takaoka Construction Company, São Paulo

Colombia

Gustavo Zafra Roldon, vice-minister of government, Bogotá, and former deputy mayor of Cali

Ecuador

Alvaro Perez Intriago, mayor of Quito

Mexico

Carlos Alcaraz Guzman, director, Budget and Programming, the Federal District and Metropolitan Zone of Mexico City

Paraguay

Herenio Centurion, finance secretary of the municipality of Asunción

Peru

Eduardo Orrego, mayor of Lima
Fernando Correa Miller, president of the Peruvian Builders' Bank, Lima
Francisco Leo Farje, metropolitan director of the municipality of Lima

Uruguay

Angel Brian, director of architecture and urbanism of the municipality of
    Montevideo

Venezuela

Miriam Romero, director, Planning and Budget, FUNDACOMUN (Founda-
    tion for Municipal and Community Development), Caracas
Victor Murillo, municipal councillor of the Federal District of Caracas

Appendix B

Asian Development Bank– Economic Development Institute Seminar on Metropolitan Management

Manila, January 12–16, 1981

Participants

Fazlul Huq (Bangladesh), chief executive officer, Dakha Municipal Corporation

Brian George Jenney (Hong Kong), principal assistant financial secretary, Government Secretariat

Bernard Healy Newman (Hong Kong), project manager, New Territories Development Department

Mangazhi Govindan Kutty (India), finance secretary, Finance Department, government of West Bengal

Mrinal Kanti Mukharji (India), secretary to government of India, Ministry of Works and Housing

Har Mohinder Singh (India), vice-chairman, Madras Metropolitan Development Authority

Wisnu Indradjit Oemar (Indonesia), head, Planning Subdivision, Directorate General of Housing, Building, Planning, and Urban Development, Ministry of Public Works

Marzuki Usman (Indonesia), director of investment and state properties, Directorate General for Domestic Monetary Affairs, Ministry of Finance

Tokue Shibata (Japan), professor, Department of Economics, Tokyo Kcizai University

Kiyotaka Hayashi (Japan), chief, Development Control Unit, City Planning Bureau, Nagoya

Hyung Suk Park (Korea), director, Budget Division, Seoul City Government

Sun Jin Chang (Korea), assistant director, Urban Transport Bureau, Ministry of Transportation

Abd. Razak Noordin Bin (Malaysia), director, Development and Coordination Unit, Kuala Lumpur

Shamsul Haq (Pakistan), deputy secretary, Environment and Urban Affairs Division, government of Pakistan

Asad Ali Shah (Pakistan), chief, Physical Planning, Housing and Regional Planning, Planning and Development Division

Muhammad Mashood Usmani (Pakistan), chairman, Karachi Development Authority, and district commissioner

Oscar I. Illustre (Philippines), acting general manager, Metropolitan Waterworks and Sewerage System

Nathaniel Von Einsiedel (Philippines), commissioner for planning, Metropolitan Manila Commission

Mauro Calaguio (Philippines), commissioner for finance, Metropolitan Manila Commission

Apollo Jucaban (Philippines), director, Metropolitan Manila Finance and Delivery Services

Au Eng Kok (Singapore), general manager, Urban Redevelopment Authority

Ranaweera Abeyratne (Sri Lanka), municipal commissioner, Colombo Municipal Council

R. Paskaralingam (Sri Lanka), secretary, Ministry of Local Government, Housing and Construction

Virachai Naewboonnien (Thailand), assistant director, Technical and Planning Division, Local Administration Department

Tawil Praisont (Thailand), deputy director, Bureau of Policy and Planning, Bangkok Metropolitan Administration

Resource Persons

Leslie Green (U.S.A.), international programs advisor, Institute of Public Administration

Kenneth Davey (U.K.), senior lecturer and associate director, Institute of Local Government Studies, University of Birmingham

Observers

Anthony Churchill, director, Urban Projects Department, World Bank

Sven Sandstrom, division chief, South Asia, Urban Projects Department, World Bank

Fred Temple, acting division chief, East Asia, Urban Projects Department, World Bank

Haruo Nagamine, United Nations Center for Regional Development

Course Directors

K. C. Sivaramakrishnan, Economic Development Institute, World Bank

Ronald Skeates, Social Infrastructure Department, Asian Development Bank

M. P. Perlas, project economist, Asian Development Bank

Index

Administration: bureaucracies and, 49–51, 62–65; growth of cities and public, 4–6; as institutional constraint, 49–51; integration of planning and, 59–62; manpower needs and, 75–77; metropolitan governmental conflicts and, 11; metropolitan management tasks and, 23–33; networks for, 60–61, 65–71, 83; process of, 64. *See also* Management

Bangkok, 8, 11, 31, 36, 37, 47, 48; fiscal situation in, 103–07, 115–16; government structure in, 100–03; historical sketch of, 93; metropolitan development in, 93–94; metropolitan government experiments in, 9–10; networks in, 68, 70; private sector in, 71; problem response in, 107–14; problems in, 94–100; services in, 24, 25, 102, 107; taxes and, 43, 44, 103–07, 115–16
Bangkok Metropolitan Administration (BMA), 9–10, 52, 101–03, 107, 110, 115, 116, 117–18
Bombay, 8, 11, 26, 28, 29, 35, 36, 47, 52; cost-benefit example in, 39; fiscal situation in, 131–32, 136–37; government structure in, 127–31; historical sketch of, 119; infrastructure investment in, 25; metropolitan development in, 119–20; New Bombay and, 137–38; problem response in, 133–36; problems in, 126–27; spatial planning in, 30, 31; taxes and, 43, 128, 138
Bombay Corporation's Electric Supply

and Transport (BEST), 126, 127, 128, 131, 132, 133
Bombay Metropolitan Region Development Authority (BMRDA), 9, 133–36, 137, 138
Bureaucracies, 5, 32; development and, 49–51; development administration and, 62–65
Bureau of Public Works (Bangkok), 117

Calcutta, 11, 36, 37, 47, 52, 54, 55, 56, 58, 85; cost-benefit example in, 39; cost recovery and, 43; economic development and, 28–29, 30; fiscal situation in, 151–52, 160–61, 165–67; government structure in, 149–50, 159–61; historical sketch of, 140; internal efficiency and, 41–42; international organizations and, 89; interorganizational agencies and, 85; local representation and, 86–87; manpower needs and, 77; metropolitan development in, 140–41, 155, 165; municipal reorganization and, 159–61; networks in, 69–70; private sector in, 71; problem response in, 152–57; problems in, 141–49; project uncertainty and, 55; reform and, 167; sectoral response in, 6, 7, 8; services in, 24, 25, 26, 148, 156; slums in, 25; spatial planning in, 30, 31; taxes and, 43, 151–52, 156; transport example of financial constraints and, 38–39; urban poor in, 28
Calcutta Metropolitan Development

Agency (CMDA), 85, 87, 156–59, 160; incentives and, 161–67
Calcutta Metropolitan District (CMD), 26
Calcutta Metropolitan Planning Organization (CMPO), 8, 61–62, 86–87, 150, 155
Cities (Asian): multisectoral response in, 8–9; persistent problems in, 10–12; premetropolitan phase in, 4–5; rapid growth in, 5–6; sectoral response in, 6–8. *See also names of specific cities*
Colombo, 11, 29, 36, 47, 56; development projects in, 185–86; fiscal situation in, 181–83, 184–85, 188; government structure in, 178–81, 184; historical sketch of, 171; internal efficiency and, 42; interorganizational relations and, 86; manpower needs and, 76, 77; metropolitan development in, 171–72; networks in, 66–71; new agencies in, 187; problem response in, 183–86; problems in, 172–77; purpose of development and, 50–51; spatial planning in, 30, 31; taxes and, 43, 181–82; unemployment in, 28, 172, 188
Community participation in city management, 7, 11, 52, 274–75
Construction: housing (Colombo), 186; lack of skills in, 188; manpower needs and, 76, 80; public sector (Colombo), 178, 183, 184; public sector (Jakarta), 196; services and highway, 25
Cost-benefit analysis, 39–40

Development authorities, 8–9, 11, 83. *See also* Interagency relations; *names of specific development agencies*

Economic Development Institute, 12
Efficiency (internal), 41–42
Employment: in Bangkok, 94; in Bombay, 119–20; in Calcutta, 142; in Colombo, 172, 185; creation of, 27–29; in Karachi, 210; in Madras, 233, 234; in Manila, 246
Expressway and Rapid Transport Authority of Thailand (ERTAT), 113

Financial constraints: assessing needs and resources and, 37–38; cost-effectiveness and, 40; cost recovery and, 42–43; costs and benefits and, 39–40; financial demands and, 35–36; impact analyses of investment and, 40; interagency consistency and, 36–37; internal efficiency and, 41–42; metropolitan management and, 32;

minimum needs and standards and, 40–41; resource allocation and, 34–35; resource mobilization and, 45–46; tax policies and, 42–45; transport example and, 38–39
Financial management, 270–72, 279
Financial resources, advocacy for, 45, 46, 84–85
Fiscal concerns: in Bangkok, 103–07, 115–16; in Bombay, 131–32, 136–37; in Calcutta, 151–52, 160–61, 165–67; in Colombo, 181–83, 184–85, 188; in Jakarta, 200–01, 203, 207; in Karachi, 219–23; in Madras, 237–39; in Manila, 255–59, 260
Flooding: in Bangkok, 94, 100, 110; in Calcutta, 148; in Jakarta, 197, 203; in Madras, 233; in Manila, 251, 252
Ford Foundation, 155
Fourth National Economic and Social Development Plan (Thailand), 114

Government structure: in Bangkok, 100–03; in Bombay, 127–31; in Calcutta, 149–50, 159–61; in Colombo, 178–81, 184; experiments in metropolitan, 9–10; in Jakarta, 197, 198–200; in Karachi, 215–19; in Madras, 234–37, 239–42, 244; in Manila, 252–54; political development and, 51–54

Herbert Commission, 33
Hong Kong, 26, 31, 35, 42, 48, 52, 56, 71
Housing: in Bangkok, 111–13; in Bombay, 126, 127, 129, 131, 133; in Colombo, 177, 178, 184, 185, 186, 188; cost recovery and, 42; in Jakarta, 196–97, 199, 207; in Karachi, 210, 223; in Madras, 234, 235–36, 238, 242–43; in Manila, 253, 260; services and, 25; subsidized, 111, 113
Hyderabad, 72

Income: in Bombay, 127; in Calcutta, 142; in Colombo, 172; in Jakarta, 190; in Madras, 233; in Manila, 251
India, 11, 51, 81, 84; five-year plan in, 40, voluntary groups in, 72
Industries: in Bombay, 119–20, 128–29; in Calcutta, 141; in Colombo, 179, 184; in Madras, 228
Information systems, 32–33, 269
In-migration: in Bangkok, 114; in Calcutta, 149; in Colombo, 172; in Jakarta, 190; in Karachi, 209; in Manila, 251

Institutional constraints: developing urban policies and, 47–49; management and, 32; project uncertainty and, 54–56; social and political development and, 51–54; town planning and, 56–57; urban bureaucracies and, 49–51

Interagency relations, 7–8, 36–37, 62, 84–86, 117

International agencies, 88–90

Interorganizational relations, 84–86

Investment, 33, 49; in Bangkok, 116; in Bombay, 127, 128, 132, 136, 138; in Calcutta, 157, 158, 165; in Colombo, 172, 183–84, 187; cost-benefit analysis and, 39; effective management and budget for, 83–84; in Jakarta, 203, 206–07; in Karachi, 225, 226; in Madras, 83, 237–38; in Manila, 260–62, 264; organizational fragmentation and, 37; priorities and impact determinations and, 40; project programming and, 26–27; in urban services, 25

Jakarta, 8, 9, 10, 11, 28, 48, 53, 67, 84; development projects in, 208; fiscal situation in, 200–01, 203, 207; government structure in, 197, 198–200; historical sketch of, 189; internal efficiency and, 41; metropolitan development in, 189–90; problem response in, 201–06; problems in, 196–98; services in, 24, 25, 196, 200; taxes and, 43, 44, 199, 200, 207; voluntary groups in, 72

Job creation, 28–29

JABOTABEK plans, 48, 190, 201, 202, 203, 206

Karachi, 9, 10, 11, 28, 47, 56; development projects in, 225, 226; education in, 215; financial demands and services in, 35–36; fiscal situation in, 219–23; government structure in, 215–19; historical sketch of, 209; infrastructure investment in, 25; internal efficiency and, 41–42; manpower needs and, 76, 77; metropolitan development and, 209–10, 223; networks in, 68; private sector in, 71; problem response in, 223–24; problems in, 210–15; services in, 23–24, 25, 224–25, 227; taxes and, 43, 219–20, 222, 225, 226; voluntary groups in, 72

Karachi Development Authority (KDA), 216, 222

Land speculation (Karachi), 222–23

Land use, 69; in Bangkok, 107, 115; in Bombay, 137; in Colombo, 177, 185; in Karachi, 219, 223; in Madras, 239, 242; in Manila, 251; serviced land for industry and, 29; spatial planning and, 30–32, 55–56

Land values, 36, 277

"Learning-by-doing" approach to urban problems (World Bank), 88–90

Local representation, 86–88

Madras, 8, 11, 26, 28, 29, 31, 33, 47, 48, 49, 56; cost recovery and, 42, 43; fiscal situation in, 237–39; government structure in, 234–37, 239–42, 244; historical sketch of, 228; internal efficiency and, 41–42; international organizations and, 89; metropolitan development in, 228–33, 237; problem response in, 239–42; problems in, 233–34; resource mobilization and, 46; taxes and, 43, 44, 235, 238

Madras Corporation, 237, 238, 241, 244

Madras Metropolitan Development Authority (MMDA), 52, 84, 235, 237, 241, 243, 244

Madras Urban Development Project, 235, 240, 241, 242, 244

Maintenance, 7; in Calcutta, 148; road, 117, 182, 196

Management: developing processes for, 32–33; economic development and, 27–30; financial and institutional constraints and, 10–11, 32; social and political development and, 51–54. See also Metropolitan management teams.

Manila, 9, 10, 11, 31, 33, 36, 37, 48, 49, 84, 85; fiscal situation in, 255–59, 260; government structure in, 252–54; historical sketch of, 245–46; internal efficiency and, 41, 42; international organizations and, 89; investment and, 83, 237–38; manpower needs and, 76, 77; metropolitan development in, 245–46; networks in, 69; private sector in, 71; problem response in, 259–62; problems in, 246–52; project development in, 260–61, 263–64; project programming in, 26–27; slums in, 25, 236; taxes and, 43, 44, 255, 256; transport in, 39; urban poor in, 27; voluntary groups in, 72

Manpower: administrative needs and, 75–77; training and, 77–81

Manufacturing, 34; in Bombay, 119–20,

128, 129; in Colombo, 171; in
  Madras, 228; in Manila, 246
Metropolitan development: in Bangkok,
  93–94; in Bombay, 119–20; in
  Calcutta, 140–41, 155, 165; in
  Colombo, 171–72; in Jakarta, 189–90,
  196, 202, 203, 207; in Karachi, 209–
  10, 223; in Madras, 228–33, 237; in
  Manila, 245–46; planning and
  administration and, 59–62
Metropolitan management teams:
  investment budget and, 83–84;
  organizational needs and, 82–83;
  relations with other agencies, 84–86;
  representativeness of, 86–88
Metropolitan Manila Commission
  (MMC), 27, 38, 46, 52, 53, 85, 254,
  255, 259, 262, 263, 264
Migration. *See* In-migration
Mortality rate (Jakarta), 197
Municipal Corporation of Greater
  Bombay (BMC), 127–28, 131, 134, 138
Municipal Finance Commission
  (Calcutta), 161

National Economic and Development
  Authority (NEDA, Philippines), 42,
  261, 262, 263
National Economic and Social
  Development Board (NESDB,
  Thailand), 100
Nehru, Jawaharlal, 148
Networks, administrative, 60–61, 65–71,
  83
New Bombay, 137–38
New towns, 114, 235

Planning, 11; in Bangkok, 107–10, 116;
  in Bombay, 132, 133; in Colombo,
  178, 179, 184, 185, 186–87; for
  economic development, 30;
  integration with development
  authorities and, 59–62; in Jakarta,
  202–03, 206; in Karachi, 219, 223,
  225, 226; in Madras, 237, 242, 244;
  in Manila, 259–60, 263; spatial, 30–
  32, 55–56; town, 56–57
Policymaking, 47–49, 59–60
Political development, 51–54; in
  Bangkok, 117–18. *See also*
  Government structure
Population: in Bangkok, 93; in Bombay,
  126, 137; in Calcutta, 140, 142; cities
  with more than one million, 5–6; in
  Colombo, 171, 177, 181, 188;
  increases in (as urban problem), 11;
  in Jakarta, 190, 196, 202, 203; in
  Karachi, 209; in Madras, 228, 233,

234; in Manila, 245, 246, 264; urban
  trends in, 3–4, 88
Poverty, 27–28
Project management: private sector and,
  61, 71–72, 73–74; process of, 63–65;
  public sector and, 61, 73–74
Projects (development): bureaucracies
  and administration and, 49–51; in
  Colombo, 185–86; demonstration,
  269–70; development policy process
  and, 59–60; in Jakarta, 208; long-
  term development policies and, 47–
  49; in Madras, 235, 239–44; in
  Manila, 260–61, 263–64;
  programming and, 26–27; social and
  political development and, 51–54;
  town planning and, 56–57;
  uncertainty and, 54–56
Property tax. *See* Taxes (on property)
Protection Planning Committee
  (Tennessee, U.S.A.), 62
Public sector, 7; construction
  (Colombo), 178, 183, 184; investment
  (Colombo), 172; project management
  and, 61, 73–74

Reform, municipal management
  (Calcutta), 167
Resource allocation, 34–35
Resource mobilization, 45–46, 84–85
Road maintenance, 117, 182, 196
Royal Thai Government (RTG), 100,
  102, 107, 115
Rural-to-urban migration. *See*
  In-migration

Sectoral issues: Asian cities and, 6–8; in
  Bangkok, 110, 116–18; development
  policies and, 47–48; in Madras, 241–
  42, 243; multisectoral response and,
  8–9
Services: in Bangkok, 24, 25, 102, 107;
  in Calcutta, 24, 25, 26, 148, 156; in
  Colombo, 172, 182, 185; financial
  demands and, 35–36; in Jakarta, 24,
  25, 196–97, 200; in Karachi, 23–24,
  25, 224–25, 227; labor unions and,
  24; in Madras, 234, 235; in Manila,
  251, 252, 256, 260; metropolitan
  management and provision of, 23–26;
  private sector and, 71; resource
  mobilization and, 45; training in
  management and, 80–81
Sewerage: in Bangkok, 100; in Bombay,
  133; in Calcutta, 148, 152, 155, 156,
  157, 158, 165; in Colombo, 177; in
  Karachi, 215, 216, 222, 226; in

Madras, 234, 235; in Manila, 253, 260
Shanghai, 35, 70
Shelter. *See* Housing
Singapore, 26, 31, 35, 38, 48, 52
Skills: lack of construction, 188; lack of technical, 207; manpower needs and, 75-77; training and, 77-81
Slum upgrading, 25; in Bangkok, 111, 113, 117; in Bombay, 133; in Colombo, 177; in Karachi, 223-224, 227; in Madras, 236; in Manila, 260; manpower needs and, 76, 80
Social development, 51-54
Spatial planning, 30-32, 55-56
Squatters: in Colombo, 177; in Karachi, 210, 215; in Manila, 260
Suburbanization (Bombay), 120, 126

Taxes, 68; Bangkok and, 43, 44, 103-07, 115-16; Bombay and, 43, 128, 131, 138; Calcutta and, 43, 151-52, 156; Colombo and, 43, 181-82; financial constraints and policies for, 42-45; financial resource allocation and, 34-35; Jakarta and, 43, 44, 199, 200, 207; Karachi and, 219-20, 222, 225, 226; Madras and, 43, 44, 235, 238; Manila and, 43, 44, 255, 256; on property, 115-16, 131, 161, 199, 220, 222, 226, 238; tax mapping and, 46; Tokyo and, 43, 44, 45
Technical assistance to municipalities, 267-68
Tennessee (U.S.A.), developmental system integration and, 62
Tokyo, 9, 10, 26, 38, 52, 56; cost recovery and, 42; networks in, 66, 67, 69; tax policies and, 43, 44, 45
Town planning, 56-57
Trade: Bombay and, 119-20, 129; Calcutta and, 141, 142; Karachi and, 220; Madras and, 233
Traffic: in Bangkok, 113-114, 117; in Bombay, 133; in Colombo, 177
Training, 75, 76, 77-81
Transport: in Bangkok, 113-114, 117; in Bombay, 126, 127, 129, 135, 136, 137, 138; in Calcutta, 26, 38-39, 148, 158; in Colombo, 177; cost recovery and, 42; efficiency example and, 41; financial constraints and, 38-39; infrastructure investment in, 25; in Jakarta, 189, 203-04; in Karachi,

224, 225; in Madras, 234, 236-37, 241, 242; in Manila, 246

Uncertainty (project), 54-56
Unemployment, 28; in Bangkok, 94; in Colombo, 28, 172, 188
United Nations, 81, 179; demographic assessment and, 88, 90
Urban Community Development Program (Hyderabad), 72
Urban Development Authority (Colombo), 52, 69, 179, 182, 183-85
Urban growth, 5-6; in Bangkok, 93-94, 114; in Bombay, 119-20; in Calcutta, 140-41, 155, 165; in Colombo, 171-72; in Jakarta, 189-90, 196, 202, 203, 207; in Karachi, 209-10, 223; in Madras, 228-33, 237; in Manila, 245-46
Urbanization, 31, 88; Bangkok and, 107, 114; Bombay and, 119, 126; Colombo and, 171, 179; trends in, 3-4
Urban problems: in Bangkok, 94-100, 107-14; in Bombay, 126-27, 133-36; in Calcutta, 141-49, 152-57; in Colombo, 172-77, 183-86; in Jakarta, 196-98, 201-06; in Karachi, 210-15, 223-24; "learning-by-doing" approach to, 88-90; in Madras, 233-34, 239-42; in Manila, 246-52, 259-62; persistent, 10-12

Voluntary groups, 72-73

Water supplies: in Bangkok, 94-100, 110; in Bombay, 126, 132, 133, 135, 138; in Calcutta, 148, 155, 156, 157, 158, 165; in Colombo, 177, 182; in Jakarta, 197, 199, 203; in Karachi, 215, 216, 220, 222, 225, 226; in Madras, 233, 235, 238, 241; in Manila, 252, 253, 260; sectoral response and, 7; services and, 25; water contamination and, 30
World Bank, 11, 27, 28, 39, 55; Bangkok and, 110, 113, 114; Bombay and, 126, 133, 135, 136; Calcutta and, 157, 159, 161, 165; Colombo and, 188; Jakarta and, 197-98, 202; Karachi and, 226; "learning-by-doing" approach and, 88-90; Madras and, 237, 239, 243, 244; Manila and, 260, 261, 262
World Health Organization (WHO), 155